Path Through Catholicism

Mark Link, S.J.

REVISED EDITION

RESOURCES FOR CHRISTIAN LIVING®

Executive Editor:
John L. Sprague

Book and Cover Design:
Dennis Davidson

Production:
Kevin Fremder
Laura Fremder

Nihil Obstat:
Rev. Msgr. Glenn D. Gardner, J.C.D.
Censor Librorum

Imprimi Potest:
Richard J. Baumann, S.J.

Imprimatur:
† Most Rev. Charles V. Grahmann
Bishop of Dallas

December 30, 1999

The Nihil Obstat and Imprimatur are official declarations that the material reviewed is free of doctrinal or moral error. No implication is contained therein that those granting the Nihil Obstat and Imprimatur agree with the contents, opinions, or statements expressed.

ACKNOWLEDGMENTS

Unless otherwise noted, Scripture quotations are taken or adapted from the *Good News Bible: Today's English Version* (Catholic edition). Copyright © American Bible Society 1992, 1976, 1971, 1966. Used by permission.

Excerpts from the English translation of the *Rite of Baptism for Children* © 1969, International Committee on English in the Liturgy, Inc. (ICEL); excerpts from the English translation of *Rite of Marriage* © 1969, ICEL; excerpts from the English translation of *The Roman Missal* © 1973, ICEL; excerpts from the English translation of *Rite of Confirmation,* second edition © 1975, ICEL; excerpts from *Pastoral Care of the Sick: Rites of Anointing and Viaticum* © 1982, ICEL. All rights reserved.

Excerpts taken from the *Catechism of the Catholic Church* for the United States of America, copyright © 1994, United States Catholic Conference, Inc.—Libreria Editrice Vaticana.

Excerpts from the Vatican II documents are adapted from *The Documents of Vatican Council II,* copyright © 1966, Walter M. Abbott, S.J., Gen. Ed., America Press.

Photograph credits appear on page 319.

Send all inquiries to:
RCL • Resources for Christian Living®   Toll free   877-275-4725
200 East Bethany Drive   Fax   800-688-8356
Allen, Texas 75002-3804

E-mail: **cservice@rcl-enterprises.com**
Web site: **www.rclweb.com**

Printed in the United States of America

20270   ISBN 0-7829-0971-X

3 4 5 6 7 8 9 10
04 05 06 07 08 09

Preface

Three factors profoundly influenced the revision of this text:

- The *Catechism of the Catholic Church*
- The Pontifical Biblical Commission's document "The Interpretation of the Bible in the Church"
- The Holy Father's challenge to youth at the end of World Youth Day in Denver

The first influence was the *Catechism of the Catholic Church*.

Throughout the text you will notice the letters CCC followed by a number. These are references to the *Catechism*. The text designer did a superb job of designing them to fit into the text at the right spot without giving the text a cluttered look. The references guide us to further references to the documents of Vatican II and other relevant documents.

The second influence was the PBC's *The Interpretation of the Bible in the Church*.

When it appeared in English in 1995, the late Peter Hebblethwaite called it the most important statement on the Bible since Vatican II. While affirming the importance of the historical-critical approach (the "then-and-there" meaning) it affirms that the "here-and-now" meaning is equally important. In other words, it is equally necessary to discern and communicate the meaning of the word of God for our world.

Reviewing the PBC document, *America* magazine (5/20/95) drew this bottom-line conclusion:

If the eagerness of lay Catholics to learn more about the Bible is to be fostered, there needs to be changes in how Catholic Scripture scholars and seminarians are trained.

For the present, without neglecting the historical meaning of the Bible, the priority needs to be on learning to discern and communicate the meaning of the word of God for our world today.

This important principle became a guiding norm in revising *Path Through Catholicism*.

Finally, the third factor that influenced the revision was the pope's challenge to young people at World Youth Day in Denver.

The Holy Father challenged them to lead the way for the rest of the world in (a) undergoing a personal conviction to Jesus, and (b) developing a personal relationship with Jesus.

This challenge was kept uppermost in mind in the revision of *Path*. It resulted in the many creative features of the text to its refreshing contemporary design.

One final note, a unique and labor-saving *Resource Manual* is available to enhance use of the text in classroom and RCIA settings.

Feast of the Mother of God,
the year of our Lord, A.D. 2000
Mark Link, S.J.

Contents

1

WORD
God reaches out to us

I said to the man
who stood at the gate of the year:
"Give me a light that I may tread safely
into the unknown."

And he replied:

"Go out into the darkness
and put your hand in the hand of God.
That shall be to you better than light
and safer than a known way."

MINNIE LOUISE HASKINS

LOOKING Back

One important episode up to this point in my faith journey was . . .

_____

_____

One difficulty I have experienced up to this point in my faith journey is . . .

_____

_____

LOOKING**Ahead**

Every faith journey begins with God reaching out to us and inviting us to journey together into the unknown.

Our faith journey in the weeks ahead will be divided into three stages:

- **WORD**   God reaches out to us. (Revelation)
- **WORSHIP**   We reach out to God.   (Sacraments)
- **WITNESS**   We journey together.   (Commandments)

7

Light of Faith

It was faith that made Abraham . . .
obey when God called him.
He left his own country
without knowing where he was going.

It was faith that made Moses . . .
refuse to be called
the son of the king's daughter.
He preferred to suffer with God's people
rather than enjoy . . .
the treasures of Egypt.

As for us . . .
Let us keep our eyes fixed on Jesus,
on whom our faith depends.
HEBREWS 11:8; 24–26; 12:1–2

*Faith invites me to enter
into a personal relationship with Jesus.
It invites me to open my heart to Jesus,
fix my eyes on him,
and journey through life with him.*

Tommy's faith journey

Father John Powell of Loyola University, Chicago, was watching students file into his classroom on the first day of school. That's when he met Tommy for the first time.

Tommy turned out to be his "atheist in residence." But he managed to live together with Tommy rather peacefully. After the course, Tommy asked Father somewhat cynically, "Do you think I'll ever find God?"

Father Powell decided on a little shock therapy. "No, Tommy," he said. "I don't think you'll ever find God. But I'm certain that God will find you." Tommy shrugged and left, not sure how to take Father's remark.

1 How would you take Father Powell's remark?

About a year later, Father Powell learned that Tommy had terminal cancer. Before he could get in touch with Tommy, Tommy got in touch with him. Father Powell writes:

When Tommy walked into my office,
his body was badly wasted. . . .
I blurted out,
"I've thought about you so often . . .
Can you talk about it?"
"Sure, what would you like to know?"

"What's it like to be only twenty-four
and know you are dying?"
"Well, it could be worse," Tommy said.
"Like what?" I asked.

"Well," said Tommy,
"like being fifty years old
and having no values and thinking
that booze and making money
are the real biggies in life.

"But what I really came to see you about
is something you said to me
the last day of class.
I asked if you thought I would ever
find God and you said, 'No!' which
surprised me. Then you said,
'But God will find you.'"

Tommy went on to say that after the doctors removed a malignant lump from his groin, he decided he'd start looking for God.

For the first time in his life, Tommy made a serious effort to reach out and search for the God that he had been avoiding:

"I really began banging
against the bronze doors of heaven.
But nothing happened. So I just quit."

2 How would you explain Tommy's failure to find God?

Then one day Tommy remembered something else that Father had said in class:

The essential sadness
is to go through life without loving.
But it would be almost equally sad
to leave this world
without ever telling those you loved
that you loved them.

Tommy decided to spend the time he had left reaching out to those he loved. He began with his dad. One night he said to him:

"'Dad, I love you.
I just wanted you to know that . . .'
Then my father did two things
I couldn't remember him doing before.

"First, he cried and hugged me.
Then we talked all night, even though
he had to go to work the next morning.

"It was easier with my mother and
little brother."

Tommy then explained what happened after he reached out to his family: "I turned around and God was there. You were right. God found me."

3 When we are lost, how does God go about finding us?

THINK about it

It's not dying for faith that's so hard, it's living up to it.

William Makepeace Thackeray

Our faith journey

Listen! I stand at the door and knock; if any hear my voice and open the door, I will come into their house and eat with them, and they will eat with me. REVELATION 3:20

Every faith journey begins with a knock at the door of the heart. It may take the form of a spiritual hunger in the soul, a call to love in the heart, or some unforeseen event that turns our world upside down.

If we open the door, God will take us by the hand and lead us into the unknown. Then at some memorable moment, God will surprise and bless us beyond all of our expectations.

Three faith stages

Most faith journeys follow a path that leads the believer through three faith stages:

■ **Childhood stage   Cultural faith**
■ **Adolescent stage   Transitional faith**
■ **Adult stage   Convictional faith**

Childhood stage

The childhood stage is *cultural*, in the sense that, if we were born in Iran to Iranian parents, we'd probably begin life as a Muslim; if we were born of Lutheran parents, we would probably be Lutheran.

In other words, our childhood faith is conditioned by both our cultural situation and the faith—or lack of faith—of the family into which we are born and raised.

Adolescent stage

The adolescent stage is both the most critical and the most painful.

It is the most critical because it involves making the transition from receiving the "seed" of faith in baptism to "confirming" it by personal conviction. CCC 168

It is the most painful because our childhood faith must die before our adult faith can be born. That is, we must rid our faith of any simplistic or immature notions. This is what takes place in the adolescent stage. It is this process that causes the pain.

John Kirvan's book *The Restless Believers* contains a description of how the death of our childhood faith affects us. He quotes a young person as saying:

I don't know what's going wrong. When I was in grade school, and for the first couple of years of high school I was real religious, and now I just don't seem to care.

4 Have you ever felt this way? Explain.

The death of our childhood faith can make us feel sick of heart—even guilty. This is unfortunate because the truth of the matter is that we are only experiencing growth pains, which are a part of every "faith journey."

Adolescent questioning

The adolescent stage of our faith involves a good deal of questioning. When this questioning is done constructively, it results in faith growth.

5 What do we mean by "constructive questioning"?

First, constructive questioning fosters *faith clarity*. For example, we may have a view of God that needs to be revised. This was the case of a college student who told her professor, "I no longer believe in God." The professor said, "Good!" The student said, "Now what's that supposed to mean?"

The professor explained that many of us have childhood images of God that are simplistic and need to be clarified. CCC 158

Second, constructive questioning widens *faith horizons*. For example, we may think that science and the biblical story of creation are in conflict. Exploring the question, however, we learn that if the creation story and science are understood correctly, there is no conflict at all. CCC 159

6 How is the creation story often misunderstood by people?

Third, constructive questioning deepens *faith commitment*. Take the case of God again. Before our questioning, we may have prayed to God out of habit or fear. After our questioning, we may begin praying to God out of conviction and love.

In brief, *destructive* questioning means we want to disprove a point, so we can do what we want. *Constructive* questioning means we want to learn the truth, so we can do what is right. Constructive questioning does the following:

- **Fosters faith clarity**
- **Widens faith horizons**
- **Deepens faith commitment**

7 What are some questions you have about your faith?

Adult stage

The adult stage is clearly the important one. At this stage we appropriate the faith to ourselves. In other words, we move beyond an unexamined cultural faith to an examined, personal faith. An example is the Samaritan neighbors of the "woman at the well."

Many of the Samaritans in that town believed in Jesus
because the woman had said,
"He told me everything I have ever done."
So when the Samaritans came to him,
they begged him to stay with them,
and Jesus stayed there two days.

Many more believed because of his message, and told the woman, "We believe now,
not because of what you said,
but because we ourselves have heard him,
and we know that he is really
the Savior of the world. JOHN 4:39–42

8 How does this story illustrate what needs to take place at the adult stage of faith?

A reporter asked astronaut Ed White what personal items he took along with him on his Gemini-4 flight. He said one was a Saint Christopher medal, which Pope John XXIII gave each astronaut. White said: "I took it on the Gemini-4 flight to express my faith in myself, in Jim McDivitt, my partner, and especially in God." "Faith," he said, "was the most important thing I had going for me on the flight."

■ *What do you carry or wear that expresses your faith?*

■ *What faith do you find most challenging: faith in God, others, yourself? Explain.*

THINK
about it

Faith with works is a force.
Faith without works is a farce.

E. C. McKenzie

Our faith journey is the greatest adventure we will ever embark upon. This is because it takes us beyond the natural world to the supernatural. It leads us beyond material reality to spiritual reality.

We begin our faith journey by placing our hand in the hand of God and allowing ourselves to be led by both the light of reason and the light of faith, which is the safer light. CCC 154–55 Jesus spoke of this light when he said:

*"I will ask the Father
and he will give you . . . the Spirit,
who will stay with you forever. . . .
He is the Spirit,
who . . . will teach you everything
and make you remember
all that I have told you."* JOHN 14:16

And so our journey begins and moves forward toward that awesome faith encounter that brings us face to face with the mystery of the Holy Trinity. CCC 253–56

■ **Father**   **Who created us**
■ **Son**   **Who redeemed us**
■ **Holy Spirit**   **Who graces us**

Three faith levels

The Holy Spirit graces and guides us every step of the faith journey. It unfolds gradually and throughout our lives at three levels:

■ **Mind level**   **Openness to truth**
■ **Heart level**   **Openness to love**
■ **Soul level**   **Openness to grace**

Mind level

At the *mind* level, the Holy Spirit helps us to better grasp the truths of our faith. For example, we deepen our knowledge of God. The Russian mystic, Leo Tolstoy, had this in mind, by saying:

*When a savage
ceases to believe in his wooden God,
this does not mean there is no God,
but only that the true God
is not made of wood.*

In other words, by opening our minds to truth, we get a better grasp of who God is and what God is really like.

Heart level

At the *heart* level, the Holy Spirit leads us beyond our childhood world—with its focus on love of self—to an adult world, which looks to love of other people. In other words, by opening our hearts to a love of other people, we open our hearts to God.

We discover what Tommy realized; namely, that a failure or inability to find God is often traceable to a failure or inability to open our hearts to love other people and to receive love from them.

9 *What keeps me from opening my heart more fully to love—especially family love?*

Soul level

Lastly, there is the *soul* level. If our soul is open, the Holy Spirit will grace us abundantly, prepare us for faith, invite us to faith, and embrace us every step of the faith journey. CCC 153–54 This journey involves a mystery of:

- **Gift**   **God's contribution**
- **Freedom**   **Our contribution**

Faith is a gift from God. It cannot be "merited" or "won." Jesus himself made this clear. One day he said:

JESUS   *Who do people say I am?*

APOSTLES   *Some say John the Baptist. . . .*

JESUS   *What about you?*
                Who do you say I am?

PETER   *You are the Messiah,*
                the Son of the living God!

JESUS   *Good for you, Simon, son of*
                John. For this truth did not
                come to you from any human
                being, but it was given to you
                directly by my Father.
                MATTHEW 16:13–17

10 *How does this dialogue make it clear that faith is a gift from God?*

Faith involves "freedom" on our part. Although God graces us and guides us on our faith journey, God does this in a way that respects our free will. In other words, God leaves us free to accept or to reject the gift.

Three faith realities

This leads us to three realities that we must be prepared to embrace on our faith journey:

- **Loving trust**   **Risk**
- **Ongoing effort**   **Recommitment**
- **Suffering darkness** **Growth times**

Loving trust

An example of the kind of "loving trust" that faith requires is marriage. When two people join hands and promise to journey together on the road of life, there is no guarantee that each will remain faithful should a major crisis arise.

This is where loving trust comes in. Without it, there could be no marriage. Every marriage, by its very nature, involves a dimension of risk.

Faith is something like this. It too involves loving trust—not in the sense that God might be unfaithful (God is always faithful), but in the sense that we are not sure where our faith commitment to God will lead us. It is in this sense that faith involves risk and loving trust.

Abraham is a good example of the kind of risk and loving trust that a faith commitment to God involves. God said to Abraham:

"Leave your country,
your relatives,
and your father's home,
and go to a land
I am going to show you."
GENESIS 12:1

In other words, God was inviting Abraham to embrace a situation that involved both risk and loving trust. CCC 145–46

11 *What risk might God be asking of you?*

PRAYER
hotline

Dear Lord,
I believe in you
but I am so confused
about where I am going—
all I know
is where I've been.

I am so scared and
I have no one to talk to
but myself
and I hide my feelings
in my music.

Homeless youth. Quoted in
God, Please Save Me,
by Sr. Mary Rose McGready

John Newton was a British sea captain and slave trader. One night a great storm threatened his ship and his cargo of slaves. He promised to give up slave trade if his ship came through the storm. It did and he kept his promise. He wrote a hymn to celebrate his conversion. A part of it reads:

Amazing grace!
How sweet the sound,
that saved a wretch like me!
I once was lost
but now am found—
Was blind, but now I see. . . .

Through many dangers, toils,
and snares
I have already come;
'Tis grace hath brought me
safe thus far,
and grace will lead me home.

■ *Describe a time when you felt God's grace at work in you in a special way.*

Ongoing effort

A misunderstanding that some people have is the idea that once we "get the faith" we don't have to worry about it again. This is not the case. An example will illustrate. A person writes:

I made a five-day retreat.
On it, I committed my life to Jesus in a way that I had not anticipated.
This decision gave me deep peace and joy.

A week later,
I found myself doing something that was contrary to my faith.
I was profoundly disturbed.
How can I explain this?
Had I really committed myself to Jesus on the retreat?
Or had I merely deluded myself into thinking that I had?

12 *How would you answer these questions?*

The person's retreat experience illustrates what psychologists have always told us. The greater part of ourselves lies beneath our consciousness. It surfaces slowly and only gradually with each new experience.

This explains why faith involves *ongoing effort.* It's because we are constantly evolving and changing as persons. As a result, we must constantly recommit ourselves to God in harmony with our change and evolvement. It is by this process of recommitment that faith grows and matures. CCC 162

Suffering darkness

Finally, our faith is like the sun. Sometimes it shines brightly and everything is clear and beautiful. At other times it seems to go behind a cloud and disappear in darkness. You begin to wonder if it is even there. CCC 164–65 This darkness is usually traceable to one of three sources:

■ **Human nature**
■ **Ourselves**
■ **God**

Human nature

First, it may be caused by *human nature.* The darkness may simply reflect the natural mood swings of our human nature. On some days everything goes right and life is great. On other days everything goes wrong and life is a drag.

Ourselves

Our faith follows similar mood swings. Such swings simply go with the territory of being human.

Second, the darkness of faith may be of our own making. We can cause it by neglecting our faith. That is, we can let our faith grow weak from sin or lack of spiritual nourishment. In other words, just as our body grows weak from abuse or lack of nourishment, our soul does the same thing.

God

Third, the darkness of faith may be traceable to God. Just as God can use our physical suffering—regardless of what caused it—to help us grow and mature in our faith, so can God use spiritual suffering—like darkness—to help our faith grow and mature.

Abraham

Take the case of Abraham, again: When he was told to sacrifice his son Isaac, he was absolutely thunderstruck. The spiritual suffering this caused must have been close to unbearable.

Just as painful to Abraham was the dilemma that God's command posed. How could Abraham have descendants through Isaac—as God had promised he would—if Isaac were sacrificed?

Suddenly, Abraham felt his faith being challenged to the breaking point. Had he relied solely on the light of reason, his faith would have died right there and then.

Instead, Abraham trusted God and—in God's providence—his faith grew to a level he never dreamed to be possible. When it reached this level, God could do great things through him; and he did.

13 Which of the three sources of darkness is the most common cause of darkness? Why?

ART Connection

The great seventeenth-century Dutch painter Rembrandt spells out in living color God's command to Abraham:

*"Take Isaac,
whom you love so much,
and offer him
as a sacrifice to me."*

Genesis 22:2

LITERARY Connection

Faith darkness can cause deep spiritual agony. In his novel *The Devil's Advocate*, Morris West describes such an agony and the loss of faith that it occasioned. The character says:

*I groped for God
and could not find God.
I prayed to God. . . .
God did not answer.
I wept at night
for the loss of God. . . .
Then one day,
God was there again. . . .
I had a parent
and God knew me. . . .
I had never understood
'til this moment
the meaning of the words
"gift of faith."*

Slightly adapted

Recap   Review

The faith journey begins with God knocking at the door of the heart. The faith journey follows a path that leads through three stages:

- **Childhood stage   Cultural faith**
- **Adolescent stage   Transitional faith**
- **Adult stage   Convictional faith**

The faith journey involves *gift* and *freedom* and unfolds at three levels:

- **Mind level   Openness to truth**
- **Heart level   Openness to love**
- **Soul level   Openness to grace**

The faith journey also involves:

- **Loving trust   Risk**
- **Ongoing effort   Recommitment**
- **Suffering darkness   Growth times**

Constructive faith questioning:

- **Produces clarity   I see better**
- **Widens horizons   I see more**
- **Deepens commitment   I act more lovingly**

 1 Explain (a) the three stages through which faith passes as it grows, and (b) why the second stage is the most critical and painful.

2 List and explain the three ways constructive questioning fosters faith growth.

3 List and explain the threefold awesome mystery that we encounter and affirm on our faith journey.

4 List the three levels at which our faith journey takes place and what each level involves.

5 Explain in what sense faith involves the mystery of gift and freedom.

6 Explain in what sense the faith journey calls for: (a) loving trust, (b) ongoing effort, and (c) suffering darkness.

7 List and explain three sources to which the times of darkness on the faith journey are traceable.

Reflect

1 Ludolf Ulrich writes:

One night I was standing in the rain,
waiting for the bus. Up comes a man
who had had a bit too much to drink.
Tapping me on the chest
with an empty beer bottle, he asked,
"Do you believe in God?"

What a question to ask! Was it a joke?
Was he putting me on?
I ignored him, hoping he'd move on.
But he persisted.
Finally, I said, "Yes."
At this, I was ready for the worst—
a remark like, "Explain to me why!"

But he just stood there unsteadily,
looked me in the eye, and said,
"Man! Are you ever lucky!"

(PARAPHRASED)

■ *In what sense was the man right in saying,*
"Man! Are you ever lucky!"?
■ *What are some reasons you believe*
in God?

2 Dan Wakefield has won many awards for his writing (e.g., *TV Guide*, NBC TV, etc.). But none of these awards filled the void that he experienced after he had left God behind in college. To numb the pain caused by the void, he turned to drugs. When he began to turn back to God, the "return" road was not easy. A couple of times he turned back to drugs. In his book *Returning*, he writes:

Throughout all this I never lost faith in God,
never imagined he was not there.
It was just that his presence was obscured.
Then the storm broke like a fever,
and I felt in touch again. . . . I was grateful,
but I also knew that such storms . . .
would come again.

■ *How do you explain the "faith storms" that so*
many Christians seem to experience?
■ *How are you handling your own storms?*

3 The final day of school had ended. The students had gone home, and the building was as quiet as a tomb. A teacher was in her classroom picking up a few books that had been carelessly left behind. Randomly, she picked up a book that still looked useable. It opened to this quote by Morris West:

The sanctions of being a man
are so horrendous,
that it seems madness to try to relate them
to any kind of divine plan.
A cancer will eat your guts . . .
a drunken fool with an automobile
will mow you down . . .
The believers are the lucky ones . . .
But belief is a gift . . .
If you have not the gift,
you are thrust back on reason.

In the margin the student wrote, "Tell me how to go about getting this gift. I really need it."

■ *How would you answer the student?*

PRAYER TIME
with the Lord

Lord, I don't know if I know you or not.
They say you're closer to me
than I am to myself.
But that's not the way it seems to me.

Is this, perhaps, where I lose the trail?
Looking for you the way I picture you,
rather than the way you are?

Should I even look—
can the eye ever see the eye?
Could it be that while I walk in flesh,
you will never be a destination—
only a journey?
What if I found you?
That would be heaven!

But can heaven be on earth?
When does the quest cease to be
a question and become the answer?

Or, perhaps, that is it:
The question is the answer;
the search is the discovery.

For in searching, I am already there—
as "there" as any searcher can ever be. M.L.

■ *Compose a similar prayer to God. Begin with this sentence: "Lord, there's a question I'd like to ask you."*

PRAYER Journal

Each year nearly 50,000 homeless teenagers show up at some 20 Covenant Houses seeking housing, counseling, medicine, or food. Frequently, they leave prayers in the house chapel. Here is an example of one of the prayers found there:

Help me, Dear Lord,
as I travel towards You.
There are many detours
which will try to distract me from you. . . .

Help me, though I may fall,
to continue my journey towards You.
Help me, Dear Lord.
I want so much to be with You.
PLEASE HELP ME, GOD, Sister Mary Rose McGready

■ **Compose a prayer to God about some problem you are experiencing with, for example, faith, family, failure, the future.**

_____

_____

_____

_____

_____

_____

_____

_____

_____

_____

_____

_____

_____

_____

SCRIPTURE Journal

1	Opening to grace	John 1:35–51
2	Closing to grace	Matthew 19:16–26
3	Trusting in God	Genesis 22:1–19
4	Trusting in Jesus	Luke 5:1–11
5	Moments of darkness	Luke 24:13–35

■ *Pick one of the above passages.*
Read it prayerfully and write a short statement to Jesus expressing your feelings about it.

_____

_____

_____

_____

_____

_____

_____

Divine Revelation

Many people have done their best to write a report of the things that have taken place among us.

They wrote what we have been told by those who saw these things from the beginning and who proclaimed the message. . . .

Because I have carefully studied all these matters from their beginning, I thought it would be good to write an orderly account for you. LUKE 1:1–3

Divine revelation is the Trinity's response to the hunger in the human heart, to know God and God's plan for us. Revelation began with creation, reached completion in Jesus, and is passed on by Tradition and Scripture.

Ways of knowing God

A sailor was assigned to the gun crew on a small ship. He was given heat-resistant gloves and instructed to catch eighteen-inch shell casings as they ejected after each firing from the gun.

The reason for the gloves was that the casings were hot. The reason for catching them was to keep them from rolling around the gun pit and endangering the gun crew.

Suppose you were walking through a factory with a friend and you saw a workman wearing large gloves carrying a chunk of metal.

Your friend says, "I wonder why he's wearing such large gloves to carry such a small piece of metal." You explain to him that it's probably because the metal is hot. Your friend argues, "That metal certainly doesn't look hot. There must be another reason for the large gloves."

1 *What are three ways you could settle the argument?*

The argument about the large gloves leads to another argument that people have. To what extent can we apply the same "three ways of knowing whether or not metal is hot" to God? In other words, to what extent can we know God by:

- **Experiencing God**
- **Reasoning to God**
- **Believing another**

2 *How would you answer this question?*

Experiencing God

When astronaut James Irwin and his two team members blasted off for the moon on Apollo 15, he thought their goal was merely "to get some moon rocks and to take pictures of the moon's landscape."

What happened on the moon, however, changed his life forever. He writes in his book *To Rule the Night:*

*I wish I had been a writer or a poet
so that I could convey
more adequately the feeling of this flight.
It has been sort of a
slow-breaking revelation for me.*

*The ultimate effect
has been to deepen and strengthen
all the religious insight I ever had.
It has remade my faith. . . .*

*On the moon
the total picture of the power of God
and his Son Jesus Christ
became abundantly clear to me.*

Later, Irwin said in a public lecture:

*God became closer and closer to us
as we ventured
deeper and deeper into space. . . .
I felt the power of God
as I never felt it before.*

Because of the life-changing impact this experience had on Irwin, he was personally convinced that he had *experienced* God's hand touching his life.

Like Irwin, other people have had spiritual experiences that have had a life-changing impact on them. Similarly, they too believe they experienced the touch of God.

3 *What would be some reasons why you would/would not agree that Irwin had experienced God?*

The human heart was born with a "longing" or "hunger" for God. How did this longing get into the heart?

In *Man Does Not Stand Alone,* A. Cressy Morrison cites an example that points to a possible answer.

He tells how eels swim thousands of miles from Europe and America to Bermuda. There they breed, give birth, and die. Then some instinct or "inner longing" prompts their offspring to swim back across the same ocean in search of the river or lake from which their parent came.

The eel's "inner longing" for its true "home" is not unlike the "inner longing" that leads the heart to search for God who created it and put the "inner longing" in it.

■ *How do people experience a longing for God?*

THINK
about it

Follow the longing
in your heart.
It will lead you to Jesus,
just as the star
led the Magi to Jesus.

Reasoning to God

Wernher von Braun has been dubbed "the twentieth-century Columbus" of space travel. More than any other scientist, he was responsible for putting us on the moon.

Born in Germany, he and his team of scientists surrendered to the Allies near the end of World War II. They were sent to the United States. There he became the director of Alabama's Marshall Space Flight Center. Before he died, he wrote:

*The natural laws of the universe
are so precise that we have no difficulty
building a spaceship to fly to the moon,
and we can time the flight
with the precision
of a fraction of a second. . . .
Anything . . . so precisely balanced . . .
can only be the product of a Divine Idea.*
UNPUBLISHED LECTURE

Von Braun's words echo the inspired words of Saint Paul in his letter to the Romans. He comes to a similar conclusion:

*Ever since God created the world,
his invisible qualities,
both his external power
and his divine nature,
have been clearly seen;
they are perceived in the things
that God has made.* ROMANS 1:20

Faith in God

Many people believe that we can know God from experience and reason. Others are not so sure. Most,

however, agree that the surest way to know God is through God's own revelation to the human race. CCC 31–38

Dr. Warren Weaver, the author of several books on mathematical science, says:

*I think a scientist
has a real advantage in any struggle
to conceive and believe in God.
For he is expert in seeing the unseeable and
in believing in the essentially undefinable.*

Weaver gives this example to illustrate: No scientist has succeeded in seeing or really defining an electron. For a while they thought of it as a particle, and then as a wave. Now they think of it as both or either. "Electron," says Dr. Weaver, "is simply the name for a consistent set of things that happen in certain circumstances."

4 *Do you tend to be more comfortable with experiencing God or reasoning to God? Why?*

Divine revelation

The word *revelation* is derived from the Latin word meaning "to unveil." Divine revelation is the "unveiling" of God and God's plan to the human race. CCC 50–67

*This plan, which God will complete
when the time is right,
is to bring all creation together,
everything in heaven and earth
with Christ as head.* EPHESIANS 1:10

Revelation began in Old Testament times through such figures as Abraham and Moses. It reached completion in New Testament times in the life and teaching of Jesus. Saint Paul summed up God's revelation to us this way:

God spoke to our ancestors many times
and in many ways through the prophets;
but in these last days,
he has spoken to us through his Son.
HEBREWS 1:1–2

Before ascending to heaven, Jesus gave this commission to his disciples:

"Go . . . to all peoples everywhere
and make them my disciples:
Baptize them in the name of
the Father, the Son, and the Holy Spirit,
and teach them everything
I have commanded you." MATTHEW 28:19–20

With the coming of the Holy Spirit, the life and teaching of Jesus became the foundation and norm for our own Catholic faith. It is this divine revelation that the apostles, guided by the Holy Spirit, passed on to their successors, the bishops of the Church. CCC 74–79

Handing on revelation

We may think of divine revelation as having two stages: immediate and mediate.

By immediate revelation we mean the unveiling or communication of God and God's plan to God's people in biblical times.

By mediate revelation we mean the transmission of divine revelation to future generations. This is done in two ways, by:

- **Sacred Tradition**   **Oral word**
- **Sacred Scripture**   **Written word**

Sacred Scripture and Sacred Tradition are like two rails of a railroad track. They are inseparable, working together at all times to transmit God's Word to all people of all ages. CCC 80–83

Let us now take a closer look at Sacred Tradition, the oral communication of divine revelation.

Margaret Mehren

Margaret Mehren was 15 when she joined the Nazi youth movement in Germany. After the war she learned of the Nazi atrocities and was shocked. She realized that Hitler was not the glorious leader she thought he was.

It was in this frame of mind that she also began having doubts about her atheism. One night she picked up a Bible to read. But it made no sense, so she put it down. Some time later, she picked it up again. This time she opened to the Gospels. She wrote:

Something happened to me
when I read the words of Jesus.
I knew he was alive. . . .
I knew he was there in the room
with me,
even though I couldn't hear
or see anything. Jesus was real,
more real than anything
around me—
the furniture, my books,
the potted plants.
I was no longer alone.

A few years later, at age 21, she became a Franciscan nun and missionary to Africa.

Terry Anderson was kidnapped by Shiite Muslim extremists in 1985. He spent the next seven years in Lebanon in windowless cells, often in chains and in pain.

In December 1987, he nearly lost it, banging his head against a wall until blood oozed out. After his release in 1992, he remarked that some cynics deny God's existence, saying:

We made him up out of our need.
I only say that once in
my own need.
I felt a light and warm
and loving touch
that eased my soul
and banished doubt
and let me go on to the end.

It is not proof—there can be none.
Faith is what you have when
you're alone and find you're not.

Media interview

■ **Explain the two points in the last paragraph.**

■ **What is the closest thing to such an experience that you've had?**

Sacred Tradition

Toward the end of his gospel, Saint John refers to Sacred Tradition this way:

There are many other things that Jesus did. If they were all written down one by one, I suppose that the whole world could not hold the books. JOHN 21:25

In other words, not everything that Jesus did or taught got written down. Saint Paul makes the same point about his own teaching. Some things he taught through word of mouth (preaching) and some things through writing (letters). He writes:

Hold on to those truths
which we taught you,
both in our preaching [Tradition]
and in our letter [Scripture].
2 THESSALONIANS 2:15

The first community of Christians began with no written gospels. They simply passed on God's Word orally.

This brings us to the written form of communication of divine revelation.

Sacred Scripture

At first, the things that Jesus said and did were passed on almost entirely by word of mouth. Only later were they written down. This is clear from the Gospels themselves.

For example, Saint Matthew says that after Jesus rose from the tomb on Easter morning, the guards were paid to say that the disciples stole his body while they were asleep. He then adds: "And so that is the report spread around by the Jews to this very day." MATTHEW 28:15

5 *How does the final sentence indicate a significant time lapse between the event and the recording of it?*

And so, the four Gospels passed through three stages in the process of

reaching the form they now have today. CCC 126 These stages are:

■ **Life**   **What Jesus said and did**
■ **Oral**   **What apostles preached**
■ **Written**   **What evangelists wrote**

John refers explicitly to all three stages when he writes in his First Letter:

What we have seen [life stage] . . .
we announce to you [oral stage]. . . .
We write this in order [written stage]
that our joy may be complete.
1 JOHN 1:3–4

An analogy might help to illustrate these three stages: life, oral, and written.

The ocean floor is littered with thousands of seashells. In time some of these *floor* shells wash up onto the beach.

One day an artist is out walking and sees the *beach* shells. She picks up the most beautiful ones, takes them home and shapes them into a lovely *vase*.

6 *Which gospel stages do the following shells correspond to and why: floor, beach, vase? Explain.*

Divine inspiration

The novel *The Last Temptation of Christ,* by Nikos Kazantzakis, portrays Matthew sitting at a table with an open notebook. Jesus enters. Matthew shows him the notebook, saying, "Rabbi, here I recount your works."

After reading a few lines, Jesus asks, "Who told you these things?" Matthew replies, "The angel." Jesus asks, "What angel?" Matthew replies, "The one who comes each night, as I take up my pen to write. He dictates what I should write."

This brings us to the question of divine inspiration. CCC 100–106 Saint Paul says, "All Scripture is inspired by God." 2 TIMOTHY 3:16 When we think of divine inspiration, we have to avoid two extremes.

We should not imagine that the Holy Spirit dictated to the biblical writer as an executive might dictate an important letter. Nor should we imagine that the Holy Spirit has acted simply as a kind of "watchdog" keeping the biblical writers from making mistakes as they wrote.

Rather, we should envision inspiration as the Holy Spirit working in and through the personal talents of the biblical writers to communicate all and only what God wanted to say through them.

7 *In what sense may we say Sacred Scripture is "the Word of God in the Words of Men"?*

Inerrancy of Scripture

Although Sacred Scripture contains many accurate historical facts and descriptions that reflect the times and events of the day, this was not its goal.

Rather, guided by the Holy Spirit, its goal was to interpret the spiritual meaning of the events of the day. As a result, like Sacred Tradition, it is free from religious error, that is, *in matters related to salvation.* CCC 107–8

THINK about it

**A thumbprint in the Bible
is more important
than a footprint on the moon.**

E. C. McKenzie

ART Connection

This seventeenth-century painting was done by Italian painter Caravaggio. It portrays Saint Jerome translating the Bible into Latin.

BIBLE Connection

People ask, "Do we have the original biblical manuscripts?" The answer is no.

Remarkably, the oldest copies we have were found in caves near Qumran on the northwest corner of the Dead Sea. The discovery of these "Dead Sea Scrolls" reads like a novel.

While searching for a stray goat, a boy came upon a hole in a hillside. When he threw a stone through it, he heard something break. It turned out to be a tall jar containing an ancient scroll of the Book of Isaiah.

The boy's discovery touched off a hunt for more scrolls in more caves. Between 1947 and 1956, eleven caves yielded 800 documents (mostly fragments). Some 200 were documents of practically every book of the Hebrew Bible.

Interpretation of Scripture

Shortly before ascending to his Father in heaven, Jesus made a remarkable promise to his disciples. He said:

*"When . . . the Spirit comes,
who reveals the truth about God,
he will lead you into all the truth."*
JOHN 16:13

By these words, Jesus assured his disciples that the Holy Spirit would assist them in interpreting, recording, formulating, and transmitting divine revelation to future generations.

This brings us to the important task of interpreting God's Word.

The Church, or community of Jesus' followers, gave birth to Sacred Scripture, so to speak. Therefore, the awesome responsibility of preserving and interpreting Scripture falls to the Church, guided by the Holy Spirit. CCC 109–19

8 *From a purely natural point of view, why is it logical that the Church be the interpreter of Sacred Scripture?*

Canon of Scripture

As used in the Bible, the word canon refers to the official list of books inspired by God. Therefore, these books are the "measuring stick," or norm, for our Christian faith.

The same Holy Spirit who guided the writing of Scripture also guided the Church in the selection of the biblical canon. CCC 120 Most Christian Churches agree on the New Testament canon, but not fully on the Old Testament canon. The reason goes back before Jesus' birth.

Between 300 and 150 B.C., the Old Testament was translated into Greek. This was because many Jews living outside Israel no longer spoke Hebrew. The Greek translation was called the *Septuagint* ("seventy") after the number of Jewish scholars legend says were involved in the project.

Christians (most of whom spoke Greek) adopted the Septuagint as their accepted Old Testament text. New Testament writers—like Matthew, Mark, Luke, and John—quoted from it over three hundred times.

The Septuagint contained seven books and parts of two others that modern Jews omit from their official canon:

- **Judith**
- **Tobit**
- **1–2 Maccabees**
- **Wisdom**
- **Sirach**
- **Baruch**
- **Esther**
  (long version)
- **Daniel**
  (long version)

Ancient Jews living in Israel gradually distanced themselves from Jews who spoke only Greek and from the Septuagint as well.

Decades after Jesus' ascension, the Jews in Israel adopted a new canon, omitting the books listed above. Modern Jews and modern Protestants follow the later Palestinian listing; Catholics follow the original Septuagint listing.

Around A.D. 400, Saint Jerome translated the Septuagint into Latin. The first complete English translation of the Bible came in the fourteenth century.

ARCHAEOLOGICAL
Connection

This scroll fragment from the Book of Isaiah was found in a cave near the Dead Sea. It dates from long before Jesus' birth.

Stitch marks (right side) show where the segments (made of animal skin) were joined and sewn.

Recap

Review

Divine revelation is God's self-communication to the human race:

- **Immediately**   **To people in biblical times**
- **Mediately**   **To people of all times**

Mediate revelation involves the "handing on" of God's Word through:

- **Sacred Tradition**   **Spoken word**
- **Scripture**   **Written word**

Mediate and immediate revelation take place under the guidance of the Holy Spirit and, therefore, are:

- **Inspired**   **The Word of God in the words of human beings**

- **Inerrant**   **Free from religious error in matters relating to salvation**

1 List and briefly explain the three ways by which we can learn things.

2 What made astronaut James Irwin conclude that his spiritual experience on the Apollo 15 mission was truly an experience of God?

3 What convinced Werhner von Braun that the universe was created by God?

4 Explain (a) divine revelation, (b) immediate revelation, and (c) mediate revelation.

5 List and briefly explain the two ways divine revelation is transmitted to future generations.

6 How are (a) Sacred Tradition and (b) Sacred Scripture like the two rails of a train track, and how does Paul refer to each?

7 List and briefly explain (a) the three stages the four Gospels passed through to reach the form they now have today, and (b) how John refers to them.

8 List and briefly explain (a) the two extremes to avoid in how we envision divine inspiration, and (b) how we ought to envision it.

9 From what error is Scripture free?

10 What is the Septuagint, and how does it help to explain why the Catholic Bible differs from the Protestant Bible?

Reflect

1 It was a peaceful evening.
My mom and brother and sister and I
Were on our way
To a high school basketball game. . . .
It was quiet in the car. . . .
I was just looking out the window
at the still night, enjoying the stars . . .
happy to be on my way to the game.
The happiness that I was feeling
grew deeper and . . . I noticed that tears
were rolling down my cheeks.
This was really weird. . . . Then I understood.
This was how full joy could be . . .
a joy that comes only from God.

JACQUE BRAMAN, QUOTED IN *HOW CAN I FIND GOD?*

A study showed that certain situations were more likely than others to trigger a religious experience in us (e.g., awareness of God's presence). Four such situations were:

a. Reading the Bible
b. Contemplating nature
c. Meditating quietly
d. Listening to music

■ *List the above four situations in the order that you have found they are more apt to trigger an awareness of God in you.*
■ *List one or two other situations that tend to do it.*
■ *Describe a situation when this happened.*

2 Father Francis F. Buckley, S.J., teaches theology at the University of San Francisco. He writes:

One of the ways
my students have surprised me
is that they find God in failure
more than in success or beauty.
The death of a parent or relative,
the breakup of a love affair,
the loss of a game or a job are
for them windows of discovery.

■ *Why would failures lead students to God more than success or beauty?*
■ *To what extent is this true of you? Explain.*
■ *Describe a concrete time when a major failure or tragedy helped you to find God or led you to experience God in a special way.*

3 Suppose a TV camera crew got into a time machine and flew back into history to Jesus' time. Suppose the crew filmed Jesus' entire life, fed it into a computer, and programmed it. By keyboarding the name of any event, you could bring it up on a monitor and see and hear exactly what the Apostles saw and heard.

Now suppose you are given this choice. You can trade the four printed Gospels (as we now have them) for the computerized film. If you traded, however, the human race would lose the four printed Gospels forever. They would be totally destroyed and replaced by the film.

■ *Why would/wouldn't you make that trade?*
■ *List some of the advantages and disadvantages that a film of Jesus' life would have.*

PRAYER TIME
with the Lord

In flights of wild fantasy,
I've streaked across the sky,
tunneled the clouds,
and touched the stars.

In daring flights of ecstasy,
I've fled my craft,
danced on the wind,
and painted rainbows in the sky.

I've stowed away on meteors,
explored the Milky Way,
and planted my own flag
on the moon.

I've talked with eagles
and followed flights of birds
to worlds you've never dreamed of.

Laughing in symphony with thunder,
and skipping rope
with lightning bolts,
I've fled my skin and walked
and talked with God. M.L.

■ *Compose a few paragraphs about what you would say to God in a situation like this.*

PRAYER *Journal*

Cardinal John Henry Newman wrote a prayer that focused on God's intimacy in dealing with us:

God knows what is in me,
all my peculiar feelings and thoughts . . .

God sympathizes with me in my hopes
and temptations. . . .

God hears my voice,
the beating of my heart and my breathing.

I do not love myself
more than God loves me.

I cannot shrink from pain
more than God dislikes my bearing it.

SLIGHTLY ADAPTED AND TRANSPOSED
INTO THE FIRST PERSON.

■ **Write a similar prayer about God. Make it as practical and down-to-earth as you can.**

SCRIPTURE *Journal*

1	Reasoning to God	Romans 1:20–25
2	Experiencing God	Genesis 3:1–17
3	Believing in God	John 20:24–29
4	Recording Scripture	Luke 1:1–4
5	Scripture is inspired	2 Timothy 3:14–4:5

■ *Pick one of the above passages.*
Read it prayerfully and write a short statement to Jesus expressing your feelings about it.

I n the beginning,
when God created the universe,
the earth was formless and desolate.
The raging ocean that covered everything
was engulfed in total darkness, and
the Spirit of God
was moving over the water.

Then God commanded,
"Let there be light"—and light appeared.
GENESIS 1:1–3

**The Old Testament
begins with the Trinity
creating the universe,
placing in it people with free will,
and inviting them
to share their life and love forever.
When sin disrupts that plan,
the Trinity sets in motion
an even more incredible plan.**

Interpreting the Bible

T he Bible begins with the story of
creation. It unfolds over a period
of seven days. Typical of the poetic way
it is described, is the first day:

God commanded,
"Let there be light"—
and light appeared.
God was pleased with what he saw.
Then he separated
the light from the darkness,
and he named the light "day"
and the darkness "night."
Evening passed and morning came—
That was the first day. GENESIS 1:3–5

When we continue reading and come
to the fourth day, an interesting question is raised. The fourth day reads:

Then God commanded,
"Let lights appear in the sky
to separate day from night . . .
and it was done. . . .
And God was pleased with what he saw.
Evening passed and morning came—
That was the fourth day. GENESIS 1:14–19

The question is this: If God did not
create the "lights in the sky" until the
fourth day, how could there be light on
the first day?

**1 How would you respond to this
question?**

As we continue reading the creation story, we come to the sixth day. It portrays God creating people last, after having created all other things.

Moving on to the second chapter of the Book of Genesis, we run into another problem. The second chapter opens with a "second creation story." It portrays God creating people first, contradicting the "first creation story." The second story reads:

When the LORD God made the universe, there were no plants on the earth and no seeds. . . .

Then the LORD God took some soil from the ground and formed a man. . . . Then the LORD God planted a garden. . . .

Then the LORD God said, "It is not good for the man to live alone. I will make a suitable companion for him."

So he took some soil from the ground and formed all the animals and birds. Then he brought them to the man to see what he would name them; and that is how they all got their names.

So the man named all the birds and all the animals; but not one of them was a suitable companion to help him. Then God formed the woman out of [a rib taken from the man].
GENESIS 2:1–8, 18–21

This raises two questions: Which of the two creation stories is correct? Did God create people first or last?

2 *How would you answer this question?*

Apparent contradictions in the Bible, like the two mentioned above, led one woman to say, "The Bible is responsible for more atheism and agnosticism than any other book ever written."

The question of "apparent contradictions" raises the subject of biblical interpretation.

We may divide Bible readers into two main groups: *literalists* and *contextualists*.

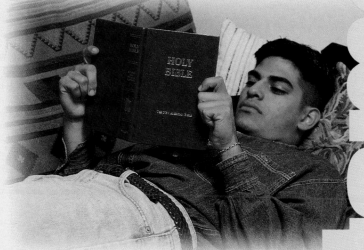

Literalists

Literalists focus exclusively on the *text* of the Bible. They say the Bible "means exactly what it says." There is some disagreement, however, among these literalists.

For example, members of the Church of God say that we must interpret the word *day* to mean exactly twenty-four hours. Jehovah's Witnesses, on the other hand, say that we may interpret *day* to mean "era"—as in the *day* or *era* of Lincoln.

Thus, Church of God members, following a strict biblical timetable, hold that creation took place in the year 4004 B.C. People ask: "How can you hold this when science proves the earth is millions of years old?"

Many books of the Old Testament are hard to classify. Nevertheless, using the classification of the New American Bible, we may list its 46 books (45, if we combine Jeremiah and Lamentations) as follows:

Pentateuch—5

(plus 3 special books)

Genesis

Exodus	Special books
Leviticus	Joshua
Numbers	Judges
Deuteronomy	Ruth

Wisdom—7

Job	Song of Songs
Psalms	Wisdom
Proverbs	Sirach
Ecclesiastes	

Historical—13

1, 2 Samuel	Ezra
1, 2 Kings	Tobit
1, 2 Chronicles	Judith
1, 2 Maccabees	Esther
Nehemiah	

Prophetic—18

Isaiah	Habakkuk
Obadiah	Daniel
Jeremiah	Zephaniah
Jonah	Hosea
Lamentations	Haggai
Micah	Joel
Baruch	Zechariah
Nahum	Amos
Ezekiel	Malachi

Literal interpreters answer: "The very first paragraph of the creation story holds the key. It suggests that the heavens and the earth *already existed* before God began his six days of work. The six days, therefore, refer to the preparation of earth for human habitation."

Even if we grant this interpretation, which most scholars will not, this still leaves a problem. How do we explain the existence of fossils and bones that scientists say are millions of years old? Shouldn't they also be 6,000 years old, if God created them?

Literalists give various answers. Among them is the blunt statement: "The scientists are wrong!"

3 *How do you feel about all this?*

This brings us to the second group of readers and how they interpret the Bible.

Contextualists

Contextualists say we must focus on both the text and the context of the Bible. For example, we must take into account the historical context in which a certain story or passage was written. This is especially true of the early chapters of the Book of Genesis. CCC 109–114

These early chapters deal with *prehistory,* that fuzzy era between the appearance of people and the recording of their stories.

Let us now take a closer look at how contextualists interpret the first creation story.

Creation

As we read the description of each day of creation, we find that each description follows relatively the same fourfold pattern:

- **Command**   Let there be light
- **Execution**   Light appeared
- **Reaction**   God was pleased
- **Conclusion**   Evening passed

4 *What does this fourfold pattern suggest about the writing style used by the biblical author and how he intended us to interpret his account?*

What is true of each day is true also of each week of creation. It, too, follows a pattern:

- **Three days**   **Creation & Separation**
  (light/darkness, water/water, water/land)
- **Three days**   **Creation & Population**
  (sky, water, land)
- **One day**   **Celebration**
  (rest & blessing)

These literary patterns suggest that we are dealing with a special kind of writing. It is not the kind you will find in a science book or a newspaper report. CCC 337 Rather, it is the kind of *poetic* writing you will find in children's books. Poetic stories are enjoyable to listen to, easy to remember, and easy to repeat.

It is this kind of poetic writing that the Genesis writer used to teach people about God and creation. (Recall that most ancients could not read or write. They learned by listening.)

Four religious truths

A study of the creation story reveals that it teaches four *religious* truths that would have been considered revolutionary at the time the Bible was composed:

- **God is one**
- **God planned creation**
- **God created everything good**
- **God made the Sabbath holy**

5 *In what sense do you think these four truths were revolutionary at the time the Bible was composed?*

God is one

L et us take a look at the *first* religious truth and why it was revolutionary. We need to consider not only the biblical *text*, but also the historical and cultural *context* in which it was written.

The first creation story was recorded at a time when people worshiped many gods. The Old Testament refers to this, saying:

"Do not sin by making for yourselves
an idol in any form at all—
whether man or woman,
animal or bird, reptile or fish.
Do not be tempted to worship and serve . . .
the sun, the moon, and the stars."

DEUTERONOMY 4:15–19

T im Anderson and two friends were driving home from Connecticut to Chicago during one of the coldest winters on record.

Tim dropped off a friend in Fort Wayne and took a back road to the tollway. Miles from nowhere, his car died. No lights could be seen anywhere. As the cold invaded the car, the two boys began to pray. Suddenly, lights appeared: a tow truck. It took them back to Fort Wayne.

Tim ran in to get cash for the tow fee. When he came out, no tow truck was in sight—and only tire tracks in the snow were their own. To this day the boys believe an angel answered their prayer.

The Church teaches that angels are part of God's *unseen* creation. We pray at Mass: "We believe in one God . . . maker of heaven and earth, of all that is seen and unseen." Scripture portrays angels as God's *servants* and *messengers*. Thus, an angel stops Abraham from sacrificing Isaac. GENESIS 22:11 "What are angels, then? They are spirits who serve God and are sent by him to help those who are to receive salvation." HEBREWS 1:14

This brings us to Satan and "fallen" angels. They were created good, but became evil by choice. 2 PETER 2:4 They opposed Jesus throughout his ministry, trying to keep him from replacing "Satan's kingdom" with "God's Kingdom."

MARK 3: 20–27

One summer night Abraham Lincoln and Gilbert Greene were out walking. Greene later wrote: "As we walked along, Lincoln turned his eyes to the sky full of stars and told me their names." Lincoln ended up saying:

I never behold them
that I do not feel
that I am looking
in the face of God.
I can see
how it might be possible
to look down upon earth
and be an atheist,
but I cannot conceive
how he could
look up into the heavens
and say there is no God.

■ *Where do you see God's "face" easiest in our world? Explain.*

Earth's crammed with heaven,
And every common bush
aflame with God;
And only he who sees
takes off his shoes—
The rest sit round it
and pluck blackberries.

E. B. Browning, Aurora Leigh

The biblical writer portrays the one true God creating the false "gods" that ancients worshiped.

His point is clear. If God created them, they cannot be God. Rather, there is only one God, the one who created them. CCC 293, 338 We may sum up the first biblical teaching this way:

■ **Old teaching**   **Many gods**
■ **New teaching**   **One God**
■ **How taught**   **God creates gods**

God planned creation

This brings us to the *second* religious truth and why it was so revolutionary. To appreciate this, we need to recall that the creation story was written at a time when people believed the world happened by chance. (Some people still believe this.)

Against this background the biblical writer portrays God creating the world in an orderly way. CCC 295, 299

The writer's point, again, is clear. God created the world by plan, not by chance. We may sum up the second teaching this way:

■ **Old teaching**   **Creation by chance**
■ **New teaching**   **Creation by plan**
■ **How taught**   **God follows plan**

6 *From a practical viewpoint, what convinces you most that the world is not the product of chance?*

God created everything good

To understand the *third* truth, we need, again, to consider its *context*. It was recorded at a time when many people believed parts of creation were evil.

For example, they believed the human body was evil because it seemed to war against the human spirit.

Against this background, the biblical writer has God affirm the goodness of all things, including the human body. CCC 299, 339 We may sum up the third truth this way:

■ **Old teaching**   **Creation part good**
■ **New teaching**   **Creation is all good**
■ **How taught**   **God says it is good**

7 *In what sense does the human body seem to war against the human spirit?*

God blessed the Sabbath

Finally, the story was written at a time when the Sabbath was treated as any other day. Against this background, the biblical writer portrays God as blessing the Sabbath and resting on this day. CCC 345–49

His point is this: God fashioned the Sabbath to be a day of rest and prayer:

■ **Old teaching**   **Sabbath is ordinary**
■ **New teaching**   **Sabbath is special**
■ **How taught**   **God blesses it**

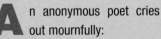

Second creation story

This brings us back to the second creation story and the questions it raises concerning the order in which God created people: first or last.

The key lies in how the Bible came to be recorded. From the Bible itself we learned that parts of it were passed on orally long before they were written down.

Clearly, there were two creation stories that were handed down orally. When the time came to record them, the biblical writer simply recorded both.

A closer study of the two creation stories shows that the biblical writer preserved both stories for a very good reason. They complement each other. They do this, especially, in two ways.

The second story, as we saw earlier, portrays God creating man much as a potter goes about making a vase. We read: "The LORD God took some soil from the ground and formed a man."

When God succeeded in forming the body exactly the way he wanted it, God breathed into it "life-giving breath." GENESIS 2:7

This image stresses the intimate relationship between God and humans. CCC 299 It is a relationship that is more intimate than the relationship of a mother to a child. The LORD says:

"Even if a mother should forget her child, I will never forget you! I have written your name on the palms of my hands." ISAIAH 49:15–16

The second story ends portraying God making woman from the side of man. Like many ancient societies, Hebrew society was dominated by men. Women were valued primarily as bearers of children (especially males: workers and warriors).

Many contextualists read the second story as a correction of the ancient social structure. CCC 383 It affirms the equality of men and women. They share the same flesh and bone. GENESIS 2:23

Thus, the second creation story complements the first story in two ways. It affirms:

- **The intimacy of God and people**
- **The equality of the sexes**

An anonymous poet cries out mournfully:

In the beginning was the earth, and the earth was beautiful. But the people living on it said, "Let us build skyscrapers and expressways." So they paved the earth with concrete and said, "It is good!"

On the second day, the people looked at the rivers and said, "Let us dump our sewage into the waters." So they filled the waters with sludge and said, "It is good!"

On the third day, the people looked at the forest and said, "Let us cut down the trees and build things." So they leveled the forests and said, "It is good!"

On the fourth day, the people saw the animals and said, "Let us kill them for sport and money." So they destroyed the animals and said, "It is good!"

On the fifth day, the people felt the cool breeze and said, "Let us burn our garbage and let the breeze blow it away." So they filled the air with carbon and said, "It is good!"

On the sixth day, the people saw other nations on earth and said, "Let us build missiles in case misunderstandings arise." So they filled the land with missile sites and said, "It is good!"

On the seventh day, the earth was quiet and deathly silent, for the people were no more. And it was good!

Years ago there was a popular TV program called Mork and Mindy. Mork, played by Robin Williams, was an alien who had remarkable power.

One day he shared some of this power with a few of his friends on earth. Touching his fingertips to theirs, he transferred just a little bit to them. Right away they began using it to make people do ridiculous things, like turn cartwheels and leap up and down.

Mork was horrified and shouted, "Stop! You're misusing the power. Give it back!" That episode is a good illustration of what sin is—misusing the power and talents that God has shared with us.

■ *List some ways you see your friends misuse their talents or abuse God's gifts. What are some ways you yourself do this?*

De-creation

The famous naturalist Henry David Thoreau was watching loggers level a forest of beautiful trees. He later wrote: "Thank God, they cannot cut down the clouds."

8 What do you think Thoreau had in mind?

In many parts of our world, commercial interests are threatening our environment. For example, in certain areas, industrial wastes are pouring into the earth's atmosphere to the point that clouds are producing acid rain.

Similar wastes are pouring into the earth's upper atmosphere at such a rate that its ozone layer is eroding. This

erosion has reached such an extent that it could become a threat to the future of our planet. CCC 2414–18

This devastation of our planet has been referred to as "de-creation," the physical destruction of God's creation. But tragic as it is, there is an even worse de-creation taking place: a spiritual one.

This "de-creation" has its origin in the human heart. It consists in misusing the free will that God gave us. Traditionally, we refer to spiritual de-creation as sin.

Sin

People are reluctant to talk about sin today. They are even more reluctant to admit that they sin. This reluctance has a lot of people concerned.

9 Why would so many people today be reluctant to talk about sin? To admit sin?

We will discuss sin in more detail later. For the present, it will help to make some preliminary observations. We may describe sin as a fracture or a total break in our love relationship with God and God's people. CCC 1849–52 We may think of sin as falling into two general categories: personal and social.

Personal sin

In John Steinbeck's novel *East of Eden,* one of his characters says:

*A man, after he has brushed off
the dusts and chips of life,
will have left only one hard clean question:
Was it good or was it evil?
Have I done well or ill?*

Steinbeck is talking about *personal* sin: the free act of a single individual. CCC 1868 This act takes two forms:

- **Commission**   **Doing bad**
- **Omission**   **Not doing good**

10 *Do you think people sin more through omission than through commission? Why?*

Social sin

The second category of sin is called social sin because it involves the collective behavior of a group of people, like a nation. CCC 1869 It also takes two forms: commission and omission.

A social sin of commission occurs when a group of people discriminates against a minority group in its midst. A social sin of omission occurs when a nation ignores its poor and homeless or lets industry pollute the environment.

Social sin is especially destructive because no one person feels responsible for it. Social sin is something "society" does, not something "I" do. Touching on this attitude, Dr. Martin Luther King said: "Whoever accepts evil without protesting against it is really cooperating with it."

Social evil is tolerated for many reasons. For example, people excuse themselves from responsibility, saying that their isolated opposition is too tiny to make a difference.

11 *How would you respond to this excuse?*

Regardless of the excuse, the bottom line on social sin is this: The responsibility to oppose it rests with individuals. Whoever shirks this responsibility is guilty of a *personal* sin of omission.

Origin of sin

Lance Morrow of *Time* magazine suggests there should be a TV character called "Dark Willard." This "sick" newscaster would begin each morning reciting the morning "evil" report. On the wall behind Willard would be a big map with ugly blotches. These blotches would indicate the places where "evil" defeated "good" during the night: crime in America, floods in India, war in the East.

The widespread presence of evil in our world poses a vexing question: If God created everything good, where did evil come from?

12 *What answer would you give to this question?*

The Bible answers the question with a series of "sin stories." We may call them the "de-creation" stories—stories of the victory of evil over good.

The biblical writer begins these sin stories with the account of a snake tempting Adam and Eve. The snake talks them into "eating" a fruit that God forbade them to eat, explaining:

"When you eat it, you will be like God
and know what is good
and what is bad . . ."
As soon as they had eaten it,
they were given understanding and
realized that they were naked. . . .

So the LORD God
sent them out of the Garden of Eden
and made them cultivate the soil
from which they had been formed.
GENESIS 3:5, 7, 23

Years ago, Dr. Norman MacDonald addressed a group of anthropologists gathered in Chicago from around the world. In the course of his address, he gave this gloomy assessment of human nature:

*Man has been violent
since his remote ape-like
ancestors descended from trees
and there is little prospect
that his innate desire to kill
for dominance
will ever change. . . .*

*We have to face the truth
and accept one basic,
unpleasant fact. . . .
Biologically, man is a killer. . . .*

*From the time he fashioned
a club as his first weapon,
man has insisted on developing
more powerful weapons. . . .
that now, instead of killing
individuals or groups,
he can annihilate a planet.*

■ *To what extent do you agree or disagree with MacDonald's assessment?*

■ *Which of the following statements best expresses your feelings about people and why? They are:
(a) basically evil, but society civilizes them;
(b) basically good; society corrupts them.*

Symbolic story

Contextualists interpret this story the same way they interpret the creation story. Like the parables that Jesus told, it is a *symbol* story.

This particular story was created by the biblical writer to answer the question "How did evil enter the world?" The key to the story lies in understanding two major symbols:

■ **The snake**
■ **Eating of the forbidden fruit**

The key symbol is the snake. To understand it we must keep in mind the context in which it was written.

Symbolic meaning

Archaeology reveals that snakes played a bizarre role in the worship ceremony of the Canaanites. Thus, the snake became a symbol of evil to the Hebrews, who looked upon Canaanite worship as an abomination. And so the snake symbolizes the *devil*.

To understand the second symbol, recall that the snake told the woman that if she *ate* the fruit, she would *know* good from bad. The snake makes a connection between *eating* and *knowing*.

Because most ancient peoples could not read, *experience* became a major source of *knowledge* for them. This explains the connection between *eating* and *knowing*.

"To eat" means "to know by experience." It is a symbolic way of saying that the first couple *learned* about evil by *experiencing* it. They "tasted" evil. They became evil. They sinned.

The biblical writer's answer to the question about how evil entered the world is this: It entered the world through the first sin of the first human couple. CCC 397–98

Sin dooms us

After the first couple sinned, the Bible says they were *aware* that they were naked. GENESIS 3:7 To understand this statement, we need to go back to the creation story. There we read, "The man and the woman were both naked, but they were not embarrassed." GENESIS 2:25

The couple's *awareness* of nakedness *after* they sinned symbolizes that sin did something to them. They were no longer at ease with themselves. Something went wrong inside them. Sin "flawed" them.

The symbolic sin story ends with the first couple being expelled from the Garden of Eden. The point of the expulsion is obvious. The first couple is now separated from God.

The first sin not only introduced evil into the world but also "flawed" the first couple and "separated" them from God. The first sin did even more. CCC 399–405 It opened the floodgates of sin. CCC 401 Soon sin engulfed the world. GENESIS 11:1–9 The human race was *doomed*. The tragic condition that the first sin produced in the world is referred to as the *state of original sin*. The first sin:

- **Introduced evil into the world**
- **Flawed the human race**
- **Doomed it to destruction**

Ray of hope

The story of the first sin ends with God confronting the three guilty parties: the woman, the man, and the snake.

To the *woman,* God says, "I will increase . . . your pain in giving birth." GENESIS 3:16

To the *man,* God says, "You will have to work hard all your life to make [the ground] produce food." GENESIS 3:17

To the *snake,* God says: "You will crawl on your belly. . . . I will make you and the woman hate each other; her offspring and yours will always be enemies. Her offspring will crush your head, and you will bite her offspring's heel." GENESIS 3:14–15

13 *In what sense might you interpret the final sentence God addresses to the snake as a ray of hope?*

New Testament writers viewed God's remarks to the snake as a ray of hope. They viewed them as a "prophecy" that God would rescue the human race from its sinful condition. CCC 410–12

These writers interpreted the expression "hate each other" to refer to an ongoing state of "spiritual warfare" between the devil and the human race. They interpreted the expression "her offspring will crush your head" as a "prophecy" that the human race will win.

It is in this sense that God's remarks to the snake are viewed as a ray of hope. CCC 410–11 Jesus, the noblest offspring of the human race, will eventually defeat the devil. 1 JOHN 3:8

Re-creation

Mark Twain once wrote a story about a group of people who get trapped in a hopeless situation. It was like having them on a plane ten feet away from crashing into a cliff. He didn't want these people to die, but he didn't know how to save them in a credible way.

So he ended his story, writing, "I don't know how to save these people; if you think you do, you are welcome to try."

Thousands of years ago the world was in a similar hopeless situation. Sin was like a tidal wave threatening to destroy everyone in its path. But God had a plan to save the world. This brings us to the "re-creation story."

We may think of God's plan as a stage play in three acts:

- **Creation**   **God creates**
- **De-creation**   **Sin destroys**
- **Re-creation**   **God saves us**

Covenant with Abram

God's plan to save the world begins with a man named Abram. One day God says to him:

"Leave your country, your relatives, and your father's home, and go to a land that I am going to show you. . . .

"I make this covenant with you: I promise that you will be the ancestor of many nations. Your name will no longer be Abram, but Abraham, because I am making you the ancestor of many nations. . . .

"You must no longer call your wife Sarai; from now on her name is Sarah. I will bless her, and I will give you a son by her. . . . You will name him Isaac.
GENESIS 12:1, 17:4–5, 15–16, 19

In biblical times, names were more than arbitrary identification tags. They said something significant about the person. Thus, a name change often accompanied a destiny change.

14 *Can you give some examples of this practice even today?*

A covenant is a sacred pact between two parties. God's covenant with Abram changed his life in a remarkable way. It gave him:

- ■ **New identity** **God's chosen person**
- ■ **New destiny** **Father of nations**

Eventually, Sarah gave birth to Isaac. He grew up, married Rebecca, and they had two sons: Esau and Jacob. After Isaac's death, God said to Jacob: "Your name is Jacob, but from now on it will be *Israel*." GENESIS 35:10

Israel became the father of twelve sons, forerunners of the twelve tribes of Israel, who became known as *Israelites.* Jacob's favorite son was Joseph. GENESIS 37:3

One day Joseph's jealous brothers sold him into slavery in Egypt. There he rose to prominence by foretelling a famine and preparing Egypt for it.

Joseph invited his family to come to Egypt. They came, prospered, and grew into a great people. After Joseph died, however, they fell into disfavor and were enslaved by the Egyptians. Eventually, a leader named Moses arose to lead them out of Egypt to freedom.

Covenant with Israel

Moses led the Israelites out of Egypt to the foot of Mount Sinai. There God made a covenant with them, giving them:

- ■ **New identity** **Chosen people**
- ■ **New destiny** **Priestly people**

The Israelites became God's Chosen People in the sense that God chose them to prepare all the nations of the world for the re-creation of the human race. CCC 1961–64

After making a covenant with the Israelites, God schooled them in the desert and, eventually, led them into the land promised to Abraham.

After preparing the people for entry into the land, Moses died. Joshua succeeded him, led the people into the land, and divided the land among the twelve tribes of Israel.

15 *Moses is the first in a long line of great people who fathered a great cause but died without seeing it realized. Who were some others?*

When Joshua died, leaving the Israelites without a strong leader, the tribes periodically drifted from the covenant. To deal with these situations, God used popular leaders, called judges, to bring them back to their senses.

In time, a holy man named Samuel anointed Saul to be Israel's first king. Saul began well but ended badly.

After Saul became king of Israel,
he fought all his enemies everywhere . . .
He fought heroically . . .
He saved the Israelites from all attacks.
1 SAMUEL 10:1; 14:47–48

But success has a way of turning a person's head. Soon Saul began to follow his own mind; he grew insensitive to the spirit of Yahweh.

The LORD said to Samuel,
"I am sorry that I made Saul king;
he has turned away from me
and disobeyed my commands."
1 SAMUEL 15:10–11

Covenant with David

When Saul died in battle, a young shepherd named David was anointed king. Under his brilliant leadership, Israel began its "glory years." David made Jerusalem the center of government and worship.

Then came a remarkable moment. One night while David was praying in the sacred tent (the forerunner of the Temple), God made a covenant with David. CCC 709–16 Through the prophet Nathan, God promised David:

"You will always have descendants,
and I will make your kingdom last forever.
Your dynasty will never end."
2 SAMUEL 7:16

This prophecy is the most important in the Bible. It begins a series of prophecies called the "messianic prophecies." They point to the coming of a king (Messiah) from David's line, whose kingdom (God's Kingdom) will last forever.

At Mount Sinai the covenant was set up in a general way between God and the people. Now it is linked specifically with the Davidic kings, who represent the kingdom and are responsible for its welfare.

New Testament writers saw God's promise of a Messiah fulfilled in Jesus. CCC 436–40 In announcing Jesus' birth to Mary, an angel says of Jesus:

ART Connection

Michelangelo (1475–1564) created this masterpiece of David from a flawed block of marble abandoned by another artist. It was completed in 1504.

David

In the streams of Israel, you can still spot water-smooth stones, like the fabled disk that David used to kill Goliath. Fingering one of these stones helps to bridge the 3,000 years since King David lived.

As a youth, David was a shepherd. While his flocks munched grass, he practiced the shepherd's defense against unwelcomed intruders: the slingshot. Little did he realize that this skill would catapult him into the limelight of history.

The moment came when Philistine armies invaded Israel and prepared for attack. A giant warrior named Goliath issued a pre-battle challenge to duel any Israelite. David, a teenager, at the time, accepted the challenge.

Goliath was no match for the agile youth with his deadly sling. David's shepherding days were over, and his career as a warrior and king launched. Under the magic of David's leadership, Israel began her "glory years."

He will be great and will be called the Son of the Most High God. The Lord God will make him a king, as his ancestor David was, and . . . his kingdom will never end!
LUKE 1:32–33

As God's covenant moved from Abraham to Israel, it now moved to David. CCC 702–709 We may sum up the moves this way:

Abraham is given:

- ■ **New identity**   **Chosen person**
- ■ **New destiny**   **Father of many**

Israel is given:

- ■ **New identity**   **Chosen people**
- ■ **New destiny**   **Priestly people**

David is given:

- ■ **New identity**   **Chosen king**
- ■ **New destiny**   **Ancestor of Messiah**

God's people sin

After David's death, his son Solomon took over as king. Under his rule, Israel became a great world power.

But his most important achievement was fulfilling his father's dream and building a great Temple in Jerusalem.

Unfortunately, however, like Saul, he began nobly but ended tragically (turning from God and worshiping foreign gods).

16 *How do you account for the fact that so many people seem to follow the pattern of beginning nobly and ending tragically? Can you think of any examples?*

After Solomon died, civil war broke out. The nation split in two: Israel (north) and Judah (south). This tragic split began a flood of personal and social sins against God and the covenant.

In the face of these sins, God raised up prophets like Elijah, Amos, and Hosea to warn the nation of Israel (north) to reform. But their words fell on deaf ears. In 722 B.C. Assyria invaded and destroyed Israel.

Ironically, the southern kingdom (Judah) did not learn from the tragedy. It soon drifted into some of the very same evils that doomed the north: idolatry, religious formalism, exploitation of the poor and the powerless.

17 *Give an example from modern life of each of the following sins: idolatry, religious formalism, exploitation of the poor.*

Prophets like Isaiah and Jeremiah warned the people, but to no avail. Finally, their "days of glory" ended in a "day of drums." Babylonian armies destroyed Jerusalem and the Temple and led the people away into slavery. CCC 710

God's people suffer

For decades the people lived in exile in a foreign land. Their faith flickered and, at times, nearly went out. Among the prophets God sent them were Ezekiel and another spiritual giant called Second Isaiah. Scholars give him this name because his writings are appended to those of the earlier "great Isaiah."

Finally, the day came when Babylon fell to the armies of Cyrus of Persia. He freed Judah and allowed the Jews to return to Jerusalem. In time, under leaders like Nehemiah and Ezra, they rebuilt the city and the Temple. But further difficulties lay ahead.

Around 313 B.C. Alexander the Great conquered Judah. In the centuries that followed, the people isolated themselves from the world. In the process of doing so, they began to lose their spiritual focus. They began to make the creator of the universe into a national God who cared only about them.

Into this critical situation stepped prophets like Malachi and the unknown author of the Book of Jonah. These prophets helped the people regain their focus.

But another great challenge lay ahead. Around 200 B.C. a Syrian king conquered Judah and tried to destroy its ancient faith. Years of persecution followed. Into this crisis stepped the prophet called Daniel. Like prophets before him, he faced the problem of communicating a message of hope to a simple people. To do this, he used two literary devices: folktales and visions.

Typical of the visions is one in which Daniel saw a mysterious figure in the clouds. Jesus would refer to it when asked if he were the Messiah.

"I am," answered Jesus,
"and you will all see the Son of Man seated at the right side of the Almighty and coming with the clouds of heaven!"
MARK 14:62

Typical of the folktales is God's protection of Daniel in the lions' den. If God could save Daniel, God could save Judah.

God's people wait

The religious inspiration of Daniel and the political leadership of the Maccabees pulled the people through this threatening period. But Judah's joy was short-lived. In 63 B.C. the Romans conquered Judah.

The people cried out in profound anguish: "What happened to God's covenant with us? What happened to the promised Messiah? What happened to the promised kingdom?"

These questions are reflected in books like Ecclesiastes and Job. Together with the Book of Psalms, they act as a window through which we glimpse the anguished hearts and souls of Jews waiting for further revelation from God.

So, by their own admission, the Hebrew Scriptures end "unfinished." They end with faithful Jews, especially "the poor," waiting for the Messiah—praying for God to complete the work of re-creating the world. CCC 716

Recap

Review

To interpret the Old Testament correctly, we need to consider both:

- **Text**   **What it says**
- **Context**   **Literary, cultural, historical**

The *content* of the Old Testament may be divided into the following three themes:

- **Creation**   **God makes us**
- **De-creation**   **We sin**
- **Re-creation**   **God saves us**

The creation stories teach four *religious* truths that were revolutionary in the biblical era:

- **God is one**
- **God planned creation**
- **God created everything good**
- **God made the Sabbath holy**

The de-creation stories begin with the first sin by the first couple. It opened the floodgates of evil. The tragic condition that the first sin produced in the world is referred to as the *state of original sin*. The first sin:

- **Introduced evil into the world**
- **Flawed the human race**
- **Doomed it to destruction**

The *re-creation* story involves three important covenants with the following:

- **Abraham**   **Father of nations**
- **Israel**   **Chosen people**
- **David**   **Promise of a Messiah**

God's covenant with David began a series of prophecies called the *messianic* prophecies. They point to a king (Messiah) from David's line.

The Hebrew Scriptures end with faithful Jews waiting and praying for the Messiah to come and complete the work of "re-creation."

1 List and briefly explain: (a) the two major groups into which Bible readers split, (b) two contradictory details in the two creation stories.

2 List and briefly explain: (a) the pattern used to describe each day of creation in the first creation story, (b) the pattern used to describe the week of creation, (c) what these patterns suggest about the kind of writing we have in the story.

3 List and briefly explain (a) each of the four new teachings contained in the first creation story, (b) what old teaching each new teaching replaced, and (c) how the new teaching was communicated.

4 Briefly explain and give an example of the following sins: (a) personal, (b) social, (c) commission, and (d) omission.

5 Explain the following points concerning social sins: (a) why it is especially bad, (b) one reason why we tolerate it, (c) the bottomline on where the responsibility to oppose it rests.

6 Explain the following symbols in the de-creation story: (a) snake, (b) eating the fruit, (c) awareness of nakedness.

7 Describe what we mean by original sin. List (a) the threefold impact it had on the human race, and (b) how God's remarks to the three guilty parties (woman, man, and devil) served as a "prophecy" that God would rescue the human race.

8 Explain the new identity and destiny conferred by the following covenants: (a) Abram, (b) Sinai, (c) messianic.

9 Briefly identify: Solomon, Judah, Israel, Elijah, Amos and Hosea, Isaiah and Jeremiah, Cyrus of Persia, Nehemiah and Ezra, Alexander the Great, Daniel.

Reflect

1 The movie *Lili* is a delightful fantasy about a girl who is a member of a traveling carnival in France. She becomes depressed one day because she thinks no one cares about her, especially the carnival's bashful puppeteer. Her only friends are the puppets of the young puppeteer. She decides to run away. Before leaving, however, Lili says good-bye to the puppets. As they hug her and weep, Lili suddenly feels them trembling. Only then does she make the connection between the puppets and the puppeteer.

■ *How is this sequence in the movie a kind of parable of God and the human race? In other words, whom do the following stand for: Lili, the puppeteer, the puppets?*
■ *Describe a time when you felt like leaving home.*

2 In Avery Corman's book, *Oh God!* someone rebukes God for not lifting a finger to destroy the evil in the world, saying, "So you've decided to just let us stumble along and never do a thing to help?" God replies:

Such a smart fella and you missed the point. . . .
I set all this up for you and made it so it can work.
Only the deal is you have to work at it.

■ *Explain God's point.*
■ *What evil in the world are you most concerned about and why?*

3 When Joseph's father arrived in Egypt, Joseph threw his arms around him and "cried for a long time." GENESIS 46:29 This moving scene stands in contrast to the way many modern parents and children greet one another. For example, a parent wrote Ann Landers:

The greatest regret of my life
is that I kept my son at arm's length.
I believed it was unmanly for males
to show affection for one another.
I treated my son the way my father treated me,
and I realize what a terrible mistake it was.

■ *On an unsigned sheet of paper, answer these questions:*
(a) When was the last time your father and you hugged one another? Your mother?
(b) Would you like to have a more openly affectionate relationship with your parents?
(c) On a scale of one to ten, how would you rate your relationship, in general, with your father? Your mother?
■ *What do you think is the biggest obstacle to a better relationship?*

PRAYER TIME
with the Lord

David was a skilled musician. Under his leadership, the Book of Psalms was begun around 1000 B.C. It was completed around 400 B.C. It was Israel's songbook and prayerbook. Today, Catholics pray the psalms at every Mass. Here's a favorite:

The LORD is my shepherd;
I have everything I need.
He lets me rest in fields of green grass
and leads me
to quiet pools of fresh water.

He gives me new strength.
He guides me in the right paths,
as he promised.

Even if I go through
the deepest darkness,
I will not be afraid, LORD,
for you are with me.
Your shepherd's rod and staff protect me.

You prepare a banquet for me,
where all my enemies can see me;
you welcome me as an honored guest
and fill my cup to the brim.

I know that goodness and love
will be with me all the days of my life;
and your house will be my home
as long as I live. PSALM 23

■ *Some modern songs have spiritual messages, just as the psalms do. Identify one. Explain its message.*

PRAYER Journal

One form of prayer is to speak to God from the heart, holding nothing back. It is telling it like it is. Here is an excerpt from such a prayer by the prophet Jeremiah:

LORD, everyone makes fun of me;
they laugh at me all day long. . . .
I am ridiculed and scorned all the time
because I proclaim your message. . . .

I hear everybody whispering. . . .
Even my close friends
wait for my downfall. . . .

Why was I born?
Was it only to have trouble and sorrow,
to end my life in disgrace? JEREMIAH 20:7–8, 10, 18

■ **Pick out some problem from your life or from our world. Compose a prayer to God about it. Speak from the heart as Jeremiah did. Here are some suggestions for opening lines: (a) Lord, life is really unfair. (b) Lord, why did you make growing up a hassle? (c) Lord, why do you let drug pushers wreck people's lives?**

SCRIPTURE

1	**In praise of the Creator**	**Psalm 104**
2	**Covenant with Abram**	**Genesis 15**
3	**Sinai Covenant**	**Exodus 19–20**
4	**Davidic Covenant**	**2 Samuel 7**
5	**Re-creation**	**Revelation 21:1–8**

■ **Pick one of the above passages. Read it prayerfully and write a short statement to Jesus expressing your feelings about it.**

4 New Testament

In the beginning the Word already existed;
the Word was with God,
and the Word was God. . . .
The Word was the source of life. . . .

The Word became a human being, and . . .
lived among us. We saw his glory . . .
as the Father's only Son. . . .

No one has ever seen God.
The only Son, who is the same as God . . .
has made him known.

JOHN 1:1, 4; 14, 18

The Old Testament is like the radio;
you hear God's Word.
The New Testament is like television;
you not only hear God's Word
but also see it come alive in Jesus.

Birth of Jesus

Darrel Dore was inside a room in the platform of an oil rig in the Gulf of Mexico. Suddenly, the rig and its platform capsized. It began to sink into the sea. The lights of the room flickered and went out. Soon the room Dore was in began to fill with water—except for a big air bubble in the corner of the ceiling.

Dore plunged his head inside the air bubble. For twenty hours, he shivered and prayed inside it. Then when he had just about lost hope, a tiny glow of light appeared in the murky darkness of the water. It was a light on a diver's helmet. Rescue had arrived.

1 *Some people observe that there is a close resemblance between this story and the Christmas story. What do you think they have in mind?*

Birth narratives

The centuries before Jesus' birth were dark times for Jews. Powerful nations took turns occupying their land. Many Jews began to wonder whether God's promise of a Messiah to prophets would be fulfilled:

The LORD says, "The time is coming
when I will choose as king
a righteous descendant of David. . . .
He will be called
'The LORD Our Salvation.' "
JEREMIAH 23:5–6

Interestingly, only Luke and Matthew begin their Gospels with the birth of Jesus.

2 How do the Gospels of Mark and John begin?

Luke situates Jesus' birth within the context of world history. He begins his description this way:

At that time Emperor Augustus
ordered a census to be taken
throughout the Roman Empire. LUKE 2:1

Matthew, on the other hand, situates the birth of Jesus against the background of Jewish history. Moreover, he is at pains to show how Jesus' birth fulfills the prophecies concerning the coming of the promised Messiah. Matthew writes:

This is how
the birth of Jesus Christ took place.
His mother Mary was engaged to Joseph,
but before they were married,
she found out
that she was going to have a baby.
MATTHEW 1:18

Joseph was confused and shocked until an angel of the LORD appeared to him and said:

"Do not be afraid
to take Mary to be your wife.
For it is by the Holy Spirit
that she has conceived.
She will have a son, and
you will name him Jesus—
because he will save his people
from their sins." MATTHEW 1:20–21

Emperor
Augustus

Matthew then adds:

All this happened in order to
make come true what the Lord
had said through the prophet,
"A virgin will become pregnant and
have a son, and he will be called
'Immanuel' (which means,
'God is with us')." MATTHEW 1:22–23

The birth of Jesus takes place in Bethlehem, where Joseph and Mary had to go to register for the Roman census. CCC 522–534

3 Explain how the two different backgrounds against which Luke and Matthew situate the birth of Jesus, suggest the kind of audience each had in mind at the time they wrote.

Nathaniel Hawthorne was dead. On his desk lay the outline to a story he never got a chance to write.

It concerned an important person who was coming to a certain place. People dreamed about his coming. They prepared for it; they waited for it, but he never came.

Nathaniel Hawthorne's unfinished story is like the Old Testament. It centered around a promised Messiah for whom everyone was preparing and waiting. But he never came.

■ *I imagine I am an old Jew, living a few months before Jesus' birth. All my life I've waited for the Messiah. What are my thoughts as I prepare to die without any sign of his coming?*

Ministry preview

Shortly after Jesus' birth, Magi show up in Jerusalem and ask, "Where is the baby born to be king of the Jews?" King Herod calls his advisers and asks: "Where will the Messiah be born?" The advisers say:

In the town of Bethlehem. . . .
For this is what the prophets wrote:
"Bethlehem, . . .
from you will come a leader
who will guide my people Israel."
MATTHEW 2:5–6

The Magi go on to Bethlehem. When they see Jesus, they kneel down and present him with gifts of gold, frankincense, and myrrh. Early Christian writers saw these gifts as being prophetic and symbolic:

■ **Gold**   **"King" of metals**
     (Points to Jesus' *kingship*)
■ **Frankincense used in worship**
     (Points to Jesus' *divinity*)
■ **Myrrh**   **used for burial**
     (Points to Jesus' *humanity*)

After the Magi depart, an angel appears to Joseph in a dream and warns him that Herod is plotting to kill Jesus.

Joseph got up,
took the child and his mother,
and left during the night for Egypt,
where they stayed until Herod died.
This was done to make come true
what the Lord had said through the prophet,
"I called my Son out of Egypt."
MATTHEW 2:14–15

Herod's hostile reaction to Jesus stands in contrast to the Magi's reverent reaction. It previews how people will react to Jesus in the days ahead. Many Jews will reject him; many Gentiles will accept him.

Four Gospels

A TV director was planning a series called *San Francisco: A Tourist's View.* He decided to present the city through the eyes of four tourists, as they approached it for the first time by:

■ **Rail**   **Train**
■ **Road**   **Car**
■ **Water**   **Boat**
■ **Air**   **Plane**

Thus, viewers would get four different views of San Francisco.

4 *How would each approach and view be different from the other three? Why?*

Similarly, the New Testament writers provide their readers with four views of Jesus. CCC 514–15 Three (Mark, Matthew, Luke) are quite similar, while John's view is quite different.

One reason for the difference is that John writes at a later date for a more mature Christian audience. Thus, John presumes some knowledge of Jesus.

For example, he identifies Jesus immediately as the Messiah and goes on from there. John 1:41 John also substitutes the expression "eternal life" for the expression "Kingdom of God."

Because each evangelist wrote for a different audience, each stresses a different facet of Jesus:

- **Mark**   **Suffering Messiah**
- **Matthew**   **Teaching Messiah**
- **Luke**   **Compassionate Messiah**
- **John**   **Life-giving Messiah**

5 Why might Matthew, writing primarily for Jews, stress the "teaching Messiah"?

Baptism of Jesus

Matthew does a "fast forward" from the story of the Magi to the baptism of Jesus. CCC 535–37 Without any introduction, he writes:

At that time, John the Baptist came to the desert of Judea and started preaching. "Turn away from sins," he said, "because the Kingdom of heaven is near!" Matthew 3:1–2

Matthew then adds:

John was the man the prophet Isaiah was talking about when he said . . . "Someone is shouting in the desert, Prepare the road for the Lord. . . ." People came to him from . . . all over. . . . They confessed their sins, and he baptized them in the Jordan. Matthew 3:3, 5–6

One day, to John's surprise, Jesus waded into the Jordan to be baptized. John said to Jesus:

"I ought to be baptized by you. . . ." But Jesus answered him, "Let it be so for now." Matthew 3:13–15

After Jesus was baptized, a remarkable thing happened.

While he was praying, heaven was opened, and the Holy Spirit came down upon him in bodily form like a dove. And a voice came from heaven, "You are my own dear Son. I am pleased with you." Luke 3:21–22

Three striking images stand out in this brief description:

- **The sky opens above Jesus**
- **A dovelike form descends upon Jesus**
- **A heavenly voice identifies Jesus**

To understand these images, we need to consider them within their historical and cultural context.

6 What is meant by a historical context? A cultural context?

ART Connection

This fifteenth-century Italian wood carving portrays Saint Luke composing his Gospel. Unaware that books did not appear until 150 years after Luke lived, the artist portrays the evangelist writing in a book, not a scroll.

Thomas Merton

Thomas Merton was orphaned at 16. The summer after graduating from high school, he backpacked his way across Europe. What happened that summer eventually led him to become a Catholic and a priest. In *The Seven Storey Mountain* he writes:

I don't know how it began—
I found myself looking into
churches. . . .

For the first time in my life
I began to find out
something of . . . this Person . . .
called Christ.
The saints of those forgotten
days had left upon the walls
of their churches
a word [I could understand]. . . .

But above all, the most real
and most immediate source . . .
was Christ himself
present in those churches.
It was he
who was teaching me . . .
more directly
than I was capable of realizing.

ART
Connection

This church door contrasts the "tree of forbidden fruit" (de-creation) with the "tree of the cross" (re-creation). The first Adam and the first Eve are contrasted with Jesus (the new Adam) and Mary (the new Eve).

New era

First, let us consider the image of the sky opening above Jesus. Ancient Jews viewed the universe as being made up of three worlds stacked one upon the other, like pancakes:

■ **World of God**   **Top world**
■ **World of the Living**   **Middle world**
■ **World of the Dead**   **Bottom world**

After Adam sinned, a tidal wave of sin flooded the "world of the living" (middle world). People prayed to God to come down and set things right. Thus, the psalmist prayed, "O LORD, tear the sky open and come down." PSALM 144:5

It is within this context that we must interpret the image of the sky opening above Jesus. God has heard the prayer of the people and is coming down, in the person of Jesus, to set things right.

The opening of the sky symbolizes that a *new era* in history is beginning.

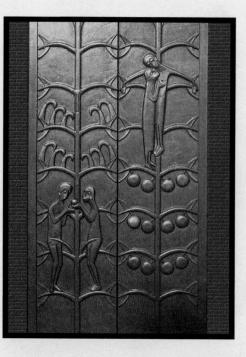

New creation

The context for the "dove" image is the Book of Genesis. There it describes the "power of God . . . moving over the water" just prior to the creation of the universe. GENESIS 1:2

Ancient rabbis compared God's power moving over the water to the image of a dove hovering over its newborn. CCC 695, 701 Thus, the dove hovering over Jesus signifies that a *new creation* is about to take place. This fulfills what Isaiah foretold:

The Lord says,
"I am making a new earth. . . .
Be glad and rejoice forever
in what I create." ISAIAH 65:17–18

New Adam

This brings us to the final image: the voice from heaven saying to Jesus, "You are my own dear Son."

The Book of Genesis portrays God creating Adam as the "firstborn" of the human family. Thus, the voice identifies Jesus as the *new Adam*. He is the "firstborn" of the *new creation* (re-creation).

Saint Paul draws this comparison between the first Adam and "last Adam" (Jesus):

The first man, Adam,
was created a living being;
but the last Adam [Jesus]
is the life-giving Spirit. . . .

The first Adam,
made of earth, came from the earth;
the last Adam came from heaven. . . .
Just as we wear the likeness
of the man made of earth, so we will wear
the likeness of the Man from heaven.
I CORINTHIANS 15:45, 47, 49

THINK
about it

Why not let Jesus take over my life?
He can do more with it than I can.
Anonymous

Paul Stookey was in a popular singing group, "Peter, Paul, and Mary." In spite of his success, he was not at peace with himself.

One day he told singer Bob Dylan about it. Dylan told Stookey to go back to his old high school for a visit and start reading the Bible. Later, Stookey wrote:

*All the truths I sought
were contained
in the life of this man. . . .
It was fantastic. . . .
He set a good example,
but it never occurred to me
that he could really be
the Son of God.*

Then one night during a concert in Austin, Texas, he met a young man. Stookey writes:

*Somehow this guy
made all the reading
in Scripture make sense . . .
and I asked Jesus to come in
and take over my life.*

That was the start of a new life for Paul Stookey.

And so the three events that take place at Jesus' baptism signify the following:

- ■ **Sky opens**   **New era**
- ■ **Dove comes down**   **New creation**
- ■ **Voice speaks**   **New Adam**

7 *Besides revealing the "new creation," how do the three events at Jesus' baptism act as a revelation of the Trinity?*

Let us now turn to the life and teaching of Jesus in the four Gospels.

Miracles of Jesus

A speaker on a Miami radio station startled a lot of listeners. He said that if he had the power to work miracles, he would use it far differently than Jesus did:

*I would not cure one person of blindness;
I would make blindness impossible.
I would not cure one person of leprosy;
I would abolish leprosy.*

The speaker's remarks raise an important question. What was the purpose of Jesus' miracles? Did he heal the blind and the lepers because he pitied them? Did he heal them because they asked him to? MARK 1:40–41 Or was there another reason?

8 *What is your reaction to the speaker's remarks? What was the purpose of Jesus' miracles? For example, why do you think he healed people?*

Miracles are signs

To understand the purpose of Jesus' miracles, we need to understand that Jesus' baptism sets in motion the "re-creation" of the world.

The *first step* in this "re-creation" process is the coming of the Messiah and the Kingdom of God. This is where the miracles of Jesus enter the picture. They are signs announcing the arrival of these two great events.

The four evangelists, who wrote in Greek, used three different Greek words in referring to the miracles of Jesus:

- **Teras**   **Something marvelous**
- **Dynamis**   **Something powerful**
- **Semeion**   **Important sign**

The favorite word for "miracle" in John's Gospel is *semeion*. John favored this word because it underscored the most important point about Jesus' miracles. They were signs announcing the arrival of the:

- **Messiah of God**
- **Kingdom of God**

Signs of the Messiah

To understand how miracles announced the Messiah, we need to keep in mind that the prophet Isaiah had foretold that certain events would signal the arrival of the Messiah:

*The blind will be able to see,
and the deaf will hear.
The lame will leap and dance.* ISAIAH 35:5–6

One day some people asked Jesus, "Are you the one John said was going to come, or should we expect someone else?" Jesus said:

*"The blind can see,
the lame can walk . . .
the deaf can hear."* LUKE 7:22

By his reply, Jesus makes it clear that the signs foretold by Isaiah are now taking place. Jesus is the promised Messiah.

This brings us to the second main purpose of Jesus' miracles. CCC 541–50

Signs of the Kingdom

Before Adam and Eve turned their backs on God, there was no sin, sickness, or death in the world. All of this changed with their sin. It ushered in the "Kingdom of Satan" and from that moment on, those three evils held the human race in slavery.

It is against this background that we must read the Gospel accounts of Jesus' power over each of these three evils. Jesus:

- **Forgives sin**   **Luke 5:17–26**
- **Heals the sick**   **Mark 1:29–31**
- **Raises the dead**   **Luke 7:12–16**

Jesus' mastery over sin, sickness, and death is a dramatic sign pointing to the beginning of the demise of the "Kingdom of Satan" and the rise of the "Kingdom of God."

9 If the Kingdom of God has arrived, why is there still so much evil in the world? Why do we still pray in the Lord's Prayer, "Thy Kingdom come"?

Jesus compared the coming of God's Kingdom to the planting of a seed. It takes time to grow and bear fruit. MARK 4:26–29 Jesus' point is that the coming of God's Kingdom isn't going to be an instant occurrence, but a gradual and painful process.

This is why there is still so much evil in the world. This is why we still pray in the Lord's Prayer, "Thy Kingdom come!" Meanwhile, the "Kingdom of Satan" continues to wreak havoc in the world. It has not yet been destroyed. It is only under the sentence of death, and it will not die without a fight.

Signs inviting faith

But the miracles of Jesus do more than merely announce the coming of the Messiah and the Kingdom. They invite us to faith and action. CCC 543–46 How so?

The healing of the blind beggar invites us to *open our eyes* to what Jesus does. The healing of the deaf man invites us to *open our ears* to what Jesus says. The raising of the dead man invites us to *open our hearts* to Jesus and begin a new life in God's Kingdom.

People responded to Jesus' invitation in four ways. Jesus used this parable to illustrate each of these ways:

A farmer sowed seed in his field. (Ancient farmers sowed seed atop the soil and then plowed it under.)

Some seed fell on a path by the field. Birds stole it and ate it instantly.

Some fell on soil-covered rocks. It sprouted quickly but died when the sun baked the layer of soil.

Some blew into thorn bushes that fenced in the field to keep out animals. It sprouted but was choked to death by the thick thorns.

Finally, some seed fell on good soil and bore abundant fruit.

Jesus compared the four fates of seed to the four ways that people respond to his invitation:

Seed's fate	People's response
Fails to sprout	Reject
Sprouts but withers	Accept but falter
Sprouts but chokes	Accept but forget
Sprouts and grows	Accept and grows

10 *What is your response to Jesus' invitation? Explain.*

LITERARY Connection

The novel *Father Malachy's Miracle* was made into a Hollywood movie. It is a fanciful story of a priest in Scotland who gets the idea of praying for a miracle so powerful that it will leave no doubt about the truthfulness of God and religion.

"One spectacular miracle," he tells a friend, "and we shall prove to the world . . . that we have the Light and the truth."

And so he prays that on a certain night an evil nightclub will take flight and be carried off to a barren island off Scotland's coast.

The miracle takes place. But it backfires. Instead of convincing people of the truth, it is turned into a big publicity stunt by the nightclub's owner.

The story ends with a wiser Father Malachy realizing that you can't make people believe. You can only invite them to open their hearts to the gift of faith.

The film *The Ox Bow Incident* concerns town leaders who bypass the law and hang three people without a trial. Later they learn the terrible truth. The three people were innocent.

Before being hanged, one young man asks to write a letter to his wife. After he is hanged, someone reads it. A part of it reads:

*I suppose there's
some good men here,
only they don't realize
what they're doing.
They're the ones
I feel sorry for,
'cause it'll be over for me
in a little while, but they'll
have to go on remembering
the rest of their lives.*

■ **How do you account for the young man's lack of anger and calmness?**

Arrest and Trial

Jesus' claim to be the Messiah and to inaugurate God's Kingdom brings him into sharp conflict with the Jewish religious leaders of his time. More and more, they see Jesus as a threat to their authority and their own beliefs and teachings.

As a result, the gap between Jesus and the leaders widens day by day and week by week.

Finally, it reaches the breaking point, when Jesus raises Lazarus from the dead. The news of this miracle spreads everywhere. The religious leaders panic and say:

*What shall we do?
Look at all the miracles
this man is performing!
If we let him go on this way,
everyone will believe in him,
and the Roman authorities will take action
and destroy our Temple and our nation!*
JOHN 11:47–48

From that fateful day, the religious leaders plot to do away with Jesus. JOHN 11:53 The day arrives when Jesus is arrested, tried, and sentenced to crucifixion.

Death of Jesus

An Associated Press news release might have described Jesus' crucifixion on Good Friday something like this:

JERUSALEM (AP)—
*Jesus of Nazareth was executed today
outside the walls of this ancient city.
Death came at about three o'clock.*

*A freak thunderstorm
scattered the crowd of curious onlookers
and served as a fitting climax
to the brief but stormy career
of the controversial preacher
from the hill country of Galilee.*

*Burial took place immediately.
A police guard was posted at the grave site
as a precautionary measure.
The Galilean is survived by his mother.*

The events of Good Friday left Jesus' followers in a state of shock. Their faith was shaken to the foundation.

Weren't Jesus' miracles *signs* that he was the Messiah? Weren't they *signs* that he was inaugurating God's Kingdom? How, then, could all this be reconciled with his death on the cross? CCC 599–630

Suddenly, all their dreams seemed buried with Jesus.

The Crucifixion,
by Tintoretto.

Way of the Cross

Catholics have always been devoted to Jesus in his Passion (suffering and death). One form their devotion takes is "The Way of the Cross." It involves journeying with Jesus to Calvary and contains 14 stations.

The procedure for meditating on each station is as follows: (1) think about it; (2) speak to Jesus about it; (3) listen for Jesus' reply to you in the depths of your heart.

1 Jesus is condemned to death.
Love your enemies, do good to those who hate you. LUKE 6:27

2 Jesus takes up his cross.
If you want to come with me, forget yourself, take up your cross every day, and follow me. LUKE 9:23

3 Jesus falls the first time.
"Do not be discouraged for I, the LORD your God, am with you." JOSHUA 1:9

4 Jesus meets his mother.
Jesus saw his mother and said to the disciple, "She is your mother." JOHN 19:26

5 Jesus is helped by Simon.
"When you refused to help another, you refused to help me. . ." MATTHEW 25:45

6 Jesus' face is wiped by Veronica.
"When you did this for another, you did it for me. . ." MATTHEW 25:40

7 Jesus falls a second time.
Happy is the person who remains faithful under trials. JAMES 1:12

8 Jesus comforts the women.
"Don't cry for me, but for yourselves and for your children. . ." LUKE 23:28

9 Jesus falls a third time.
Those who trust in the LORD will be renewed in strength. ISAIAH 42:16

10 Jesus is stripped of his clothes.
"I was naked and you clothed me." MATTHEW 25:36

11 Jesus is nailed to the cross.
What we suffer now cannot be compared to the glory to come. ROMANS 8:18

12 Jesus dies on the cross.
"If you lose your life for my sake, you will save it. . ." LUKE 9:24

13 Jesus is taken down from the cross.
"I have set an example for you; do what I have done for you. . ." JOHN 13:15

14 Jesus is laid in the tomb.
". . . I will be put to death, but I will be raised to life. . ." MATTHEW 16:21

LIFE Connection

I carry a crucifix
in my pocket . . .
It's not for . . .
all the world to see.
It's simply an understanding
Between my Savior and me . . .

It reminds me to be thankful
For my blessings day by day
And strive to serve him better
In all I do and say . . .

Reminding no one but me
That Jesus Christ is
Lord of my life
If only I'll let him be.

Author unknown

A canoeist saw a water beetle crawl up the side of his canoe, hook its talons in the wood, and die.

Three hours later he glanced down again. The beetle had dried in the sun, and the shell was cracking open. From it emerged a lovely dragonfly. The canoeist nudged the shell; it was like an empty tomb.

The dragonfly fluttered above the other beetles in the water. They saw it but didn't recognize it.

■ *List several similarities between the beetle's transformation and Jesus' transformation.*

Resurrection of Jesus

Some women went to visit the tomb on the Sunday after Good Friday. They were not prepared for what they found. It was empty! As they stood there totally bewildered, two men in white appeared and said:

Why are you looking among the dead for one who is alive? He is not here; he has been raised. LUKE 24:5–6

The women did not know what to make of their discovery. They ran back to tell the apostles what they had found.

Peter got up and ran to the tomb; he bent down and saw the grave cloths but nothing else. Then he went back home amazed at what had happened. LUKE 24:12

Jesus was alive! He had risen from the dead.

11 *Didn't Lazarus and Jairus' daughter die and come back to life? Explain.*

The word *resurrection* does not mean resuscitation. It is not a restoration to one's previous life, such as what happened to Lazarus and the daughter of Jairus. It involves far more. Resurrection involves complete transformation. It involves a quantum leap forward into a totally new life. It is something that no human being before Jesus had yet experienced.

To put it another way: The body of Jesus that rose on Easter Sunday was totally different from the body that was buried on Good Friday. CCC 631–66

Paul compares the body *before* resurrection to a seed planted in the soil and then compares the body *after*

resurrection to the plant that emerges from the dead seed plant. He writes:

*Someone will ask,
"How can the dead be raised to life?
What kind of body will they have?" . . .
When you plant a seed in the ground,
it does not sprout to life unless it dies.*

And what you plant is a bare seed . . .
not the full-bodied plant
that will grow up. . . .
That is how it will be
when the dead are raised to life.

When the body is buried, it is mortal;
when raised, it will be immortal.
When buried, it is ugly and weak;
when raised, it will be beautiful and strong.
When buried, it is a physical body;
when raised, it will be a spiritual body.
1 CORINTHIANS 15:42–44

Promise of the resurrection

The resurrection of Jesus is a promise that if we follow Jesus' teaching, we too will be raised to life on the last day. Jesus himself promised this:

"Those who eat my flesh and
drink my blood have eternal life, and
I will raise them to life on the last day."
JOHN 6:54

The resurrection of Jesus invites us to open our hearts to his presence among us. It invites us to let Jesus do for us what he has done for so many.

It invites us to love again after our love has been rejected and we are tempted to hate; to hope again after our hopes have been dashed and we are tempted to despair; and to believe again after our belief has been shaken and we are tempted to doubt.

The resurrection of Jesus is the good news that he has defeated death and wants to give us the power to do the same. The resurrection is the promise that nothing can destroy us: not pain, not rejection, not sin, not even death.

Spirit of Jesus

After the resurrection, Jesus enjoyed a totally new relationship with his brothers and sisters on earth. He was now glorified. He was now able to carry out his promise to send upon them the Holy Spirit. Luke describes the coming of the Holy Spirit this way in the Acts of the Apostles:

When the day of Pentecost came,
all the believers
were gathered together in one place.

Suddenly,
there was a noise from the sky. . . .
Then they saw what looked like
tongues of fire which spread out
and touched each person there.
They were all filled with the Holy Spirit.
ACTS 2:1–4

The sound of the noise was so loud that a huge crowd gathered outside to find out what was going on. Peter addressed them, saying:

Fellow Israelites!
Let me tell you what this means. . . .
This is what the prophet Joel spoke about:

"This is what I will do in the last days,"
God says: "I will pour out
my spirit on everyone."

"Turn away from his sins and
be baptized in the name of Jesus Christ . . .
and you will receive . . . the Holy Spirit."
ACTS 2:14; 16–17, 38

The coming of the Holy Spirit formed the disciples of Jesus into the Church, the "body of Christ." It empowered them to bring to completion God's Kingdom on earth, the re-creation of the world. 1 CORINTHIANS 12:1–29

Recap

The coming of Jesus and the Magi fulfill the Old Testament prophecies.

The baptism of Jesus marks the beginning of a new era, new creation, and new Adam. Jesus' miracles point to:

■ **God's Messiah**   **They fulfill prophecies: blind see and deaf hear.**

■ **God's Kingdom**   **They show power over sin, sickness, and death.**

Jesus' miracles invite us to:

■ **Open our eyes**   **Healing the blind**
■ **Open our ears**   **Healing the deaf**
■ **Begin a new life**   **Raising the dead**

Jesus compared the four ways people respond to his invitation of faith to the four fates of a seed that a farmer planted in his field.

Seed's fate	People's response
Fails to sprout	Reject
Sprouts but withers	Accept but fall
Sprouts but chokes	Accept but forget
Sprouts and grows	Accept and bear fruit

Jesus' resurrection is a promise that we will also be raised to life on the last day, if we walk with him in this life. It is also an invitation to open our hearts to Jesus' presence among us to let him do for us what he's done for so many.

The coming of the Holy Spirit formed Jesus' followers into the Church, Christ's body, and empowered them to complete his work on earth.

Review

1 The Gospels give us four approaches to Jesus. List (a) which Gospel was different from the other three, (c) why it was different, and (d) one example of how it differs from the others.

2 Against which background does Matthew situate Jesus' birth?

3 Who was responsible for giving Jesus his name, and what does the name *Jesus* mean?

4 List the three gifts the Magi presented to Jesus, and explain the symbolism of each.

5 List (a) the three events that take place at Jesus' baptism, and (b) what each signified.

6 What was John's favorite word for a miracle and why?

7 Explain how miracles announced the arrival of (a) the Messiah of God, and (b) the Kingdom of God.

8 Explain how the following miracles acted as an invitation to faith and action: (a) healing of the blind, (b) healing of the deaf, and (c) raising of the dead.

9 Briefly explain (a) the four different fates of the seed in Jesus' Parable of the Sower, and (b) how these fates correspond to the four different responses of people to Jesus' teaching.

10 Explain (a) the difference between resurrection and resuscitation, (b) in what sense the resurrection of Jesus is a promise to those who follow him faithfully, and (c) Paul's comparison to death and resurrection to a seed planted in the earth.

11 List the twofold effect the coming of the Holy Spirit had on Jesus' disciples.

Reflect

1 There was once a handsome prince who had a crooked back. It kept him from being the kind of prince he was meant to be. One day the king had a sculptor make a statue of the prince, portraying him with a straight back. The king put the statue in the prince's private garden.

In the days ahead, the prince found himself sitting in front of the statue daily, studying it and desiring to be like it. Months passed, and the people began to say, "The prince's back isn't as crooked as it once was." When the prince heard this, he grew excited. Now he began spending more time studying the statue.

One day a remarkable thing happened. The prince stood as straight as the statue.

■ *Who/what do the following stand for: (a) king, (b) prince, (c) crooked back, (d) statue, and (e) studying the statue?*

2 A London newspaper carried this ad in the early 1900s: "Wanted: Persons for dangerous journey. Small wages, bitter cold, long months of complete darkness, constant danger, safe return doubtful, honor and recognition if successful."

Over 5,000 applicants answered. From these Sir Ernest Shakleton chose twenty-eight for his polar expedition. All returned safely to honor and recognition.

Today, there is a great need for courageous, dedicated people in Christian ministry: priests, nuns, brothers, lay ministers.

Why do/don't you think more young people would address this need if they were approached frankly and straightforwardly, as Shakleton did in his ad?

■ *Have you ever thought of dedicating your life to Christian ministry? Explain.*
■ *List the pros and cons to Christian ministry as you see them.*

3 You are a reporter for the *Jerusalem Daily News*. The editor wants you to interview Jesus or someone closely connected with him. Select one of the following for the interview. List the questions you asked and the responses to them.

■ *A Magi on his visit to Jesus*
■ *Peter on Jesus' calming of the sea*
■ *A soldier on his crucifixion of Jesus*

Pencil meditations are ideal ways to pray. Simply imagine yourself to be a person in some Gospel scene and write out your feelings. Here is a pencil meditation by a Chicago student on the healing of the paralytic in Luke 5:17–26:

When my friends reached the house
where Jesus was, it was so packed that
we couldn't get in. So they got the idea to
hoist me to the roof and lower me from there.
As they dropped me down,
I felt everyone's eyes fixed on me.

There was one pair of eyes, however,
that I felt more than all the others.
They had an enormous presence about them.
It reminded me of when as a child,
I saw Herod for the first time.
Yet, this presence was far greater.

Suddenly, I began to feel badly about
what I'd done in my life. I had the feeling that
this man Jesus knew everything about me.
Then he spoke. It was a voice that could shake
the foundations of a building,
yet calm a frightened child. He told me,
"Your sins are forgiven."

I felt joy surge through my body and my mind.
Even my legs tingled. Yes! My legs tingled.
Then he told me, "Get up and walk." And I
did! I did! I had a great feeling of being born
again. I ran off to shout the news to my family.
But I forgot to thank him. Oh God!
How could I forget to thank him?

■ **Compose a similar "pencil meditation" on the crucifixion of Jesus.**

PRAYER Journal

In the Cathedral of Saint Peter in Lisieux, France, is a life-sized crucifix. Next to it are these words:

*I am the road
and you do not follow me.
I am the truth
and you do not believe me. . . .
I am your master
and you do not listen to me.
I am your leader
and you do not obey me.
I am your God
and you do not pray to me.
I am your best friend
and you do not love me.*

ANONYMOUS

■ *Compose a similar prayer of your own.*
■ *Or write a response to Jesus explaining why you find it hard to do these things.*

SCRIPTURE Journal

1	**Birth of Jesus**	**Luke 2:1–20**
2	**Temptations of Jesus**	**Luke 4:1–15**
3	**Two major miracles**	**Luke 8:40–56**
4	**Death of Jesus**	**John 19:28–41**
5	**Doubting Thomas**	**John 20:19–29**

■ *Pick out one of the above passages. Read it prayerfully and write a short statement to Jesus expressing your feelings about it.*

5 God the Father

Philip said to Jesus,
"Lord, show us the Father . . ."
Jesus answered . . .
"Whoever has seen me
has seen the Father . . .
Do you not believe, Philip, that
I am in the Father
and the Father is in me? . . .

"Those who love me will obey my teaching.
My Father will love them, and
my Father and I will come to them
and live in them.
JOHN 14:8–10, 23–24

Scripture contains
many portraits of God.
Three stand out, like stars in the night.
God is a Trinity of persons:
Father, Son, and Holy Spirit.
God is our Creator,
who called us into being.
God is our Father,
who loves us more than
we love ourselves.

Parable of God

The movie *Laura* is about a young woman who is mysteriously killed in her apartment. A young detective named Mark MacPherson is assigned to the case. He spends hours in Laura's apartment looking for clues. He leaves no stone unturned, even reading her diary.

The more Mark learns about Laura, the more he finds himself attracted to her. He finds himself falling in love with her. Then, late one night, Mark is seated in Laura's apartment thinking about her. Soon he nods and falls asleep.

Suddenly, something awakens him. He opens his eyes; and there, standing in the doorway, is a lovely young woman. It's Laura! Then an amazing story unfolds.

1 *Can you guess what could have happened?*

Laura had gone to the country for a weekend to rest. In all that time, she was out of contact with any news. The murder victim was an acquaintance, who had asked Laura to use her apartment that weekend.

The movie ends with Laura and Mark falling in love, marrying, and living happily ever after.

Commenting on the movie, one critic observed that it could be used as a kind of "modern parable of God's plan for us."

2 *Can you explain what this person probably had in mind?*

Plan of God

The movie mirrors the situation of all of us. Like Mark, we find ourselves in God's "apartment"—the universe. From its order and beauty, we get a clue of God's greatness.

Moreover, as Mark learned about Laura by studying her apartment, so we learn about God by studying the universe. Finally, as Mark's study attracted him to Laura, even though he'd never seen her; so our study of creation attracts us to the invisible God.

Hopefully, our story will also end happily, as did that of Mark and Laura.

Portraits of God

Ever since God created the world,
his invisible qualities,
*both his eternal power
and his divine nature,
have been clearly seen.* ROMANS 1:20

But the beauty and order of the universe is only a glimmer of God's glory and greatness. Reason cannot "paint a portrait" of God. Only Scripture can do that.

And so we turn to Scripture for a "word portrait" of God. First, we go to the Old Testament.

The Old Testament was written at a time when people lived close to nature. Thus, it uses many images from nature to speak about God. Consider a few of these images.

God is a mother eagle. She nourishes her young and teaches them how to fly. DEUTERONOMY 32:11

God is a shepherd. He protects his flock for wild animals, cares for the sick, and goes in search of the stray. EZEKIEL 34:16

God is the creator. He "set the earth firmly on its foundations" and decorated it with seas, and mountains. PSALM 104: 5–8

This brings us to the New Testament.

Here we find Jesus speaking of God in a variety of images also.

God is a loving Father. He knows our needs and takes care of them without our asking. LUKE 12:30

One afternoon a musician was standing on the tower that marks the highest peak of the Mohawk Trail in the Berkshire Mountains.

Three great states—New York, Connecticut, and Massachusetts—lay before him with their lakes, forests, and valleys. He was so moved by the grandeur of it all that he ran to his car, grabbed his cornet, and climbed back up the tower.

There he played with all his heart—for his joy, the joy of the tourists, and the glory of God.

Retold from Ardis Whitman

■ **What do we mean by the expression "give glory to God"? List some ways that you can give "glory" to God in your situation.**

God is a forgiving Father. He runs out to meet his repentant son and smothers him with a hugs and kisses. LUKE 15:20

Finally, God is a mystery of Unity and Trinity: Father, Son, and Holy Spirit. JOHN 14:10, 15:26

3 Which of these images do you find most appealing and why?

Let's take a closer look at three of these images of God: Creator, Father, and Trinity.

God created all

Recall that in 1968, four days before Christmas, Apollo lifted off with astronauts Frank Borman, Bill Anders, and Jim Lovell aboard.

As they rounded the moon on Christmas Eve, they sent greetings to earth, taking turns reading the story of creation from the Bible. The story portrays God creating the universe over a six-day period, much as an artisan works.

The point of this quaint imagery is to teach us that creation did not occur by chance or accident. It came into being by the creative act of a loving God.

God sustains all

God's work did not stop with creating the universe and everything in it. God also continues to hold it in existence. CCC 301 An example will illustrate.

Think of the things God created as being like images on a movie screen.

Think of God as being like the movie projector that put them there.

Just as the images owe their existence to the projector, so creation owes its existence to God.

Furthermore, just as the images on the movie screen would vanish into nothingness if the projector withdrew its light from them, so creation would vanish into nothingness if God withdrew his power from it.

But this is not all.

God is present in all

Late one hot afternoon, archaeologist Gene Savoy became lost in a jungle in Peru. A sickening feeling came over him. In panic, he began to run around feverishly, searching for the trail he had used to enter the jungle.

Suddenly, he realized that this frantic running was only making matters worse. Then he stopped and stood perfectly still. As he did, a strange thought flashed across his mind: God was in this jungle. It is God's house.

Gene had been introduced to the beauties of nature when he was a boy in Oregon. His parents taught him that God had created the universe, sustains it, and resides in it.

Why had he closed his eyes to God's presence in the jungles of Peru?

Didn't God create them also? Doesn't God sustain them also? Doesn't God reside in them also?

Instantly, Gene relaxed and put all his trust in God, in whose house he was. He said later:

I looked up
into the beautiful emerald world
of wild orchids and fragrant blossoms
where hummingbirds hovered.
Yes, God was there, too.
My heart quieted.

At that moment, something deep within him seemed to say, "Walk a few paces to the left." He did. And there was the tiny trail! He said later:

I am proud
of my archaeological discoveries.
But my greatest discovery, I believe, was
in recognizing God's presence everywhere.

4 *How might we explain the "voice" Gene heard deep within him? Which explanation fits best?*

God's presence

Let us go back to the example of the movie projector. Its light gives the images a real presence on the movie screen. So, too, the projector's light gives the projector a real presence on the screen.

In a similar way, God's creation gives God a real presence on earth. CCC 300 Saint Paul refers to this when he says of us, "In God we live and move and have our being." ACTS 17:28

A small boy was trying to lift a rock, but with no success. His father, who was watching nearby, asked: "Todd, are you sure that you're using all the strength you have?" The boy began to cry.

His father said gently, "Todd, you haven't asked me to help you. And I want to help you more than you could ever guess."

■ *What keeps me from asking my heavenly Father for help when I can't do something alone?*

THINK
about it

Like a human parent,
God will help us
when we ask for help,
but in a way that will make us
more mature, more real,
not in a way
that will diminish us.

Madeleine L'Engle

This brings us to a very important point. God is present to us in different ways and degrees. For example, God is present through:

■ **Creation** **Which God made**
■ **Scripture** **Which God inspired**
■ **Jesus** **Who is God's Son**

An example may help to clarify these different kinds of presence.

A little boy can be present to his mother in different ways and degrees. For example, he can be present through:

■ **A drawing** **Which he made**
■ **A letter** **Which he sent**
■ **In person** **Visiting his mother**

In a similar way, God can be present to us in different ways and degrees.

5 *What are some other ways and degrees the boy can become present to his mother?*

God's presence in different ways and degrees inspired the Hebrew psalmist to sing:

*Where could I go to escape from you?
Where could I get away
from your presence? . . .*

*If I flew away beyond the east
or lived in the farthest place in the west,
you would be there to lead me,
you would be there to help me.*
PSALM 139:7, 9–10

God as Father

The entire lower half of Lois Olson's body was in a cast. She lay in a bed unable to move. One night a tornado struck, and Lois began to panic. Just then her father appeared and carried her to safety. As he struggled under the weight of the cast, Lois could see sweat breaking out on his forehead and blood vessels bulging from his temples. This unforgettable experience gave Lois Olson a deep appreciation of God as Father.

Jesus used this image "Father" of God over 170 times. The Gospel According to Luke portrays Jesus addressing God as Father in his first and his last recorded words.

6 Can you recall the first and the last recorded words of Jesus in Scripture?

The word for "Father" that Jesus used in his own prayer was *Abba.* MARK 14:36 Literally, it means "Daddy."

Early Christians imitated Jesus and used the word *Abba,* also, in praying to God. ROMANS 8:15, GALATIANS 4:6

This means they addressed the infinite and all-powerful creator of the universe with the tender love and trust of a child, addressing a parent as "Mommy" or "Daddy." Thus, God says through the prophet Isaiah:

"Can a woman forget her own baby
and not love the child she bore?
Even if a mother should forget her child,
I will never forget you." ISAIAH 49:15

But God's love is infinitely different and greater than human love. Peter van Breeman explains the difference this way:

We are divided in our love.
We like a person very much (90%)
or in an ordinary way (50%). . . .

God does not measure love. . . .
If we think God is a person
who can divide love,
then we are thinking not of God
but ourselves. . . .
We have love, but God is love.
AS BREAD THAT IS BROKEN

Some people ask, "How can we reconcile the statement 'God is love' 1 JOHN 4:16 with Jesus' statement that God is to be 'feared'?" LUKE 12:5

7 How would you answer this question?

Poet Rod McKuen reconciled the paradox of love and fear with this analogy: "I love the sea, but that doesn't make me less afraid of it." In other words, the sea's beauty attracts him; but, at the same time, its awesome power makes him afraid of it.

8 How validly might this analogy be applied to God also? Explain.

Jean Webster's story "Daddy Long Legs" concerns an orphan girl who received many gifts from a person she never knew or met.

As a result she grew up blessed with remarkable opportunities that she would otherwise never have had. Often she would try to imagine what her benefactor was like, but she had no way of knowing if her image was correct.

Then one day the magic moment came: she met her benefactor. He exceeded her wildest dreams.

■ *To whom might we compare Daddy Long Legs? For what gifts from God am I especially grateful? Explain.*

THINK
about it

God wants spiritual fruit, not religious nuts.

E.C. McKenzie

God as Trinity

This brings us to the most incredible image of God that emerged from the life and teaching of Jesus: the mystery of God as Trinity.

It is the central mystery of our Christian faith. In the one, true God, there are three distinct persons: Father, Son, and Holy Spirit. CCC 266

Had God not revealed this mystery to us in Scripture, we could never have dreamed it. CCC 237

John's Gospel, especially, refers to God as Trinity: Father, Son, and Spirit. For example, Jesus tells his disciples:

"Whoever
has seen me has seen the Father. . . .
I will ask the Father,
and he will give you the Spirit."
JOHN 14:9, 16–17

The best-known reference to the Trinity is found in Matthew's Gospel. There Jesus tells his disciples:

"Go, then, to all peoples everywhere,
and make them my disciples,
baptizing them in the name of the Father,
the Son, and the Holy Spirit."
MATTHEW 28:19

The most graphic reference occurs in Luke's Gospel, as we saw, at the baptism of Jesus:

■ **Son**   **Jesus stands in the water.**
■ **Spirit**   **A dove hovers over Jesus.**
■ **Father**   **A voice says, "My Son."**

A beautiful reference to the Trinity is found at the end of Paul's Second Letter to the Corinthians. Paul uses it as a blessing upon his readers:

The grace of the Lord Jesus Christ,
the love of God,
and the fellowship of the Holy Spirit
be with you. 2 CORINTHIANS 13:13

9 *Which of the above Scripture references to the Holy Trinity do you find the clearest and the most helpful? Explain.*

Image of the Trinity

Some years ago, environmentalist Denis Hayes wrote a book entitled *Ray of Hope: The Transition to a Post-Petroleum World.*

The *Ray of Hope* is the sun. Its rays already light and heat our planet. Hayes writes that it is now time to let the sun's rays energize our planet even more than they currently do. He is referring to a more efficient use of solar energy.

Hayes's observation inspired some people to see the sun as an image of the Trinity:

Its *light* is an image of the Father who created the world, saying, "Let there be light!" And there was light.

Its *heat* is an image of Jesus, who saved us by the warmth of his love.

Its *energy* is an image of the Holy Spirit, who energizes us with grace.

And so the rays of the *one* sun bless us in *three* ways—lighting our planet, heating our planet, and energizing our planet—and in the process, serve as an image of the Trinity.

10 Can you recall other images of the Trinity? Which image do you find most helpful and why?

Saint Augustine was walking along a beach and meditating on the Trinity. "How can God be three and one at the same time?" he kept saying over and over to himself.

Suddenly, his attention was drawn to a little girl carrying a small container of water from the sea to a hole she had dug on the beach. "What are you doing?" he asked her. With childlike simplicity, she replied: "I'm emptying the sea into this hole."

Saint Augustine stopped dead in his tracks and thought: "I am trying to do what that little girl is doing. I'm trying to crowd the infinite God into the finite structure of my mind."

11 To which member of the Holy Trinity can you relate and pray most easily? Which one is hardest to pray to? Why?

HISTORICAL Connection

Father Paul Schulte offered Mass on the giant dirigible Hindenburg on its sixty-two-hour maiden voyage from Germany to Lakehurst, New Jersey, May 18, 1936. In his homily, he said:

*Glory to God the Father
who created the earth;
and to God the Son
who redeemed the earth;
and to God the Holy Spirit
who hallowed the earth.*

*Let the "Amen" be pronounced
by the skies and the marvelous
clouds which surround us,
by the ocean over which we are
hovering, by the sun, the
breeze, and the stars.*

*Let the "Amen"
be spoken by the motors,
the wonderful airship,
the crew, the passengers.
Glory be to thee today,
tomorrow,
and in all eternity. Amen.*

Quoted by John M Scott, S.J., in *Journeys Into Space: Scientific and Spiritual Events*, Liguorian, July–August 1999

Recap

Reason alone cannot give us a "portrait" of God. Only Scripture can do that.

Scripture uses a variety of images to paint a vivid and beautiful portrait of God. Among these images are the following:

- **Eagle**   **Mothers her young**
- **Shepherd**   **Protects his flock**

Of all the scriptural images of God, however, there are three that stand out above all the others.

- **Creator**   **Resides in us**
- **Father**   **Loves us infinitely**
- **Trinity**   **One God; three persons**

A modern image of the Trinity is the sun, whose rays bless our planet with:

- **Light**   **Father**   **(Creator)**
- **Heat**   **Son**   **(Redeemer)**
- **Energy** **Spirit**   **(Sanctifier)**

Review

1 Briefly explain how the movie *Laura* serves as a parable of God's plan for us.

2 List two Old Testament images and two New Testament images that the Bible uses to "paint a word portrait" of what God is like.

3 Using the example of a movie projector, explain what we mean when we say that God (a) created everything, (b) sustains it, and (c) resides in it.

4 List and briefly explain three ways God is present among us.

5 Early Christians imitated Jesus and used the word *Abba* to address God. Briefly explain (a) what the word means, literally, and (b) how we can reconcile God's love for us with Jesus' words that we should fear God.

6 Explain the difference between God's love and human love.

7 What is the central mystery of Christianity and what does it say?

8 Give two references to this mystery in the New Testament.

9 Explain how some people view the sun as an excellent image of the Trinity.

Reflect

1 Estlin Carpenter served as a chaplain at Harvard University. The surprising thing about him was that during his school days he was apathetic about God and religion. What happened to change him?

One afternoon, while out for a walk, he felt an incredible presence of God all around him. It was as if God suddenly began walking along with him just as Jesus did with the disciples returning to Emmaus.

That experience impacted him dramatically. His attitude toward God and religion did an about face. He said, "I could now not only believe in God with my mind, but also love him with my heart." Carpenter was never the same again after that afternoon.

■ *Why should only a few people be blessed with such a spiritual presence?*
■ *What is the nearest thing you have had to Carpenter's experience? Be as detailed as you can be.*

2 For years, a small statue of Cupid stood in the entrance hall of an old New York City mansion. Its arms and face were badly damaged; but the statue had a charm about it that made it a good conversation piece.

One day it caught the attention of Professor Brandt of New York University. It matched the description of a lost work of Michelangelo. Sure enough, it was. The story of the statue makes a good parable of God.

Like the statue, God is present in our midst, but unrecognized by the majority of people. But every once in a while, someone claims to recognize God's presence with the same surprise and certitude that Professor Brandt experienced when she recognized Cupid.

■ *How can we distinguish between a graced experience of God and an imaginary one?*

3 Sunday morning, May 18, 1980, the volcano Mount Saint Helens exploded. Photographer David Crocket of KOMO-TV, Seattle, was caught at the foot of the volcano when it blew. He was nearly buried by the flying debris and tons of suffocating volcanic ash.

David remained motionless for the next several hours to conserve air amidst the dust and ash that engulfed the site like a huge cloud.

Then a miraculous thing happened. A Coast Guard helicopter spotted David and rescued him. After his ordeal, he wrote in *Guideposts* magazine:

During those ten hours
I saw a mountain fall apart.
I saw a forest disappear. . . .
I saw that God is the only one
who is unmovable, unshakable, infallible.

I feel somehow
that I'm being allowed to start over
whatever is in his master plan for me.

■ *To what extent do you agree that God has a master plan for the human race and each of us has a part to play in it?*
■ *Describe your closest brush with death and how it affected you as it did David.*

PRAYER TIME
with the Lord

A practical way of praying daily to the Holy Trinity is called the "three-minute replay method. Here's how it works:

First minute: Replay your day. Pick out a high point: a good thing you did. Talk to the Father about it and give thanks.

Second minute: Replay your day again. Pick out a low point: a bad thing that you did. Talk to Jesus about it. Ask him to forgive you.

Third minute: Look ahead to a critical point: a hard thing you must do. Talk to the Holy Spirit about it and ask for help.

Here's a sample three-minute replay:

High Point: I got an e-mail from a friend. Father, I really like this person. Thank you for hearing from him and help our friendship grow.

Low Point: I yelled at my mother. Jesus, I can't imagine you ever yelling at your mother. Please forgive me and help me to make it up to her.

Critical Point: I have a problem. Holy Spirit, I have a friend who is using drugs. Help me to know how to deal with this problem.

■ *Write out a three-minute replay of your own.*

PRAYER Journal

An excellent way to begin your "Prayer Time with the Lord" is by beginning with the following prayer to the Trinity.

*Father, you created me
and put me on earth for a purpose.
Jesus, you died for me
and called me to complete your work.
Holy Spirit, you help me
to carry out the work
for which I was created and called.*

*In your presence and name—
Father, Son, and Spirit—
I begin my meditation.
May all my thoughts and inspirations
have their origin in you
and be directed to your glory.*

■ *Compose a brief letter to God the Father concerning his purpose in creating you.*

_____
_____
_____
_____
_____
_____
_____
_____
_____
_____

SCRIPTURE Journal

1	Loving Father	Hosea 11:1–4
2	Loving host	Psalm 23
3	Loving creator	Psalm 8
4	Forgiving Father	Luke 15:11–32
5	Forgiving Jesus	John 8:1–11

■ *Pick one of the above passages. Read it prayerfully and write a short statement to Jesus expressing your feelings about it.*

_____
_____
_____
_____
_____

6 God the Son

*We write to you about the Word of Life,
which has existed from the beginning.
We have heard it, and we have seen it,
and our hands have touched it. . . .*

*What we have seen and heard
we announce to you, also,
so that you will join us in the fellowship
that we have with the Father
and with his Son, Jesus Christ.
We write this in order that your joy
may be complete.* 1 JOHN 1:1–4

**Jesus is Son of God,
both human and divine.
He is also the Word of God.
He reveals God to us;
and he reveals what we can become,
if we open ourselves to the Spirit,
which he sent upon us.**

Image of God the Son

A young man pulled into a parking lot. Above the rear bumper of his car were the letters I CH TH Y S, shaped like a fish. Someone asked, "What's the meaning of the fish-shaped word?"

The young man explained that they were the first letters of the Greek expression that is translated "Jesus, Christ, Son of God, Savior."

In Greek the letters spell "fish." This explains why the image of a fish became the secret sign for Jesus during times of persecution in early Christianity.

The words "Jesus," "Christ," "Son of God," and "Savior" sum up four titles we give to the second person of the Trinity.

- **Jesus**
- **Christ**
- **Son of God**
- **Savior**

Jesus

The most personal thing we own is our name. It identifies us as a member of the human family. It is the way our friends address us; and it is the way that people speak about us. The name "Jesus" did the same thing for the Son of God.

In biblical times, names often did more than just identify a person. They also revealed something about the person. Jesus' name did that also.

Jesus received his name from an angel, who said to Joseph, "You will name him Jesus—because he will save his people from their sins." MATTHEW 1:21

The name "Jesus" not only identifies him as a member of the human family, but also as having a saving mission from God. CCC 430–35

Trapped

Three high school boys set out on a four-day climb up Mount Hood in Oregon. They were fairly experienced climbers, but they were not prepared for what happened about 9,000 feet up the mountain.

A giant blizzard struck. Unable to move up or down the mountain, they tunneled into a snowbank to make a snow cave in which to wait out the storm.

A week passed and the blizzard still raged on. The three were now growing frightened. Fortunately, there was just enough light in the snow cave to read by, so they took turns reading aloud from a pocket Bible, which one of the boys happened to have in his pack.

As the blizzard raged into the second week, their food supply ran out. Now they began to lose hope that they'd survive or be rescued. As they read the Bible and prayed, they began to see a parallel between their situation and that of the Jewish people before the birth of Jesus. They, too, were beginning to lose hope as they waited and waited for the Messiah.

On the sixteenth day, the weather cleared. The students crawled out of the cave, barely able to stand up. As they looked around, one of them saw a rescue team coming up the mountain. The glorious feeling that the students felt as they saw the rescuers was overwhelming.

1 *What parallel might we draw between the students waiting for rescue and faithful Jews waiting for the Messiah?*

Cordell Brown

Cordell Brown was a cerebral palsy victim. He was invited to speak at a pre-game chapel service in the clubhouse of the Philadelphia Phillies. Why? What did he, living in a world of pain and deformity, have to say to athletes?

He began by putting the players at ease. He said: "I know I'm different; but by the grace of God I am what I am." Then for the next twenty minutes he talked of God's goodness to him.

He concluded by answering the question: "What could he say to a group to superstars?" He said in a loving way:

*You may hit three-fifty
for a lifetime
and get $5 million a year,
but when the day comes
that they close
the lid on that box,
you won't be any different
than I am.
That's one time when
we'll all be the same.
I don't need what you have,
but one thing is for sure:
You need what I have:
Jesus Christ.*

Retold from Pat Williamson (slightly adapted)

Christ

This brings us to the second title of the second person of the Holy Trinity. One day Jesus asked Peter, "Who do you say I am?" Peter replied, "You are the Messiah, the Son of the living God." MATTHEW 16:15, 16

The Hebrew word *Messiah* means "the anointed." It is translated into Greek as *Christos*—from which we get our English "Christ." The title "Christ" identifies Jesus as the long-awaited Messiah. CCC 436–40, 711–16

Thus, the words *Messiah* (Hebrew), *Christos* (Greek), and *Christ* (English) are simply different ways to refer to the same person: the descendent of David, promised by God through the prophets.

Old Testament kings, priests, and, in some cases, prophets were anointed—consecrating and empowering them to carry out their mission from God. CCC 436

How much more appropriate was it then that the promised Messiah be anointed king, priest, and prophet. And this is precisely how Jesus identified himself in the synagogue in Nazareth, saying:

*"The Spirit of the Lord is upon me,
because he has chosen [anointed] me
to bring good news to the poor . . .
to proclaim liberty to the captives
and recovery of sight to the blind . . .
and [to] announce that the time has come
when the Lord will save his people."*
LUKE 4:18–19

And so the title "Christ" identifies Jesus as the long-promised Messiah, whose reign will extend to all peoples of all times. CCC 727–30

Cold and Confused

One Christmas day, a woman was seated in front of her fireplace thinking about the birth of Jesus. She asked herself, "Why would the Creator of the world choose to be born on earth and live among us as a man?" The whole thing seemed absurd.

Just then she heard a strange sound outside. Going to the window, she saw a half-dozen geese staggering about in the snow. They had apparently wandered off from a warm barn and were now cold and confused.

She went outside, opened the door to her warm garage, and tried to get the geese to go in. But the more she tried, the more frightened they became—and the more they scattered. Finally, she gave up. She realized that the geese had no idea that she was trying to help them.

At that moment, a strange thought crossed her mind: "If for one minute I could become a goose, I could explain to them that what I was trying to do was for their good!" Then it struck her. That's what Christmas is all about!

2 *How does the woman's experience shed light on what Christmas is all about?*

Son of God

This brings us to the most important title that is given to Jesus: "Son of God." CCC 441–45

In the Old Testament, the title "Son of God" is applied to a wide range of people. For example, it is given to Israel's kings (2 SAMUEL 7:14). It is also given to Israel as a whole (EXODUS 4:22). In this case, it signifies God's "adoption" of Israel as the "Chosen People."

In other words, the title is used in the Old Testament not in the *literal* sense of the words, but in a kind of *figurative* sense, much as we might refer to a good person as an "angel."

In the New Testament, we find the title "Son of God" used of Jesus over a hundred times. More importantly, we find it used of Jesus in the *literal* sense of the words. Thus, John writes near the end of his Gospel:

These [things] have been written in order that you may believe that Jesus is the Messiah, the Son of God, and that through your faith in him you may have life. JOHN 20:31

Similarly, Matthew has Peter use the title in the full *literal* sense when he says of Jesus, "You are the Messiah, the Son of the Living God." Jesus acknowledges the literal use of the title, saying to Peter:

"This truth did not come to you from any human being, but it was given to you directly by my Father in heaven." MATTHEW 16:17

There are two solemn moments, especially, when the title applied to Jesus in the literal sense. In both cases, the title comes from God the Father. The first is at Jesus' baptism. Matthew writes:

As soon as Jesus was baptized, he came up out of the water.

ART Connection

This painting of the *Baptism of Jesus*, by the Italian painter Paolo Cagliari, was completed about 1570.

Mike Moran was a Navy helicopter pilot. One day, while explaining his "chopper" to his parents, he said, "As complex as those machines are, their whirling rotors are held in place by one simple hexagonal nut." Then turning to his mother he said, "Guess what that nut is called, Mom?" She shrugged. He smiled and said, "It's called a 'Jesus Nut.'"

■ *To what extent does Jesus hold my life together?*

■ *What is one area of my life that is still not under his control?*

■ *What is one step I might take to change this?*

PRAYER
hotline

O Lord, help me understand that nothing can come my way that you and I together can't handle.

Author unknown

Then heaven was opened to him, and he saw the Spirit of God coming down like a dove and lighting on him.

Then a voice said from heaven,
"This is my own dear Son,
with whom I am pleased.
MATTHEW 3:16–17

The second of these solemn moments occurred at the transfiguration of Jesus on the mountain, in the presence of Peter, James, and John. Matthew writes:

As they looked on,
a change came over Jesus:
his face was shining like the sun,
and his clothes were dazzling white.
Then the three disciples
saw Moses and Elijah talking with Jesus.

So Peter spoke up and said to Jesus,
"Lord, how good it is that we are here! . . .
While he was talking,
a shining cloud came over them,
and a voice from the cloud said,
"This is my own dear Son,
with whom I am pleased—listen to him!"

When the disciples heard the voice,
they were so terrified
that they threw themselves
face downward on the ground.
MATTHEW 17:2–6

So Jesus the Son of man is also the Son of God. Within his person he harmonizes two natures: our *human* nature and God's *divine* nature. Jesus is true God and true man. CCC 442–45, 479–83

3 *Why is/isn't it easier for you to think of Jesus as "true God" or "true man"?*

Rescued

There's a story about a man who dove into a raging river to save a ten-year-old from drowning. A few days later, the ten-year-old and his mother went to see the man.

The child said to the man, "How can I thank you for what you did for me?" The man put his arm around the ten-year-old and said, "Son, the best thanks you can give me is to live your life in a way that will have made it worth saving."

4 *If you asked Jesus, your Savior, what this means in terms of living your life, what might he say?*

Savior

This brings us to the fourth title of the second person of the Holy Trinity.

One day, Jesus met a woman at a well outside a village. She was so impressed with Jesus that she hurried back to her village. Describing Jesus to the villagers, she said, "Could he be the Messiah?" JOHN 4:29

The villagers went to Jesus and invited him to teach them. After listening to him for two days, they said to one another, "He really is the Savior of the world." JOHN 4:42, CCC 457

Jesus impacted other people in the same way. For example, Saint John writes:

What we have seen and heard
we announce to you also . . .
that the Father sent his Son
to be the Savior of the world.
1 JOHN 1:3, 4:14

To appreciate Jesus' title, the "Savior of the world," recall the first sin. CCC 413–21 The sin of Adam unleashed a tidal wave of evil across the world. The human race was doomed. Saint Paul says: "Death has spread to the whole human race because everyone has sinned. ROMANS 5:12

Paul then goes on to describe how Jesus' death and resurrection saved the human race:

So then,
as the one sin condemned all mankind,
in the same way the one righteous act
sets all mankind free
and gives them life. ROMANS 5:18

Paul sums the mystery of the second person of the Holy Trinity becoming man this way:

Jesus always had the nature of God,
but he . . . appeared in human likeness.

He was humble
and walked the path of obedience
all the way to death—death on the cross.

For this reason
God raised him to the highest place above
and gave him the name
that is greater than any other name.

And so in honor of the name of Jesus
all beings in heaven, on earth,
and the earth below
will fall on their knees
and all will proclaim
that Jesus Christ is Lord,
to the glory of God the Father.
PHILIPPIANS 2:6–11

5 *Explain the titles of Jesus in the last two lines.*

This brings us to two final titles of the second person of the Holy Trinity:

- **Lord**
- **Word of God**

HISTORICAL Connection

He never wrote a book. . . .
He never owned
a home. . . .
He never traveled two hundred
miles from the place where he
was born. . . .

While still a young man,
the tide of popular opinion
turned against him. . . .

He was nailed to a cross. . . .
When he was dead,
he was taken down
and laid in a borrowed grave. . . .

Nineteen hundred centuries
have come and gone,
and today he is the central figure
of the human race. . . .

I am far within the mark
when I say that all the armies
that ever marched . . .
have not affected
the life of man upon earth
as powerfully
as this One Solitary Life.

Anonymous

Paul Waldeman was a Jew. He fled from Nazi Germany, settled in Chicago, and married a Catholic girl. The two talked a lot about religion. Then, one day, a startling question popped into Paul's mind: Could Jesus really be the Son of God? He writes:

*My first reaction
was to dismiss it. . . .
But it kept coming back. . . .
I had to investigate. . . .
But the more I read, the more
confused . . . I became. . . .
For weeks on end . . .
I pleaded with God,
"Please show me
what you want me to do." . . .
But he remained silent. . . .
[Then one evening God spoke.]
I was filled with a peace and
lightheartedness
I had never known before.*

Richer Than a Millionaire: One Man's Journey to God (Liguori, Mo.: Liguori Publications, 1992), pp. 98–99, 104.

■ *Why does God let some of us struggle long and hard for the faith?*

■ *What is one thing about the faith that I am struggling with? What should I do about resolving it?*

Lord

One day, Moses was grazing his sheep. Suddenly, he saw a nearby bush on fire. There wasn't anything alarming about that. Occasionally, a dried sagebrush caught fire in the hot sun, blazed up for a moment, and went out. But this time the fire didn't go out. Moses went over to see why.

GOD   *Do not come any closer.
Take off your sandals,
because you are standing
on holy ground.
I am the God of your
ancestors. . . .*

MOSES   *When I go to the Israelites
and say to them,
"The God of your ancestors
sent me to you," they will ask me,
"What is his name?"
So what can I tell them?*

GOD   *I am who I am.
You must tell them:
"The one who is called I AM
has sent me . . .
this is my name forever;
this is what all future
generations are to call me."*
EXODUS 3:5–6, 13–15

The expression "I am who I am" introduces us to the Hebrew proper name for God. It is designated by the four Hebrew letters YHWH.

The original meaning of YHWH is uncertain, but scholars suggest the translation "I am who I am," that is, "I cannot be named or defined." CCC 206

6 *Why do/don't you think it is significant that John used a number of "I am" titles of Jesus in his Gospel: I am the Good Shepherd, I am the Light of the World, I am the Bread of Life?*

Since New Testament times, YHWH has been translated into Greek as *Kyrios*, which means "Lord" in English. New Testament writers used this title to refer both to Jesus and the Father. By giving the name "LORD" to Jesus, early Christians made it clear that the same "power, honor, and glory" due to the Father was due also to Jesus. CCC 446–51 They made it clear that Jesus is divine: one with the Father and the Holy Spirit. And this is how Peter used the title in his speech to the people on Pentecost. He said, "This Jesus, whom you crucified, is the one that God has made Lord and Messiah!" ACTS 2:36 This is also the same way that Paul used the title in his letter to the Romans, saying:

*If you confess Jesus is Lord
and believe that God raised him from
death, you will be saved.* ROMANS 10:9

This brings us to the final title of the second person of the Holy Trinity.

Word of God

John begins his Gospel somewhat as a musical composer begins a symphony: with a beautiful overture that previews what is to follow. He writes:

*In the beginning the Word already existed;
the Word was with God,
and the Word was God. . . .
The Word was the source of life,
and this life brought light to people.*
JOHN 1:1, 4

John is speaking, of course, of Jesus, the "Word of God" made flesh. This is what we mean when we speak of Jesus as the "Incarnate Word" of God. CCC 461–63

We may think of Jesus as being the Word of God in a twofold sense. He tells us:

■ About the Father
■ About ourselves

Let's take a look at each. We begin with Jesus, the Word of God, who tells us about God the Father.

One day Jesus was speaking to his apostles about his Father in heaven. At a certain point in the discussion, Philip said:

"Lord, show us the Father . . ."
Jesus answered . . . "Whoever has seen me
has seen the Father. . . .
Believe me when I say
that I am in the Father and
the Father is in me.
If not, believe because
of the things I do." JOHN 14:8, 9, 11

Jesus is the "Word of God" in the sense that he reveals God to us. He does this not only by what he says about the Father, but also in what he is— compassionate, merciful, loving. CCC 238–42 The Letter to the Hebrews does not hesitate to say of Jesus:

He reflects
the brightness of God's glory and
is the exact likeness of God's own being.
HEBREWS 1:31

Besides telling us about God the Father, Jesus also tells us about ourselves. He reveals to us what God intended for us to become when he created us.

One day a missionary began her class on Jesus, saying to the children:

Today I want to tell you
about someone you must meet.
He is a person who loves you and
cares for you even more
than your own family and friends.
He is a person who is kinder
than the kindest person you know.

The missionary noticed that a little boy was getting more and more excited as she talked. Suddenly, the boy blurted out, "I know that man! He lives on our street."

The second way Jesus is the Word of God is that he reveals to us what every Christian can become, if we open

ourselves to the Holy Spirit. CCC 459–60, 520 Each of us can become a living image of the Word of God. Jesus says the way for us to live in order that we be worth saving is to imitate him.

Jesus sums it up in one sentence: "Love one another, just as I love you." JOHN 15:12 In other words, we are called to:

■ Love our enemies
■ Forgive those who persecute us
■ Befriend outcasts of our society
■ Be a "light" to our world

7 *Which of these would you find the most difficult to do? Why?*

FAITH Connection

Jesus and I were riding
a tandem bicycle.
At first, I sat in front;
Jesus in the rear.
I couldn't see him,
but I knew he was there.
I could feel his help
when the road got steep.

Then, one day,
Jesus and I changed seats.
Suddenly,
everything went topsy-turvy.
When I was in control,
the ride was predictable,
even boring.

But when Jesus took over,
it got wild!
I could hardly hold on.
"This is madness!" I cried.
But Jesus just smiled
and said, "Pedal!"

And so I learned to shut up
and pedal—and
trust my bike companion.
Oh, there are still times
when I get scared
and I'm ready to quit.
But Jesus turns around,
touches my hand, smiles,
and says, "Pedal!" M.L.

Inspired by and
modeled after an unknown author

Recap

Review

The Greek word *I CH TH Y S* was used by early Christians as a symbol of Jesus, the second person of the Holy Trinity. Standing at the center of our faith and of all human history, he is:

- **Jesus**   has a human nature
- **Son of God**   has a divine nature
- **Christ**   is the Messiah
- **Savior**   is the Savior

Scripture gives two final titles of Jesus to complete our picture of the second person of the Holy Trinity. He is the:

- **Lord**
- **Word of God**

Jesus is the Word of God in a twofold sense. First, Jesus tells us:

- **About the Father**
- **About ourselves**

1 Explain how early Christians came to use a fish to symbolize Jesus.

2 What is the origin and meaning of the name of Jesus?

3 Explain the relationship between the following: (a) Messiah, (b) *Christos* (Christ), and (c) the Anointed One.

4 By whom did Jesus say he was "anointed" and for what purpose? Where did Jesus make this announcement?

5 Explain how the Old Testament and the New Testament differ in the way they use the title "Son of God."

6 Cite one occasion when the New Testament calls Jesus the "Savior of the world."

7 Explain the connection between *YHWH*, *Kyrios,* and LORD.

8 Explain the twofold sense in which Jesus may be called the "Word of God."

Reflect

1 Recall the story in the text about the boy who was saved from drowning. After the boy recovered from shock, he threw his arms around the man and thanked him. The man said, "That's okay, son! Just make sure your life was worth saving."

■ *How is this story a parable of every person?*
■ *List three things you're considering doing with your life. After each one write one reason for and one reason against doing it.*
■ *Which possibility attracts you most and why?*

2 A woman said that if we accept the Gospels as being faithful to Jesus' claim, the following three options are open to us:

Jesus was a liar. He knew that he was not one with God the Father and deceived the people into thinking that he was.

Jesus was a lunatic. He was a sick person who was under the illusion that he was God's Son and one with the Father.

Jesus was the Lord. He was God's Son, of whom John said, "God loved the world so much that he gave his only Son, so that everyone who believes in him may not die but have eternal life." JOHN 3:16

■ *Explain to what extent you agree or disagree with Jesus Christ being (a) a liar, (b) a lunatic, (c) the LORD.*

3 Leonard Le Sourd wrote an article called "The Five Christs I Have Known." It describes how his personal relationship with Jesus developed as he grew up.

First, there was the *fanciful* Christ. This was the Christ of his childhood. This Christ was like Santa Claus or the Easter Bunny—pretty much a figment of his immature imagination.

Second, there was the *historical* Christ of his student years. This Christ was like Abraham Lincoln or George Washington: an admirable person, but someone who did not make any concrete demands on his personal life.

Third, there was the *teacher* Christ of his early adult life. This Christ was like Aristotle: a wise person whose teaching is still valid today.

Fourth, there was the *savior* Christ. This Christ was different from any other person who ever lived. He was the Son of God, the Savior of the world. After discovering this Christ, LeSourd committed his life to Jesus.

Finally, there was the *indwelling* Christ. This Christ formed Jesus' followers into one body and empowered them to go forth and transform their world. It was this same Jesus who now took control of Le Sourd's life.

■ *Briefly describe how your relationship with Jesus has changed over the years.*
■ *How would you describe it at this point in your life: growing, in a holding pattern, declining? Explain.*

PRAYER TIME
with the Lord

Saint Francis de Sales gives this advice in one of his letters:

Do not become discouraged,
if sometimes, and even quite often,
you do not find consolation
in your meditation. Persevere at it. . . .
Make use of your books. . . .
read a little and then meditate.
Keep this up until the end of your prayer.

This method of praying involves three steps:

1. reading a passage prayerfully,
2. thinking how it applies to your life,
3. speaking to Jesus about it.

Try the method on the following prayer.

Give us your love, Lord.
For sometimes people reject us,
and we are tempted to hate.

Give us your strength, Lord.
For sometimes things get tough,
and we are ready to quit.

Give us your courage, Lord.
For sometimes we are put under pressure,
and it's hard to do what is right.

Give us your forgiveness, Lord.
For sometimes we fail to do right
and we need your mercy.

Give us yourself, Lord.
For our hearts were made for you
and we will not rest until we rest in you. M.L.

■ **Write out your meditation on one of the above five verses.**

PRAYER Journal

Here is an imaginary dialogue between a wayfarer and Jesus:

WAYFARER   *We are traveling an unknown*
land to an unknown city.
The sky is dark and misty.
Soaring mountains and
turbulent seas obscure our path.
We have no map or person
to guide us.
Our hearts tremble with fear.

Jesus   *Fear not. I'll be your guide.*
I'll light up your darkness,
move mountains from your path,
help you walk on water,
calm your hearts and
teach you to sing.

■ *Compose a similar, brief dialogue with Jesus*
on trying to be his follower today.

_____

_____

_____

_____

_____

_____

_____

_____

_____

_____

SCRIPTURE Journal

1	**Lord and God**	John 20:24–28
2	**Son of God**	Mark 15:22–39
3	**Word of God**	John 1:1–18
4	**The Anointed One**	Luke 4:16–22
5	**Savior of the World**	1 John 4:13–18

■ *Pick one of the above passages. Read it*
prayerfully and write a short statement to
Jesus to express your feelings about it.

7

God the Holy Spirit

*F*or forty days after his death,
*Jesus appeared to his disciples many times
in ways that proved beyond doubt
that he was alive. . . .
He gave them this order:*

*"Do not leave Jerusalem,
but wait for the gift I told you about. . . .
In a few days you will be baptized
with the Holy Spirit. . . .
You will be filled with power,
and you will be witnesses for me . . .
to the ends of the earth."* ACTS 1:4–5, 8

*On Pentecost the Holy Spirit came
and filled the disciples
with amazing power.
Collectively, they became
temples of the Holy Spirit,
Christ's Body, the Church.
Individually, they were graced with
remarkable virtues, gifts, and fruits
to be used for the building up
of God's Kingdom.*

The maestro

A mother took her very young son, Jason, to a matinee concert by the famous pianist Ignace Paderewski. She hoped the experience would encourage his own musical efforts.

She was delighted to see how close to the stage their seats were. Then she saw an old friend sitting nearby. She got so involved talking with her that she didn't notice her son leaving to do some exploring.

Shortly, the auditorium lights dimmed, the audience hushed, and a spotlight fell on the piano on stage. Only then did the audience notice a tiny boy sitting on the piano bench, innocently picking out "Twinkle, Twinkle, Little Star." The five-year-old's mother gasped in total disbelief.

But before she could do anything, Paderewski emerged from the wings, walked over to Jason, and whispered, "Son, keep playing!"

Then, leaning over the boy, he reached out his left hand and began filling in the bass. A few seconds later, he reached around the other side of the boy, encircling him, and added a running obbligato.

Together, the maestro and the tiny five-year-old mesmerized the audience with their playing. When they finished, the audience broke into a thunderous applause.

Years later, not all present that day remembered the works that Paderewski played, but everyone remembered "Twinkle, Twinkle, Little Star."

The image of the great maestro transforming the boy's elementary musical efforts into something far beyond the boy's ability to achieve is a good image of what the Pentecost experience did for Jesus' followers.
DARREL L. ANDERSON, *LEADERSHIP* (RETOLD)

1 *In what sense was: (a) the disciples' spiritual knowledge akin to the boy's musical knowledge, (b) Pentecost's impact on the disciples akin to Paderewski's impact on Jason?*

The Holy Spirit

In his book *Meditations*, Anthony Bloom quotes a Japanese Christian saying: "In the Christian religion I think I understand about the Father and the Son, but I am confused about the honorable bird." The Japanese Christian is not alone in his confusion.

Whenever we think of the Holy Spirit, we usually think of Pentecost: the coming of the Spirit upon the disciples of Jesus. In a certain sense, however, it is dangerous to speak of the "coming of the Spirit." It can create the impression that the Holy Spirit was not around before Pentecost. This is not true. The third person of the Holy Trinity, the Holy Spirit, has been around as long as the Father and the Son. CCC 689

The Acts of the Apostles makes this crystal clear. It portrays the Holy Spirit acting in the world long before Pentecost. CCC 702–10 For example, it refers to the Holy Spirit inspiring King David and speaking through Isaiah. ACTS 1:16; 28:25

The Gospels also make it clear that the Holy Spirit was active in Jesus' life, long before Pentecost. CCC 689–90 The Spirit:

- **Anointed Jesus**   Acts 10:38
- **Empowered Jesus**   Luke 4:14
- **Guided Jesus**   Luke 4:1

Promise of the Spirit

Even though the Holy Spirit acted long before Pentecost, something unique and monumental did happen on Pentecost. Toward the end of his earthly life, while celebrating the Passover supper, Jesus said to his disciples:

"I shall not be with you
very much longer. . . .
I will ask the Father,
and he will give you another Helper. . . .
He is the Spirit. JOHN 13:33; 14:16–17

Then, just before ascending to heaven, Jesus gave his disciples this instruction:

"Do not leave Jerusalem,
but wait for the gift I told you about. . . .
John baptized with water, but in a few days
you will be baptized with the Holy Spirit."
ACTS 1:4–5

The stage was set for one of the most important events in history: the coming of the Holy Spirit on the followers of Jesus. It changed their lives forever.

When the day of Pentecost came,
all the believers
were gathered together in one place.
Suddenly, there was a noise from the sky,
which sounded like a strong wind
blowing. . . .

Then they saw what looked like
tongues of fire which spread out
and touched each person there.
They were all filled with the Holy Spirit
and began to talk in other languages,
as the Spirit enabled them to speak.
ACTS 2:1–4

The "noise from the sky" was so loud that it attracted a huge crowd to the house. The apostles went out to tell them what happened. Peter explained that it was what God had foretold through Joel the prophet:

"I will pour out my Spirit on everyone.
Your sons and daughters
will proclaim my message." ACTS 2:17

The people in the crowd had come from many different nations to celebrate the feast of Pentecost. They were amazed to hear the apostles speaking in their native tongues. They asked one another: "How is it . . . that all of us hear them speaking in our own native languages?" ACTS 2:8 Then it dawned on them. The answer lay in the Old Testament story of the Tower of Babel. It begins:

At first, the people of the whole world
had only one language
and used the same words.

*As they wandered about in the East,
they came to a plain in Babylonia
and settled there.
They said to one another . . .
"Let's build a city with a tower
that reaches the sky, so that we can
make a name for ourselves."* GENESIS 11:1–3, 4

But the LORD did not approve. He mixed up their language and "scattered them all over the earth."

*The city was called Babylon because
there the LORD mixed up the languages
of all the people, and from there he
scattered them all over the earth.*
GENESIS 11:9

Hearing the apostles speak in their own native tongue was a sign that what happened at the Tower of Babel is now being reversed.

The Holy Spirit will unite the peoples of the world, who split into hostile factions and whose sin had scattered across the earth. It is a giant leap forward in God's plan to re-create the world.

2 Why is the world still divided into hostile factions centuries after the Spirit's coming?

Pieter Brueghel (1525–1569)
Tower of Babel

Birth of the Church

Peter then went on to explain to the crowd that what had just taken place was what God had foretold through the prophet Joel:

*"I will pour out my Spirit on everyone.
Your sons and daughters
will proclaim my message."* ACTS 2:17

Peter's words moved the people profoundly. Nearly three thousand were baptized that very day. From that moment, the followers of Jesus shared not only the same belief, but also the same life of the Holy Spirit. CCC 694

The monumental event that took place on Pentecost is this: The Holy Spirit, the third person of the Holy Trinity, came upon those who believed in him, forming them into the Church: the Body of Christ and the Temple of the Holy Spirit.

Jesus and his followers now form one body, as Jesus had foretold, saying:

*I will ask the Father,
and he will give you another Helper. . . .
He is the Spirit. . . .
When that day comes, you will know that
I am in the Father and you are in me,
just as I am in you.* JOHN 14:16–17, 20

Paul experienced this amazing mystery firsthand before his conversion. He was on his way to Damascus to arrest Christians and return them to Jerusalem for punishment.

*Suddenly, a light from the sky flashed
around him. He fell to the ground and
heard a voice saying to him,
"Saul, Saul! Why do you persecute me?"*

Kathryn Koob

Kathryn Koob was one of the fifty-two Americans held hostage in the 1980s for 444 days by Iranian extremists and terrorists. Angry mobs shouted outside her room almost around the clock. One night she woke up with a start. She says: "I turned quickly, expecting to see a guard. But no one was there."

Kathryn then said that, for some reason, she was reminded of the Holy Spirit. From that scary moment on, the Holy Spirit seemed to be with her in a special way. Her attitude toward her situation and her guards changed markedly. She says: "The Holy Spirit was teaching me love . . . and new understanding."

THINK
about it

Where the human spirit fails, the Holy Spirit fills.

Anonymous

Images of the Spirit

A small boy got a toy sailboat for his birthday. He was so excited he ran to the window, looked up at the sky, and shouted, "O God! Have you seen my boat?" A long pause followed, as if the boy were waiting for God to answer. Then the boy turned to his mother and asked, "What is God like?" But before she could answer, he said, "I know! God's like the wind!"

Ancient Jews also linked God and the wind. The unseen wind's feather-like touch and its storm-like power spoke to the Jews of God's own unseen gentleness and power. It is interesting that the Hebrew word *RUAH* is used to designate both "wind" and the "Spirit" of God. CCC 691

Ancient Jews also linked God and fire. God appeared in a burning bush to Moses. And God came down in fire on Mount Sinai. Exodus 3:3–6, 19:16–18

4 What other "natural" connection do you see between God and fire?

Finally, Jews connected the Holy Spirit and water. Jesus himself said to his disciples:

"Whoever believes in me . . .
'Streams of life-giving water will pour out from his side.'" Jesus said this about the Spirit, which those who believed in him were going to receive. John 7:38–39

5 Can you think of a "natural" connection the Spirit and water have in common?

"Who are you, Lord?" he asked.
"I am Jesus, whom you persecute,"
the voice said. Acts 9:3–5

This mysterious experience changed Paul from a persecutor of Jesus to an evangelist of Jesus. He later wrote:

We are one body in union with Christ . . .
[We] have been baptized
into the one body by the same Spirit. . . .
Christ is the head of his body, the church;
he is the source of the body's life.
Romans 12:5, Corinthians 12:13,
Colossians 1:18

3 Explain the similarity between the "body of Christ" image and Jesus' "vine and branches" image.

Saint Cyril of Jerusalem, a fourth-century bishop, made this connection between water and the Holy Spirit:

Water comes down from heaven as rain, and although it is always the same in itself, it produces many different effects, one in the palm tree, another in the vine, and so on. . . .
It adapts itself to the needs of every creature that receives it.

In the same way the Holy Spirit, whose nature is always the same . . . apportions grace to each man as he wills. . . .
The Spirit makes one man a teacher of divine truth . . . enables another to interpret holy Scripture.

The Spirit strengthens one man's self-control, shows another how to help the poor . . . trains another for martyrdom. His action is different in different people, but the Spirit . . . is always the same.

De Spiritu Sancto

Life in the Spirit

Drawing upon Scripture, Christian tradition describes the day-to-day activities of the Spirit in our lives in terms of the following:

VIRTUES Faith, hope, and charity
1 Corinthians 13:13

GIFTS Wisdom, understanding, counsel, knowledge, fortitude, piety, and fear of the Lord
Isaiah 11:1–2

FRUITS Love, joy, peace, patience, kindness, generosity, faithfulness, gentleness, self-control
Galatians 5:22–23 (NRSV)

SHARE YOUR meditation

British TV celebrity Malcolm Muggeridge did an interview with Mother Teresa. Some people thought it a failure. Mother's delivery was halting and her accent was thick.

One TV official, however, felt it had a strange power and aired it on Sunday night. The response to the interview was amazing—both in terms of mail and money. What came through, said Muggeridge, wasn't clever words and wit, but "the power of the Spirit" speaking through this saintly nun.

■ *Can you recall a time when the Spirit seemed to guide you in some situation? Explain.*

PRAYER hotline

O Thou, Who art at home
Deep in my heart,
Enable me to join you
Deep in my heart.

The Talmud

Young Joseph of Cupertino labored under a learning disability and was considered dull and clumsy. When he tried to enter the religious life, he was turned down by one monastery after another.

Finally, guided by the Holy Spirit, a Franciscan group agreed to accept him. Joseph acquired enough knowledge to be ordained a priest. Eventually, many miracles were attributed to him.

■ *Why do you think the Holy Spirit frequently works through very unlikely people, like Saint Joseph of Cupertino?*

Virtues

Faith, hope, and charity are called the theological virtues. CCC 1812–13 Given to us through baptism, they relate us in a personal way to the Trinity—Father, Son, and Spirit— and are the foundation of our spiritual life.

FAITH   Empowers us to receive and accept God's revelation CCC 1814–16

HOPE   Empowers us to trust that God's plan for us will be realized CCC 1817–21

CHARITY   Empowers us to love God above all else and our neighbor as ourselves CCC 1827–29

6 *Which of the virtues do you feel most in need of at this time in your life? Explain.*

Gifts of the Spirit

The prophet Isaiah lists seven gifts of the Spirit. CCC 1830–31 Christian traditions describe them as dispositions that make us more sensitive to the touch of the Spirit. Saint Augustine points out that Isaiah lists the gifts in reverse order:

The prophet begins with wisdom and ends with fear of the Lord. . . .
He begins, therefore, by identifying the goal we are striving for and ends with the starting point where we must begin.

Thus, the Book of Proverbs repeats over a dozen different times that "fear of the Lord" is the beginning of "wisdom." Beginning with the fear of the Lord, the gifts of the Holy Spirit mount up the spiritual ladder in the following way:

FEAR OF GOD   Draws us from sin to God

PIETY   Awakens us to God's love

KNOWLEDGE   Helps us to see how all things come from God and lead back to God

FORTITUDE   Strengthens us to pursue our journey to God with joy and courage

COUNSEL   Helps us discern the right path of action, especially in difficult situations

The "fruits of the Spirit" serve as a kind of earthly preview of the spiritual harmony that will fill our lives in heaven. With this in mind, Saint Augustine composed this prayer. Read it slowly, pausing after each sentence to ponder it:

*Breathe into me, Spirit of God,
that I may think what is holy.*

*Drive me, Spirit of God,
that I may do what is holy.*

*Draw me, Spirit of God,
that I may love what is holy.*

*Strengthen me, Spirit of God,
that I may preserve what is holy.*

*Guide me, Spirit of God,
that I may never lose what is holy.*

■ *Which of these five prayerful petitions do you feel a special need for and why?*

UNDERSTANDING	Empowers us to penetrate more deeply into the meaning and beauty of God's revelation
WISDOM	Enables us to see and relish God's presence in all things and discern how they fit together

These gifts of the Spirit dispose us to be more sensitive to the touch of the Holy Spirit in our everyday lives.

7 *Which of the above gifts do you feel most in need of at this time in your life? Explain.*

Fruits of the Spirit

Christian tradition teaches us that when we live in harmony with the virtues and the gifts of the Spirit, we are blessed with a variety of fruits.

Saint Paul lists nine fruits of the Spirit. CCC 1832 He puts love at the top of the list. He puts it there for a good reason.

In a true sense, the other eight fruits are simply colors in the rainbow of love.

LOVE	God gives us life
JOY	Love sings in the heart
PEACE	Love trusts in God
PATIENCE	Love is willing to wait
KINDNESS	Love smiles and invites
GENEROSITY	Love gives itself away
FAITHFULNESS	Love never tires
GENTLENESS	Love melts hearts
SELF-CONTROL	Love stays in shape

In the words of Dwight L. Moody:

*It is love all the way;
love at the top,
love at the bottom,
and love all the way along
down this list of graces.*

*If we only just brought forth
the fruit of the Spirit,
what a world we would have!*

8 *Which of the above fruits do you feel most in need of at this time in your life? Explain.*

PRAYER
hotline

Lord,
**"Don't walk in front of me,
I may not follow.
Don't walk behind me,
I may not lead.
Walk beside me,
and just be my friend."**

Albert Camus

Recap   Review

The central mystery of Christianity is the revelation of God as Trinity. The third person of the Trinity is the Holy Spirit. With the Father and the Son, the Spirit is eternal: without beginning or end.

On Pentecost the Holy Spirit came upon the disciples, fulfilling Jesus' promise to them and filling them with amazing power. On this day, the re-creation of the world took a quantum leap forward.

Collectively, the disciples became temples of the Holy Spirit and members of Christ's body, the Church. Individually, they were graced with special:

VIRTUES	Faith, hope, and charity
GIFTS	Fear of the Lord, piety, knowledge, fortitude, counsel, understanding, and wisdom
FRUITS	Love, joy, peace, patience, kindness, generosity, faithfulness, gentleness, self-control

These virtues, gifts, and fruits were to be used not just for the disciples' own personal good, but for the good of all and for the building up and spreading of God's Kingdom on earth.

1 Give two examples from Scripture that describe the Holy Spirit at work in Old Testament times.

2 Give two examples from the Gospels that describe the Holy Spirit at work in Jesus' life.

3 What two instructions by Jesus to his disciples set the stage for the Spirit's coming on Pentecost?

4 Explain the relationship between Pentecost and (a) the prophecy of Joel and (b) the Tower of Babel story.

5 Explain why and how ancient Jews connected (a) the wind with God, (b) fire with God, (c) water with the Holy Spirit.

6 How did the crowd react to Peter's words?

7 Briefly describe (a) the monumental event that took place on Pentecost, (b) how Paul experienced this event firsthand before his conversion.

8 Explain (a) why the theological virtues are so called, (b) how they are given to us, (c) for what purpose they are given to us.

9 List and briefly describe (a) three of the seven *gifts* of the Spirit, (b) three of the nine *fruits* of the Spirit.

Reflect

1 Karen Karper rarely saw deer near her house during the day. But at night, she heard them prowling about and, in the morning, saw their footprints in her lawn. She writes:

*If you are in the right place
at the right moment, you will see deer,
perhaps even very close at hand.
But once you try to touch them, they flee.*

*It is kind of like this
with the comings and goings
of the Spirit of God.*

*If I wait quietly going about the tasks
of my day, I might glimpse a trace
of his activity in my life, a subtle sign
that he is just beyond the edge of my vision.*
WHERE GOD BEGINS TO BE

■ *Recall a time when you felt the urge to help someone or do something that resulted in something beautiful for one or both of you. In other words, recall a time when the Holy Spirit touched your life.*
■ *Describe what kind of an effect this had on you and/or the other person.*

2 A farmer had a large rock located in the center of his field. It was troublesome plowing around it each year. Worse yet, he sometimes forgot it and damaged his plow on it. He wanted to dig it out. But he kept putting it off.

Finally, he acted. To his surprise, it was totally on the surface and easily removed. He thought to himself: "Why did it take me so long to dig it up? How much grief I could have saved myself had I removed it right away!"

■ *What "fruit" of the Spirit does this story illustrate?*
■ *Describe a "rock" in your life causing you grief.*
■ *What keeps you from digging it up?*

3 Take two paper cups. Fill one with water; leave the other empty. Now take a cigarette lighter and hold it under the empty cup so that the flame from the lighter touches it. Next hold the lighter under the cup filled with water so that the flame touches it also.

■ *What happened in the case of the empty cup? Filled cup?*
■ *How might this experiment be used to illustrate the change that took place in disciples as a result of Pentecost?*

PRAYER TIME
with the Lord

Saint Basil lived in the fourth century. In his youth, he was hooked on the pleasures of life.

One day he saw all things in a totally different light. He wrote: "It was like waking from a profound sleep." Slowly but surely, he abandoned his old life and gave himself to God.

Eventually, he became a bishop. Among other things, he set up hospitals and soup kitchens for the poor, working in them himself.

He also did his share of writing. One of his works is called *On the Holy Spirit*. Here's a prayer, inspired by a portion of it:

Holy Spirit,
lift our minds and hearts to heaven.
Guide our footsteps as we walk this earth.
Bless our efforts to grow in our love of you. . . .

Give us
an appreciation of our Catholic faith,
an understanding of your Scripture,
and an openness to your spiritual "gifts."

Then, when the sun sinks
below the horizon of this life,
admit us to citizenship with the saints,
companionship with the angels, and
community with the Blessed Trinity.

■ ***Compose your own Prayer to the Holy Spirit and share it with the class.***

PRAYER Journal

Read the prayer below one line at a time. Pause after each line to meditate for ten seconds or so on its meaning:

Lord God, strengthen me by your Holy Spirit,
to carry out my mission of changing the world
or some definite part of it, for the better. . . .

Nourish in me a practical desire
to build up rather than tear down,
to go out on a limb rather than crave security.

Never let me forget
that it is far better to light one candle
than to curse the darkness.
EXCERPTED AND SLIGHTLY ADAPTED
FROM THE "CHRISTOPHER PRAYER"

■ *Write out a few of the thoughts that came to you during your meditation.*

_____
_____
_____
_____
_____
_____
_____
_____
_____
_____

SCRIPTURE Journal

1	Jesus and the Spirit	Luke 4:14–22
2	Waiting for the Spirit	Acts 1:1–8
3	Coming of the Spirit	Acts 2:14–18
4	Fruits of the Spirit	Galatians 5:16–26
5	Life in the Spirit	Romans 8:1–17

■ *Pick one of the above passages. Read it prayerfully and write a short statement to Jesus, expressing your feelings about it.*

_____
_____
_____
_____
_____
_____

8 The Church

Saint Paul writes: We are one body in union with Christ. ROMANS 12:5

We have been baptized into the one body by the same Spirit. 1 CORINTHIANS 12:13

Christ is the head of his body, the church; he is the source of the body's life. COLOSSIANS 1:18

Keep your roots deep in him, build your lives on him . . . and be filled with thanksgiving. COLOSSIANS 2:7

God's plan from all eternity was to create and invite us to share in his own divine life and love.

The heart of God's plan is the Church. Foreshadowed in creation, it was prepared in the Old Testament, instituted by Jesus, revealed by the Spirit, and will reach its perfection in heaven.

Plan of God

One Sunday morning, an old African chief was present at the celebration of the Eucharist. Tears flooded his eyes as he watched members of the Ngoni, Senga, and Tumbuka tribes worshiping side by side.

Then his mind flashed back to his boyhood, when he used to watch Ngoni warriors after a day's fighting wash Senga and Tumbuka blood from their spears and bodies.

The contrast between what he had seen then and what he was seeing now was the difference between day and night.

That morning, at the celebration of the Eucharist, the old chief understood as never before what Christianity and the Church are all about. They are about God's plan for the human race. Saint Paul describes it this way:

This plan, which God will complete when the time is right, is to bring all creation together . . . with Christ as its head. . . .

God put all things under Christ's feet and gave him the church. The church is Christ's body. . . . It is through Christ that all of us . . . are able to come in the one Spirit into the presence of the Father. . . .

*You are built upon the foundation
laid by the apostles and prophets,
the cornerstone being Christ Jesus himself.*

*He is the one who
holds the whole building together
and makes it grow into a sacred temple
dedicated to the Lord . . .
a place where God lives through his Spirit.*
EPHESIANS 1:10–11; 2:19–22

The Church

The Church is the centerpiece of God's plan for the human race. In the course of history, the Church has taken shape gradually through five stages. It was:

- **Foreshadowed in creation**
- **Prepared for in the Old Covenant**
- **Instituted by Jesus**
- **Revealed by the Spirit**
- **Perfected in glory**

Let us now take a closer look at each of the five stages of the Church's development over the course of history.

Foreshadowed

Early Christians saw the creation of the world as the first stage of the Holy Trinity's plan. In fact, first-century Christians did not hesitate to say "The world was created for the sake of the Church." CCC 760

The Trinity's plan was to create human beings who would be invited to share in the Trinity's own divine life and love.

Thus, creation *foreshadowed* or "pointed to" the Church. We may use this comparison: As blossoms on a tree foreshadow or "point to" the coming of fruit on a tree, so creation foreshadowed the coming of the Church into the world. CCC 761–62

1 Can you think of another comparison to illustrate the meaning of "foreshadowed"?

Prepared

The second stage of the Trinity's plan took place after the human race—through Adam's sin—freely chose to go its own way, rather than accept the Trinity's invitation. The Trinity showed its mercy by giving the human race a second chance.

Thus, God chose a leader called Moses, who led a group of "chosen people" out of Egypt to the foot of Mount Sinai. There God forged a covenant with them, making them the "instrument" by which the Trinity would prepare to extend its invitation of divine life to all peoples.

Instituted

The third stage took place when, in a mystery of love, the second person of the Trinity became a human being. He was named *Jesus* (which means "he will save his people from their sins"). He was also given the title *Immanuel* (which means he is "God is with us"). MATTHEW 1:21

To carry out the Trinity's plan, Jesus established the Kingdom of God. We may describe the Kingdom of God as *the power of God at work in the world*. It is the power of God gradually destroying the "Kingdom of Satan," which held the human race in slavery since the first sin.

2 *In what sense did the "Kingdom of Satan" hold the human race "in slavery"?*

This explains why we still pray "Thy Kingdom come" in the Lord's Prayer. It is because the "Kingdom of Satan" will not die without a struggle. In other words, the coming of the Kingdom of God is not an instant happening but a gradual process. It will reach completion only in heaven.

Here, it is important to note that the Kingdom of God is not something visible. Jesus said to a group of Pharisees:

"The Kingdom of God does not come in such a way as to be seen. No one can say, 'Look, here it is!' or 'There it is!' because the Kingdom of God is within you." LUKE 17:20–21

In other words, the Kingdom of God is a thing of the heart. It is present wherever God's will reigns.

This brings us back to the Church. Jesus instituted the Church to be the *seed, sign,* and the *instrument* of God's Kingdom on earth. Toward that end, Jesus chose twelve apostles, under the headship of Peter, to continue to spread and bring forth God's Kingdom on earth. CCC 763–66, 880–96

3 *In what sense is the Church the seed, sign, and instrument of God's Kingdom?*

Revealed

Jesus completed his mission on earth and ascended to heaven, but not before promising to send the Holy Spirit. With the coming of the Spirit on Pentecost, the plan of the Holy Trinity entered its final phase, namely, to:

- **Reveal the Church to the nations**
- **Empower it to disciple all nations**

To help the Church fulfill its mission to the world, the Holy Spirit endowed it with special gifts and powers.

Perfected

The Church will reach perfection in heaven when the "Kingdom of God" will be fully established. CCC 769

We might compare the five stages of the Church to the five stages of a plant's growth:

- **Seed**   **Church foreshadowed**
- **Stem**   **Church prepared**
- **Bud**   **Church instituted**
- **Bloom**   **Church revealed**
- **Fruit**   **Church perfected**

Unfinished work

Composer Giacomo Puccini wrote a number of operas. His last one, *Turandot* (Tour-en-doe) is regarded by many to be his best.

While working on it, he discovered he had a rapidly growing cancer. One day he said to his students, "If I am not able to finish this opera, I want you to finish it for me."

Shortly afterward, Puccini went to Brussels for an operation. He died two days after surgery. In the months that followed, his students completed his final opera. The world premiere was performed in Milan and directed by Puccini's favorite student, Toscanini.

Everything went well until the opera reached the place where Puccini stopped writing. Tears ran down Toscanini's cheeks. He stopped the music, put down his baton, turned to the audience, and cried out, "Thus far the Master wrote, but he died."

Then there was silence throughout the Milan opera house. No one moved; no one spoke.

After a minute, Toscanini picked up the baton, smiled through his tears, and cried out, "But the disciples finished his work." When the opera ended, the audience broke into a long and thunderous applause.

The story of the completion of *Turandot* bears a similarity to the story of the completion of the Church.

Jesus laid the foundation. But, like Puccini, Jesus died before its completion, leaving that important work to his disciples.

4 *What have you done to work for the Church's completion? What are you doing now? What ought you do in the future?*

Models of the Church

There's a well-known poem by John Godfrey Saxe. It describes six blind men from Indostan. They are standing around an elephant, trying to figure out what it's like.

One blind man feels its side and says the elephant looks like a wall. Another feels its tail and says it looks like a rope. A third feels its trunk and says it looks like a snake. A fourth feels its ear and says it looks like a fan. A fifth feels

Alexis de Tocqueville

A nineteenth-century French statesman, Alexis de Tocqueville came to America to learn the secret of its genius and greatness. After a careful study of the country, he wrote:

*I sought for
the genius and greatness
of America . . .
in her fertile fields
and boundless forests—
and it was not there. . . .*

*[I sought for it] in her rich mines
and her vast world commerce—
and it was not there. . . .*

*[I sought for it]
in her democratic Congress
and matchless Constitution—
and it was not there."*

*Not until I went
into the churches of America
and heard her pulpits
flame with righteousness
did I understand the secret
of her genius and power.*

*America is great
because she is good,
and if America
ever ceases to be good,
America
will cease to be great.*

Attributed to de Tocqueville by Dwight D. Eisenhower in his final campaign address in Boston, Mass., Nov. 3, 1952.

A girl said,
*I find it hard to believe
that the Church is Christ's Body
when I see
how some Christians act.*

A friend said,
*I felt the same way
until I recalled that
I shouldn't blame Beethoven
because of how some musicians
play his music.*

■ **What is the friend's point?**

Saint Peter's
Basilica,
Rome, Italy.

its tusk and says it looks like a sword. A sixth feels its leg and says it looks like a tree trunk. The poem ends:

*And so these men of Indostan
Disputed loud and long.
Each in his own opinion
Exceedingly stiff and strong.
Though each was partly in the right,
They all were in the wrong.*

5 How are the blind men trying to describe the elephant like people in the world trying to describe the Church?

Because the Church is a many-sided reality, it can't be described in simple terms. This explains why theologians use models to describe the Church. A *model* is an image that helps us to better understand a complex reality.

Theologians are not the only ones who use models. Scientists also use them. For example, no scientist has ever seen the complex reality known as the electron.

The word "electron" is simply a name scientists give to a consistent set of events that happen in certain circumstances.

In dealing with the electron, scientists sometimes use a *wave* as their model and sometimes a particle. What they can't explain by one model, they can usually explain by the other.

Traditionally, Christians have used three models to help us get a better understanding of the Church. Drawn from Scripture, and mirroring the Trinity, they are:

■ *People of God*
■ *Body of Christ*
■ *Temple of the Spirit*

Let us take a closer look at each one of these three models:

People of God

A persecution left a large area of Guatemala without priests in 1980. The Catholics in this area, however, continued to gather in their village churches to pray, read Scripture, and share their faith.

Once a month they sent someone to a distant part of Guatemala (where priests still functioned) to bring back the Eucharist.

The Guatemalan communities illustrate the most basic model of the Church: the "People of God." It is an "assembly" of Jesus' followers who gather in Jesus' name to witness to their common faith that "Christ has died, Christ is risen, Christ will come again."

The Guatemalan communities recall the very early Christian community described in the Acts of the Apostles. ACTS 2:44–47 Christians become members of the "People of God," not by physical birth, but by spiritual birth—faith in Christ and baptism into his Body. CCC 781–86

Peter addresses a community of the "People of God" in these exciting words:

You are the chosen race,
the King's priests, the holy nation,
God's own people, chosen to proclaim
the wonderful acts of God,
who called you out of darkness
into his own marvelous light.
At one time you were not God's people,
but now you are. 1 PETER 2:9–10

This brings us to a second biblical image of the Church:

Body of Christ

Saint Paul had come from Tarsus to Jerusalem to study under the great Jewish rabbi Gamaliel. Shortly after his arrival, he witnessed the stoning of Stephen, the first Christian martyr. ACTS 7:57–58

This episode fueled his opposition to Christianity. He sought and got authority from Jewish leaders to track down and arrest Christians.

Going from house to house,
he dragged out the believers, both men
and women, and threw them in jail.
ACTS 8:3

One day, Paul was riding to Damascus to arrest Christians. Suddenly, a light flashed and he fell to the road unable to see. A voice said:

"Saul, Saul! Why do you persecute me?"
"Who are you, Lord?" he asked.
"I am Jesus, whom you persecute. . . .

"Get up and go into the city,
where you will be told what you
must do . . ."

Saul got up from the ground
And opened his eyes,
but he could not see a thing.

So they took him by the hand
and led him into Damascus. ACTS 9:4–8

As Saul groped along in total darkness, he was confused. What did the voice mean? He and his companions were not persecuting Jesus, only his followers. Slowly, the meaning of Jesus' words dawned upon him. After his conversion to Christianity, Paul wrote:

We are one body in union with Christ. . . .
He is the head of his body, the church;
he is the source of the body's life.
ROMANS 12:5, COLOSSIANS 1:8

All of us . . . have been baptized
into the one body by the same Spirit.
1 CORINTHIANS 12:13

The Church as the body of Christ focuses on this great mystery: Christ and his followers form one body. His followers are the members of the body and Christ himself is their head and source of life.

Connection

Vatican City is a tiny, independent state located inside the city of Rome. It has the status of a nation and a full diplomatic corps. Headed up by the pope, the "Vatican" is the seat of the world Catholic community.

Like other leaders, the pope has a "cabinet" to assist him. Called the Curia, its departments are usually headed by a bishop or cardinal. "Cardinal" is an honorary title given to a bishop who has distinguished himself.

A duty of the "College of Cardinals" is to elect the pope.

Another honorary title is that of "Monsignor," usually given to a priest who has distinguished himself.

A simplified organizational chart of the Church might look like this:

Parish—served by a pastor and a staff of ordained and lay associates.

Diocese—cluster of parishes, served by a bishop and a staff of ordained and lay associates.

Archdiocese—cluster of dioceses, overseen by an archbishop.

The Church, under the image of the body of Christ, underscores this incredible reality: As Jesus shared his Father's life, the Church shares Jesus' life. Jesus said:

*"I am the vine, and you are the branches.
Those who remain in me, and I in them
will bear much fruit;
for you can do nothing without me."*
JOHN 15:5

This brings us to a final biblical image of the Church, which rounds out its trinitarian dimension.

Temple of the Spirit

In one of his homilies, Saint Augustine, the bishop of Hippo in Africa, said:

*What the soul is to the human body,
the Holy Spirit is to the Body of Christ,
which is the Church.*

The soul permeates, unites, and enlivens every part of the human body. In the same way the Holy Spirit permeates, unites, and enlivens every part of the Body of Christ, forming it into the Spirit's own Temple. CCC 797–801

Paul wrote to the Church at Corinth, "You are God's temple." 1 CORINTHIANS 3:16 He spelled out this image more completely in his letter to the Church at Ephesus, saying:

*You are . . . built upon the foundation
laid by the apostles and prophets,
the cornerstone being Christ Jesus himself.*

---

*He is the one
who holds the whole building together
and makes it grow into a sacred temple
dedicated to the Lord.*
EPHESIANS 2:19–21

6 *Which of the three images of the Church—People of God, Body of Christ, or Temple of the Holy Spirit—appeals to you most and why?*

Marks of the Church

Father Walter Cizsek was arrested in Russia during World War II. He spent twenty-three years in prison. After his release, he wrote a book entitled *He Leadeth Me*.

In it he describes how a tiny community of Catholic prisoners used to gather in secret to celebrate the Eucharist "in drafty storage shacks, or huddled together in mud and slush in the corner of a building."

At this Mass, they prayed the same Creed that we pray at each Sunday Mass. We pray: "We believe in *one, holy, catholic,* and *apostolic* Church." These four marks describe the Church's calling.

First, it is to be *one*. It is called to "unity." CCC 813–22 Jesus prayed for us to his Father, saying: "May they be in us, just as you are in me and I am in you. May they be one, so that the world will believe that you sent me." JOHN 17:21

7 *What keeps you from feeling a greater unity with the Church?*

Second, the Church is called to be *holy* because its head is "the Holy One." But its members are still struggling to become holy, including its ministers. CCC 823–29 All must admit they are sinners. 1 JOHN 1:8–10

8 *Can you recall a parable that Jesus used to illustrate the point that the Church will be a mixture of good and bad people until the end of the world?*

Third, the Church is *catholic* in the sense of being *total and universal*. It is *total* in that Jesus gave it the total *means* of salvation. It is *universal* in the sense that it carries these means to all nations. CCC 830–56

Finally, the Church is *apostolic*. It traces its origin to the apostles. The bishops are the successors of the apostles; and the bishop of Rome (pope) is Peter's successor. Under the Spirit's guidance, the bishops preserve and proclaim the teachings given them. CCC 857–62

Mystery of the Church

The Church is a mystery of the Trinity's love. Unlike any other community on earth, the Church, mirroring Christ (whose body is the Church), has two dimensions:

- **A divine dimension**
- **A human dimension**

The divine dimension is invisible. It is none other than Christ himself, who is the head and the life of his body, the Church.

The human dimension is visible. It is the members of the Church. By our witness and worship, we make Christ visibly present and active in the world.

The human dimension of the Church is like everything human: flawed. This includes not only its membership, but also its leadership. Because of this, it does not always show the "face of Christ" to the world as it should.

In other words, the Church is not unlike each one of us. It, too, is vulnerable to sin and still struggling to be what God called it to be.

As a result, the Church in its pilgrimage on earth will always be a mixture of light and darkness. There will always be enough light for those who wish to see and enough darkness for those whose disposition is otherwise. This is how it should be. The light should never overpower us. It should only invite us. That is, it should never take away our freedom.

Or to put it another way: When it comes to Jesus' presence in the Church, it will never be revealed so clearly as to leave us without questions. Nor will it be concealed so completely as to mislead the sincere searcher. It leaves open both possibilities. Jesus respects our freedom to accept or reject him.

9 *Explain why it is fitting that the light should not overpower us, but leave us with a certain number of questions.*

Recap

The Trinity's plan for the Church unfolded in five stages. It was:

- **Foreshadowed in creation**   **Seed**
- **Prepared for by the Old Covenant**   **Stem**
- **Instituted by Jesus**   **Bud**
- **Revealed by the Spirit**   **Flower**
- **Perfected in Glory**   **Fruit**

Three biblical images help to give us a clear picture of the Church's trinitarian, orientation, nature, and mission:

- **People of God**
- **Body of Christ**
- **Temple of the Spirit**

The Church bears four distinguishing marks of identity. It is:

- **One**
- **Holy**
- **Catholic**
- **Apostolic**

Finally, the Church is different from every other community on earth. It has both:

- **A divine dimension**
- **A human dimension**

Because of its human dimension, the Church is not unlike each one of us. It, too, is vulnerable to sin and still struggling to be what God called it to be.

As a result, the Church in its pilgrimage on earth will always be a mixture of:

- **Light**
- **Darkness**

There will always be enough light for those who wish to see and enough darkness for those whose disposition is otherwise.

Review

1 List and briefly explain (a) the five stages of the Trinity's plan for the Church, (b) how the five stages of the Trinity's plan parallel the five stages of a plant's growth.

2 List and briefly explain three biblical images of the Church that highlight its Trinitarian dimension.

3 List and briefly explain the four marks of the Church.

4 Explain in what sense the Church (a) mirrors Christ, whose body it is, (b) will always be a mixture of light and darkness.

5 Identify: (a) Vatican City, (b) Curia, (c) Cardinal, (d) bishop, (e) monsignor, (f) priest, (g) diocese, and (h) archdiocese.

Reflect

1 When eighty-four-year-old Dorothy Day died in 1980, the *New York Times* praised her as one of the truly great Christians of our time. She became a Catholic in her adult years and worked among New York's poor.

In her autobiography, *The Long Loneliness,* Dorothy said that the "human" dimension of the Church was often a scandal to her. Yet she loved the Church's "human" dimension because it made Christ visible to her. She compared the "human" dimension of the Church to the cross on which Christ was crucified, saying, "You can never separate Christ from his cross."

■ *Why do you agree/disagree with her on the two points relating to the Church's human dimension?*
■ *How does Jesus' Parable of the Weeds and the Wheat Matthew 13:24–30 help us understand why there is scandal in the Church and always will be?*
■ *What is one thing about the Church you find to be a scandal? How do you cope with it?*

2 Martin Luther King Jr. wrote a famous letter while confined in the Birmingham City Jail. Referring to the early Church, he said:

*In those days, the Church was not merely
a thermometer that recorded ideas
and principles of popular belief;
it was a thermostat that transformed
the mores of society.*

*If the Church of today does not recapture
the sacrificial spirit of the early Church,
it will lose its authentic ring,
forfeit the loyalty of millions,
and be dismissed
as an irrelevant social fan club
with no meaning for the twentieth century.*

■ *Explain (a) thermostat, (b) thermometer.*
■ *In what sense did Jesus intend his Church to be a thermostat?*
■ *What is one thing the Church might do to regain its sacrificial spirit and authentic ring?*

3 A survey shows that forty percent of Catholics between the ages of 15 and 29 stop practicing their faith for a period of two years or more. Seventy percent of these return to the Church. Sixty percent of those who return do so because of the positive influence of a friend, relative, or neighbor.

■ *On a scale of one (rarely) to ten (regularly), grade the frequency of your participation in the celebration of Sunday Mass. Explain.*
■ *On a scale of one to ten, grade and explain your involvement in youth activities in your parish.*

PRAYER TIME
with the Lord

Loving God,
give us an appreciation of who we are.

We are the Church
of whom your Son said to Peter,
"You are a rock and on this rock
foundation I will build my church."
Matthew 16:18–19

We are the Church
of whom your Son said to his disciples,
"Where two or three come together
in my name, I am there with them."
Matthew 18:20

We are the Church
to whom your Son said to his followers,
"Whoever listens to you listens to me."
Luke 10:16

We are the Church
to whom your Son said to his apostles,
"This is my body, which is given up for
you. Do this in memory of me."
1 Corinthians 11:24

We are the Church
to whom your Son said to his apostles
just before ascending to his Father,
"Go . . . to all peoples . . .
make them my disciples. . . .
And I will be with you always."
Matthew 28:19–20
M.L.

■ **Send an e-mail to Jesus. Share with him
three or four ideas that you think would help
people better appreciate the Church today.**

PRAYER Journal

During his visit to Peru, Pope John Paul II visited the poor. At one stop, a spokesperson for the poor said to him:

We are hungry, we live in misery,
we are sick and out of work.

Our women give birth in tuberculosis,
our infants die, our children grow weak. . . .

Despite all this . . . we continue to walk
with the Church and in the Church.

For it has helped us to live in dignity
as children of God.

■ *Imagine that the Holy Father visited your city and you acted as spokesperson for its youth. Using the above statement as a model, write out what you would say.*

_____
_____
_____
_____
_____
_____
_____
_____
_____
_____
_____
_____

SCRIPTURE Journal

1	Servant Church	Romans 12:6–21
2	Institutional Church	Matthew 16:13–19
3	Communal Church	Acts 2:43–47
4	Body of Christ	Romans 12:4–8
5	People of God	Acts 4:1–20

■ *Pick one of the above passages. Read it prayerfully and write out a brief statement to Jesus expressing your feelings about it.*

_____
_____
_____
_____
_____
_____

2 WORSHIP

We reach out to God

Athletes share "high fives"
to celebrate a victory.
Friends hug one another to share
a special moment.
They do this because in such situations,
words alone can't express their feelings.

This helps us to understand
why Jesus anointed the eyes of the blind
to heal them,
touched the tongue of the mute
to restore their speech,
and placed his hands on children
to bless them.

This also explains
why Jesus taught his disciples
to use similar actions
in similar situations.

LOOKING**Back**

One time in my life when words alone couldn't express how I felt was . . .

_____

_____

One question I have about the Liturgy of the Mass is . . .

_____

_____

LOOKING Ahead

Recall that our faith journey is divided into the following three stages:

- **WORD**   God reaches out to us. (Revelation)
- **WORSHIP**   We reach out to God.   (Sacraments)
- **WITNESS**   We journey together.   (Commandments)

In the first stage, we saw how the Holy Spirit formed Jesus' followers into the Body of Christ, the Church.

In this second stage, we will see how Jesus continues to heal, to forgive, and to teach people in our times just as he did in Gospel times.

115

9 Liturgy

Jesus took a piece of bread,
gave thanks to God, broke it,
and gave it to the apostles, saying,
"This is my body
which was given up for you.
Do this in memory of me." LUKE 22:19

James writes:
Are any among you sick? . . .
Send for the church elders
who will pray for them and
rub olive oil on them. JAMES 5:14

**Simply put,
the liturgy is "the participation
of God's people in God's work."
Through the liturgy,
especially the seven sacraments,
Jesus continues the work of salvation
that he began during his earthly life.**

Jesus' new presence

Just before Jesus ascended to his Father, he commissioned his disciples to preach the Gospel to all nations. Then he made a remarkable promise to them. He said, "I will be with you always." MATTHEW 28:18–20

At first the disciples had no idea what Jesus meant. How could he remain with them and still go to his Father? What did he mean?

1 *How would you answer their question?*

The answer to the disciples' question came after Jesus ascended and sent the Holy Spirit upon them on Pentecost.

Some time after Pentecost, a persecution of Christians broke out.

One day, one of the leaders, Saul of Tarsus—also known as Paul—was traveling to Damascus to arrest some Christians.

Suddenly a light from the sky
flashed around him.
He fell to the ground and
heard a voice saying to him,
"Saul, Saul!
Why do you persecute me?"
"Who are you, Lord?" he asked.
"I am Jesus, whom you persecute,"
the voice said. Acts 9:3–5

This experience converted Paul and made him a follower of Jesus. Later Paul wrote to other Christians:

We are one body
in union with Christ. . . .
He is the head
of his body the church;
he is the source of the body's life.
Romans 12:5, Colossians 1:18

Jesus' new actions

As the Christian community reflected upon this remarkable mystery, they began to realize something even more remarkable.

Jesus not only formed one body with them, but also began acting through them. The members of his Church body became his new arms and new voice, so to speak.

In other words, as Jesus once healed people through the members of his earthly body, he heals them now through the members of his Church body (*mystical* body). Through them he continues his work on earth.

Jesus' disciples now understood what Jesus meant when he said to them while still on earth, "Whoever listens to you listens to me." Luke 10:16

2 In what sense do we listen to Jesus when we listen to his disciples?

Jesus' disciples now understood that when they teach in his name, it is not they who teach, but Jesus who teaches through them. When they heal in his name, it is not they who heal, but Jesus who heals through them.

An example of this mystery took place one day when a crippled beggar asked Peter and John for money. Peter said to him:

"I have no money at all,
but I give you what I have:
in the name of Jesus Christ . . .
I order you to get up and walk. . . ."
At once the man . . . started walking.
Acts 3:6, 8

When the people saw this they stared in amazement at Peter. Peter said to them:

"Why do you stare at us?
Do you think that it was by means
of our own power . . . that we made
this man walk?" Acts 3:12

Rather, said Peter, it was by the power of Jesus that this man is able to walk again.

And so, we come to this very remarkable conclusion. Beginning with Pentecost, Jesus not only becomes *present* in the world through his

God's work." Through the Church's *liturgy,* Christ continues the work of our salvation, begun during his earthly life. CCC 1069

No action of the Church is more sacred than the liturgy. CCC 1070

3 Why is the liturgy the most sacred action of the Church?

And so on Pentecost, Jesus not only became *present* in the world in a new way (through his Church) but also began to *act* in the world in a new way (through its *liturgy*).

Liturgy and sacraments

Over the centuries the Church gradually discerned that *seven actions* of its liturgy surpassed all others.

It gave them the name *sacraments.* They may be grouped under the following three headings:

- **Sacraments of Initiation**
- **Sacraments of Healing**
- **Sacraments of Service**

The sacraments of initiation include Baptism, Confirmation, and the Holy Eucharist.

The sacraments of healing include Reconciliation and the Anointing of the Sick.

The sacraments of service include Marriage and Holy Orders.

4 In what sense do the sacraments under each group involve initiation, healing and service?

Church body (mystical body) but also *acts* through it. Thus, Saint Augustine could say, "When the Church baptizes, it is Christ himself who baptizes."

Liturgy of the Church

In time, Christians gave a special name to the actions of Jesus' Church body. They called them *liturgical* actions.

Technically, the word *liturgy* means "the participation of God's People in

Sacraments of initiation

The "sacraments of initiation" relate us to the Trinity in a remarkable new way. CCC 1123, 1212

Baptism gives the Trinity's divine life to us. Jesus said, "No one can enter the Kingdom of God without being born again of water and the Spirit. JOHN 3:5 Confirmation deepens the life of the Trinity within us.

Finally, the Eucharist nourishes the divine life. Jesus said, "If you do not eat the flesh of the Son of Man and drink his blood, you will not have life in yourselves." JOHN 6:53

Sacraments of healing

The "sacraments of healing" are exactly what they say. They restore, repair, and fortify divine life.

Reconciliation restores divine life when we have weakened or lost it through sin. CCC 1420–21

The Anointing of the Sick fortifies and strengthens our divine life against the vulnerabilities linked with illness or old age. CCC 1511, 1527

5 *Give an example to illustrate how bodily illness or old age could leave us spiritually vulnerable.*

Sacraments of service

The "sacraments of service" have as their purpose the growth and well-being of the Body of Christ and the spread of the Kingdom of God.

Marriage unites husband and wife in a union that mirrors the relationship of Christ with his Church. EPHESIANS 5:25, 32 It calls them and graces them to build up Christ's Body, the Church. CCC 1534

Holy Orders consecrates special members to serve the Church by teaching it, leading it in worship, and guiding it pastorally. CCC 1592

Definition of sacraments

We may define sacraments in the following fourfold manner. CCC 1131 They are:

- ■ **Efficacious signs of grace**
- ■ **Instituted by Christ**
- ■ **Entrusted to his Church**
- ■ **To give divine life to us**

First, they are *efficacious signs of grace* in that it is Christ himself who is present in them and acting through them.

THINK
about it

Our redeemer's visible presence
has passed into the sacraments.

Pope Saint Leo the Great

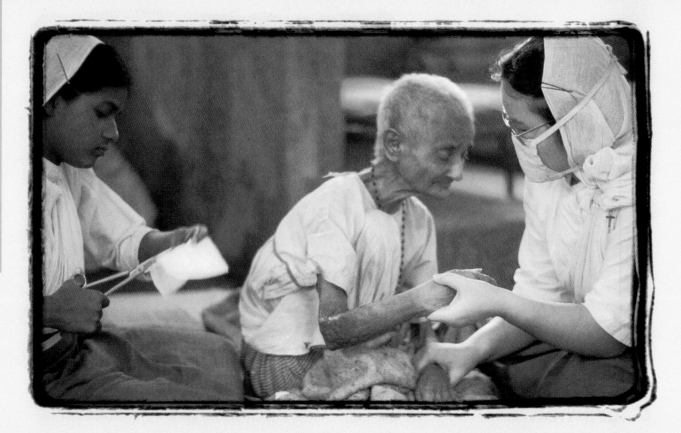

Second, they are *instituted by Christ,* but not in the sense that after anointing someone Jesus said, "What I just did was to institute the sacrament of the Anointing of the Sick."

Rather, Jesus introduced his disciples to the practice of using actions (like anointing with oil) as signs and vehicles of grace.

He instituted the sacraments in the sense that their origin and power derive from him.

We might compare the institution of the sacraments to the creation of the world. We do not know the details of how each being was created; but we do know that, ultimately, their origin comes from God and God's power.

In a similar way, each sacrament owes its origin and power to Jesus.

Third, the sacraments were *entrusted to the Church;* that is, Jesus gave to Peter the "keys of the Kingdom." MATTHEW 16:18 And he commissioned all of the Apostles to:

- **Baptize people**
- **Forgive people's sins**
- **Celebrate the Eucharist**
- **Anoint the sick**

Finally, a sacrament gives divine life to us. The communication of this life comes directly from the Holy Spirit.

In other words, the communication of divine life to us does not depend on the minister's holiness. But it does depend, to some extent, on our own holiness and openness to Jesus.

Celebration of liturgy

Elie Wiesel's story *The Town Beyond the Wall* deals with the power of friendship. In one episode Michael survives a period of torture because Pedro, his absent friend, lives on in his memory.

The power of the friendship flows not from Pedro directly, but from Michael's memory of him. This touches on a profound biblical truth. Henri Nouwen expresses it this way in his book *The Living Memory:*

Memory not only connects us
with our past, but also
keeps us alive in the present. . . .

To remember is not simply
to look back at past events:
more importantly
it is to bring these events into
the present and celebrate them
in the here and now.
For Israel, remembrance
meant participation.

Thus, when Jews celebrated the Passover, they did more than recall the event that freed them from Egyptian slavery.

By faith, they brought the event into the present, relived it, and received from it the same blessing their ancestors did.

6 *How does this shed light on what happens in our celebration of the liturgy and sacraments?*

It is with the above understanding of "memory" that Jesus said to his disciples at the Last Supper, "Do this in memory of me." When we celebrate the Eucharist, therefore, we do far more than recall what Jesus did at the Last Supper.

In some mysterious way, we bring this awesome event into the present and share in it just as really as the Apostle did. CCC 1104 The same is true for all the other sacraments.

Liturgical year

The liturgical year celebrates the great events of Christ's life. Pope Pius XII said:

The liturgical year . . .
is not a cold, lifeless representation
of the events of the past. . . .
It is rather Christ himself . . .
ever living in his Church. MEDIATOR DEI

And so the liturgical year is a *living* reality, not a dead ritual. The novelist John Steinbeck expressed the idea beautifully in his story, *The Winter of Our Discontent.* He wrote:

Aunt Deborah
read the Scripture to me
like a daily newspaper and I suppose
that's the way she thought of it,
as something going on,
happening eternally
but always exciting and new.

William Simon

William Simon was the Secretary of the Treasury under President Nixon and Ford. He was also a eucharistic minister in his own Catholic parish.

This means he brought the Eucharist to hospital patients and infirm people. While doing this, something happened to him that he hadn't anticipated. He says:

Many times I have come away from the hospital wondering if I have given the sick and infirm half of what they've given me. I feel profoundly grateful to them for helping me to strengthen my faith.

He concludes saying that when people ask, *"Where can we find God in today's world?"* one answer is: *"Almost anywhere—in fact, many times right in front of us, if we just open our eyes and hearts."*

Quotes from *How Can I Find God?:* James Martin, editor

Alvin Toffler's book *Future Shock* deals with the impact of rapid change on modern society. This change often leaves us uprooted and disorientated.

Today more than ever, says Toffler, we need a framework for our lives. We need a pattern of holidays and rotating seasonal events to remind us who we are and what we are about.

Without this pattern, we are like castaways, adrift in a boat on a trackless sea. We have no reference point to indicate where we are or the direction in which we are headed.

■ *How does the liturgical year provide a framework to remind us of who we are and what we are about?*

When I fall on my knees
with my face
to the rising sun,
O Lord, have mercy on me.

Negro Spiritual

Every Easter,
Jesus really rose from the dead,
an explosion, expected
but nonetheless new.
It wasn't 2000 years ago to her;
it was now.

This is what the liturgical year is. It is not something that happened two thousand years ago. It is something "going on now, happening eternally, but always exciting and new."

The liturgical year is made up of two liturgical seasons. The focus of the minor one is the feast of Christmas. The focus of the major one is the feast of Easter. Each season has two periods relating to the feast:

■ **Preparation** **Anticipating it**
■ **Celebration** **Reliving it**

7 *Why should Easter, not Christmas, be the highpoint of the liturgical year?*

Christmas cycle

The Church's *preparation* for Christmas is called *Advent* (which means "coming"). The *coming* for which we prepare is twofold: Jesus':

■ **1st coming**   **in history**
■ **2nd coming**   **in glory**

The *celebration* of Christmas focuses on the incredible mystery that God, in the person of Jesus, entered human history and lived among us.

The celebration of the Christmas season ends on Epiphany (coming of the Magi and, through them, Jesus' *manifestation* of himself to the non-Jewish world).

The Christmas season is followed by "Ordinary Time after Christmas." It is usually six to seven weeks long and sets the stage for the high point of the liturgical year: the celebration of Easter and the Easter season.

Easter cycle

Just as the Eucharist is the "sacrament of sacraments" of the Church's liturgy, Easter is the "feast of feasts" of the Church's liturgical year. CCC, 1169

Easter makes present and celebrates the great mystery of our faith. By Jesus' death and resurrection we "pass over" from slavery to sin to freedom as God's adopted children.

Sometimes referred to as the *passover* or *paschal mystery*, Easter celebrates our passage in Christ from spiritual death to spiritual life.

The *preparation* for Easter is called Lent ("spring"). This word underscores the fact that Easter coincides in the western world with the "resurrection" of all nature.

Lent begins with Ash Wednesday and the marking of our foreheads with ashes.

8 *What is the symbolic meaning of this action?*

Marking our foreheads reminds us that, like Jesus who died on Good Friday and rose on Easter Sunday, we must die to sin, if we are to rise to new life with Jesus.

Lent ends with Holy Week. It celebrates the final week of Jesus' life on earth, especially his Last Supper on Holy Thursday and his crucifixion on Good Friday.

The *celebration* of Easter begins with the Holy Saturday Easter Vigil service. At this time, adult converts are baptized and received into the Church.

The season ends 50 days later on Pentecost. This feast celebrates the coming of the Holy Spirit, which is the birthday of the Church.

The Easter season is followed by "Ordinary Time after Easter." About 25 weeks long, it ends with the feast of Christ the King.

This feast reminds us of our responsibility to bring to completion the Kingdom of God which Jesus inaugurated during his lifetime.

LITERARY Connection

The readings of the liturgical year are found in a book called the Lectionary. It contains all the most important readings of the Bible.

The Lectionary is arranged so that these important readings are covered every three years. The Sunday readings of the first year are called Year A; the second year, Year B; the third year, Year C.

Three readings from the Lectionary are read each Sunday. The first is from the Old Testament (Acts during the Easter season); the second is from the Letters or Revelation; the third from one of the four Gospels.

The first and the third readings at each Mass are matched and set forth the theme of the Mass. The second reading is taken consecutively from the Letters or Revelation and, thus, doesn't necessarily match the theme.

Recap

On Pentecost the Holy Spirit came upon the disciples and formed them into one body:

- **Jesus**   **Head of the body**
- **Disciples**   **Members of the body**

From that moment on, the risen Jesus not only became present in the Church but also acted through it, in the liturgy, especially the seven sacraments:

- **Initiation**   **Baptism, Confirmation, Eucharist**
- **Healing**   **Reconciliation Anointing of sick**
- **Service**   **Marriage Holy Orders**

We may define sacraments as:

- **Efficacious signs of grace**
- **Instituted by Christ**
- **Entrusted to his Church**
- **To give divine life to us**

No action of the Church is more sacred than the *liturgy*. We may describe the liturgy as the participation of the people of God in the work of God.

The "liturgical year" is a 12-month reliving of Jesus' work of salvation. It centers around two focal points or great mysteries:

- **Christmas**   **Birth of Jesus**
- **Easter**   **Resurrection of Jesus**

The celebration of each of these two mysteries involves a period of:

- **Preparation**   **Anticipating it**
- **Celebration**   **Reliving it**

Review

1 Explain the difference between Jesus' presence among his followers in biblical times and his presence among them in our times.

2 Explain the difference between the way Jesus healed and blessed in biblical times and the way he heals and blesses people today.

3 List (a) the three groups of sacraments, (b) the sacraments under each, and (c) the four elements that make up the definition of sacraments.

4 List and briefly explain: (a) the liturgical year, (b) the two major seasons of the liturgical year, (c) the main focus of each major season, (d) the three periods of each major season.

5 List the three biblical sources (books) from which the three Sunday readings are taken.

6 Identify: (a) liturgy, (b) Church body (mystical body), (c) birthday of the Church body, (d) biblical meaning of "to remember," (e) lectionary, (f) paschal mystery.

7 In which two readings is the theme of each Sunday Mass set forth?

Reflect

1 A woman had a strange dream. An angel took her to a church to worship. The woman was startled by what she saw.

The organist played; the organ's keys went up and down, but no music came from the organ. The choir sang; the singers' mouths opened and closed, but no song came from their lips. The congregation prayed; their lips moved, but no sound could be heard.

The woman turned to the angel and said, "Why don't I hear anything?"

■ *How do you think the angel answered the woman?*
Explain.

2 Some members of the French underground were arrested by the German army and sentenced to death by a firing squad. On the eve of their execution, the prisoners, mostly Catholic, asked to celebrate the Eucharist.

The Germans explained that the only priest available was German. After discussing the matter, the prisoners agreed to accept the priest. Now, one of the German guards happened to be Catholic also. He asked to join the French prisoners at Mass.

■ *How would you respond to the guard's request*
and why?

3 A little girl came home from religion class with a puzzled look on her face. She said to her mother:

"Today our teacher talked about the importance and responsibility of celebrating the Liturgy of the Mass with the Christian community at least every Sunday. Then she told us a story that didn't seem to have anything to do with celebrating the Eucharist on Sunday. She said:

A monk went to market with seven coins.
Seeing a poor beggar,
he gave him six of his coins.
The beggar thanked the monk over and over.
Then he followed the monk
until he got the chance
to steal the monk's last coin.

■ *How would you explain the teacher's story to the*
little girl?

PRAYER TIME
with the Lord

In the late 1990s Pope John Paul II presided over a rock concert of some 300,000 young people in Italy.

The performers included a host of rock stars, including a pioneer concert star, Bob Dylan. At one point the pope referred to Dylan's most famous song "Blowin' in the Wind," saying:

How many roads must a man walk down?
I answer: "one!"
There is only one road for man,
and it is the road of Jesus Christ, who said
"I am the Way and the Life." JOHN 14:6

The young people cheered.

But they saved their loudest cheers for the pope when he said that Jesus would come to them on the "road to music" as he came to two disciples on the road to Emmaus. LUKE 24:15

The concert ended with Dylan singing
"Knockin' on Heaven's Door"
and "Hard Rain's Gonna Fall."

As the Holy Father made his exit
from the concert, Dylan went to the mike
and sang "Forever Young" as a personal
tribute to the aging Holy Father.
QUOTES ARE FROM THE TABLET: OCT. 4, 1997

■ *Pick out a couple of lines from a song you like and apply it to Jesus or his teaching, the way the pope did with Dylan's song.*

PRAYER Journal

Lord Jesus,
look with love upon the human race
especially those of us who have left you
behind in a Good Friday tomb.

Surprise us on the road and
walk along with us as you did with
the two disciples going to Emmaus.
Break open the Scriptures for us
as you did for them.

Come into our house; and sit at the table
with us, as you did with them.
Take into your hands our bread;
bless it, break it, and share it.

Heal us of our spiritual blindness, as you
healed their blindness, that we, too, might
recognize you in all your risen glory. M.L.

■ *Write a similar prayer to Jesus, asking him
to help you on your faith journey.*

SCRIPTURE Journal

1 **Passover liturgy**   Exodus 12:15–28
2 **Atonement liturgy**   Leviticus 16:29–34
3 **Harvest liturgy**   Leviticus 23:15–22
4 **Liturgy of Eucharist**   Luke 22:14–20
5 **Liturgy of Word**   Luke 4:16–22

■ *Pick one of the above passages. Read it
prayerfully and write a brief statement
to Jesus expressing your feelings about it.*

Baptism

When we were baptized
into union with Christ Jesus,
we were baptized into union
with his death.

By our baptism, then,
we were buried with Christ
and shared his death. . . .

Since we have become one with him
in dying as he did, in the same way
we shall be one with him
by being raised to life as he was.

ROMANS 6:3–5

**Through the sacrament of Baptism,
the risen Jesus unites us to himself
and shares with us the new life
he won by his death and resurrection.
Thus, the sacrament achieves
what it symbolizes: a spiritual death
and rebirth of new life in Christ.**

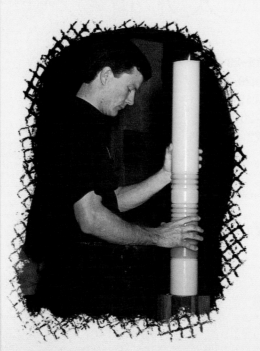

Call to life

Imagine you have been transported back in time to the year 300. Suddenly you find yourself in a large house in Rome. It is Holy Saturday night. About a hundred Christians are gathered around a pool in a courtyard.

You learn that this is the night when several people are to be initiated into the Christian community, the Church. Called *catechumens*, they have been preparing for a long time for the "sacraments of initiation."

Through these sacraments they will be united to the risen Christ and share in the new life he won by his death and resurrection. CCC 1212

1 Why didn't the Christian community meet in a church?

The celebration begins with the sacrament of Baptism. It opens with the *catechumens* renouncing sin and professing their faith. Next, a deacon escorts the catechumens down three steps into a pool. The Baptism takes place there.

After the Baptism, the catechumens are led in their white robes into a large room where the community is gathered for the liturgy of Confirmation.

It begins with the bishop calling each candidate forward by name. Next, he imposes hands on them and prays that they may be worthy to receive the Holy

Spirit. Finally, he anoints them with oil, embraces them, and welcomes them into the community.

The final sacrament is the Eucharist. The liturgy begins with singing and a procession of people carrying loaves of bread and cups of wine. The bread and wine are placed on a table in the center of the room.

The bishop then prays over them, just as Jesus did at the Last Supper. The loaves and the wine (now the Body and Blood of Christ) are shared by the entire community, including the new members.

Sacraments of Initiation

This imaginary scenario illustrates how the early Christian community celebrated the sacraments of initiation in a single ceremony.

As Christian communities began to multiply rapidly, the bishops could no longer preside over every ceremony. To stay personally involved in the initiation of each Christian, the bishops reserved to themselves the celebration of Confirmation. Thus, it became detached from Baptism and was celebrated when the bishop was available.

Similarly, as the community grew, the question of initiating infants arose. This led to the practice of initiating infants into the first stage (Baptism), but postponing the latter two stages (Confirmation and Holy Communion) until the infants reached the age of reason and could participate more personally in the liturgy. CCC 1250–1252

Thus, gradually, adult Confirmations and First Communions were separated from Baptism.

This situation lasted until modern times, when the Church restored the *Rite of the Initiation of Christian Adults* to its original form. CCC 1247–49 Now adults are normally incorporated into the Christian community at a single ceremony at the Easter Vigil.

This brings us to a closer look at the first sacrament of the initiation process.

Sacrament of Baptism

The famous anthropologist Thor Heyerdahl once had a deathly fear of water. Then something happened to change that.

One day while on military maneuvers on the Oxtongue river in Canada, his canoe capsized near a waterfall. The roaring waters pulled his body down into the murky depths of the river and carried him rapidly toward the falls. Filled with fear, he began to pray the Lord's Prayer.

Suddenly he felt a burst of energy surge through his body. Fighting his way up through the strong undertow of the river, he barely reached safety just before being carried over the falls.

That experience transformed him. Somewhere in the watery depths of the river, the old, fearful Thor died and a new, courageous Thor was born. The waters of that river were for Thor both an agent of death and an agent of rebirth.

2 In what sense were the river waters an "agent of death"? An "agent of life"?

Imagery of Baptism

Thor's death-life experience introduces us to an important theme that weaves its way through Scripture: Water is both a symbol and an agent of death and rebirth.

For example, the Book of Genesis portrays a great flood destroying all human life except for Noah's family. Thus, the flood waters act as a symbol and agent of death and rebirth—death to an "old world of sin" and rebirth to a "new world of grace."

In a similar way, the Book of Exodus portrays the Israelites fleeing Egypt through the waters of the Red Sea. Thus, water again acts as a symbol and agent of death and rebirth—death to an "old world of slavery" and rebirth to a "new world of freedom."

This brings us to the symbolism of Baptism.

Symbolism of Baptism

Water is used in baptism much as it is used in Scripture: as a *death-birth* symbol and agent. It symbolizes and achieves our passage from spiritual *death* to spiritual *life*.

Recall that the first sin doomed the human race. Paul writes:

Sin came into the world through one man, and his sin brought death with it.
As a result, death has spread
to the whole human race
because everyone has sinned. Romans 5:12

This "original" sin doomed the human race. Our only hope was that God would have mercy on us and save us. And that is just what God did.

God sent Jesus into the world to save us. The second person of the Trinity shared our humanity, died for our sins, and rose to new life. Referring to the saving act of Jesus, Paul writes:

As the one sin condemned all mankind, in the same way the one righteous act sets all mankind free and gives them life.
Romans 5:18

Through the sacrament of Baptism, the risen Jesus unites us to himself and shares with us the new life he won by his death and resurrection. Thus, the sacrament achieves what it symbolizes: a spiritual death and rebirth in Christ.

In other words, as the old Thor died and was buried in the Oxtongue river, and a new Thor was reborn, so too we are buried and reborn in the waters of Baptism.

We may sum up the sacramental and scriptural images of water this way. They both act as agents of *death* and *birth*.

■ **Scriptural   Physical death/birth**
■ **Sacramental   Spiritual death/birth**

Let us now look more closely at how the sacrament of Baptism symbolizes this spiritual death and rebirth.

The early Christians used to baptize new members by immersing them in a large pool of water—a practice the Catholic Church recommends today.

This way of baptizing better symbolizes our participation in Jesus' death and resurrection. An ancient Christian writing describes the symbolism this way:

*You were led down
to the font of holy Baptism
just as Christ was taken down
from the cross and placed in the tomb. . . .
You were plunged in the water. . . .
It was night for you
and you could not see.*

*But when you rose again,
it was like coming into broad
daylight.
In the same instant
you died and were born again;
the saving water
was both a tomb and a womb.*
JERUSALEM CATECHESIS: 3RD CENTURY

In brief, then, Baptism symbolizes our sacramental dying and rising in and with Christ:

■ **Dying   Tomb image (death)**
■ **Rising   Womb image (birth)**

Liturgy of Baptism

We may divide the liturgy of Baptism into the following three sacramental stages:

■ **Presentation of the candidates**
■ **Profession of faith**
■ **Reception of Baptism**

Presentation of candidates

The first stage begins with the candidates being called forward with their godparents and being presented to the community. This highly personal moment recalls God's call to Jeremiah to be a prophet. God said:

*I chose you before I gave you life,
and before you were born I selected you
to be a prophet to the nations.*
JEREMIAH 1:5

A native in a village refused baptism, even though his friends asked for it. The surprised missionary asked, "Is there something in your instruction that bothers or confuses you?" "No!" said the native. "The thing I want to discover now is if baptism will make a difference in the lives of my friends."

After a month of careful observation, the native returned to the missionary and said, "I am now ready to be baptized. Baptism does, indeed, make a difference. I want Jesus Christ to do for me what he has done for my friends."

■ *Why doesn't baptism seem to make a difference in the life of some people? How about my own life?*

As God called Jeremiah into existence, so God called each one of us. It is this mysterious calling that we celebrate in this opening moment of the baptismal liturgy.

The call and the presentation are followed by the praying of the Litany of the Saints over the candidates.

It is a beautiful prayer that goes back to the early days of Christianity.

It concludes by asking God to "give new life to these chosen ones" about to be baptized.

3 *Why involve prayers to the saints in the baptismal liturgy?*

Profession of faith

After the Litany of the Saints, the celebrant blesses the water to be used in baptizing the catechumens. A portion of the blessing rite reads:

*We ask you, Father, with your Son
to send the Holy Spirit
upon the water of this font.
May all who are buried with Christ
in the death of Baptism
rise also with him to newness of life.*

Then the celebrant charges the candidates to profess the faith into which they are about to be baptized.

They affirm their pledge to "refuse to be mastered by sin" and to "reject Satan, father of sin and prince of darkness."

The profession continues with an affirmation of faith in the Trinity: the Father, the Son, and Spirit.

The most sacred moment of the liturgy of Baptism now arrives.

Reception of Baptism

Each candidate approaches the baptismal font individually. The celebrant bathes each one in water three times, either by immersing them completely or pouring water over them. CCC 694 He uses this baptismal formula:

*I baptize you
in the name of the Father [first bath],
and of the Son [second bath],
and of the Holy Spirit [third bath].*

Next, the presider anoints the newly baptized with holy oil (chrism). This symbolizes and communicates to the newly baptized a share in the priestly, prophetic, and kingly missions of Jesus. (Ancient priests, prophets, and kings were anointed.) The presider prays:

*[God] now anoints you
with the chrism of salvation,
so that, united with his people,
you may remain forever
a member of Christ
who is Priest, Prophet, and King.*

The priestly mission of the newly baptized involves uniting themselves with Jesus in the sacrifice of Mass. The prophetic mission involves witnessing to Jesus in the world by word and example. The kingly mission involves actively involving oneself in the building up of God's Kingdom on earth.

Next, the godparents dress the newly baptized in a white garment. The celebrant prays:

*Receive this baptismal garment
and bring it unstained
to the judgment seat
of our Lord Jesus Christ,
so that you may have everlasting life.*

The garment symbolizes that the newly baptized is now clothed in Christ. Paul writes:

*You were baptized
into union with Christ,
and now you are clothed . . .
with the life of Christ.* GALATIANS 3:27

The Baptism concludes with the godparents lighting a small baptismal candle from the large Easter candle

(symbol of Christ) and handing it to the newly baptized. This action symbolizes the fact that in Baptism we receive the very life of God. The celebrant says:

*You have been enlightened by Christ.
Walk always as children of the light
and keep the flame of faith
alive in your hearts.*

*When the Lord comes,
may you go out to meet him
with all the saints
in the heavenly kingdom.*

4 Which of the above symbolic actions do I find most helpful and why?

Grace of Baptism

John Newton was a British slave trader. One night a storm threatened his ship and its slave cargo. He promised God that if they survived, he would give up slave-trading. They survived. Newton kept his promise, became a minister, and wrote a famous hymn. It begins:

Amazing grace! How sweet the sound—
That saved a wretch like me!
I once was lost, but now am found,
Was blind, but now I see.

Grace is, indeed, amazing. Given to us in Baptism, it "puts us right" with God by forgiving all our sins, and any punishment due to them.

In other words, if we were to die after being baptized, we would go straight to heaven. Concerning the "forgiveness of sins," Paul writes:

Everyone has sinned
and is far away from
God's saving presence.
But by the free gift of God's grace
all are put right with him
through Christ Jesus,
who set them free. Romans 3:23–24

Besides "putting us right" with God, Baptism also "puts us in possession" of God's own eternal life. Paul expresses it this way:

God poured out the Holy Spirit
abundantly on us
through Jesus Christ our Savior,

THINK
about it

Today well lived
makes every yesterday
a dream of happiness
and tomorrow a vision of hope.

Kalidasa

*so that by his grace we might . . .
come into possession of . . . eternal life.*
TITUS 3:6–7

Finally, besides putting us "right with God" and "in possession of God's life," Baptism relates us to the Holy Trinity in a deeply intimate way. CCC 1997 We become:

- **Adopted children of God**
- **Members of Christ's body**
- **Temples of the Spirit**

We become adopted children of God in this sense. Having been united with Christ by Baptism, we are now empowered to call God (through Christ) "Our Father." GALATIANS 4:5–7

Our membership in Christ's body empowers and missions us to share in and continue Christ's work of bringing forth God's Kingdom on earth. 1 CORINTHIANS 12:28

Finally, our transformation into Temples of the Holy Spirit places at our disposal the gifts and fruits of the Holy Spirit. 1 CORINTHIANS 6:4

And so we may sum up the amazing grace of Baptism as follows. It is a gift that:

- **Puts us right with God**
- **Gives us a share in God's life**
- **Relates us intimately to the Trinity**

Minister of Baptism

Ordinarily, the minister of Baptism is either a bishop, a priest, or a deacon. In an emergency, however, any person—even an unbaptized person—can baptize. This option is rooted in the "universal saving will of God." CCC 1256–61 Paul writes:

*Christ Jesus . . . gave himself
to redeem the whole human race.
That was the proof at the right time
that God wants everyone to be saved.*
1 TIMOTHY 2:6

The minister of Baptism must intend to do what the Church does as he pours water over the person while reciting:

*I baptize you
in the name of the Father,
and of the Son,
and of the Holy Spirit.*

We may sum up the heart of the liturgy of Baptism in terms of the:

- **Water ritual   Pouring/immersing**
- **Word ritual   Saying "I baptize . . ."**

On Pentecost the Holy Spirit came upon the disciples and formed them into one body:

- **Jesus**   **Head of the body**
- **Disciples**   **Members of the body**

From that moment on, the risen Jesus not only became present in the Church but also acted through it, in the liturgy, especially the seven sacraments. We may define a sacrament as:

- **An efficacious sign of grace**
- **Instituted by Christ**
- **Entrusted to his Church**
- **To give divine life to us**

We may divide the sacraments into the following three categories or groups:

- **Initiation**
- **Healing**
- **Service**

The sacraments of initiation include Baptism, Confirmation, and the Eucharist. Baptism:

- **Puts us right with God**
- **Gives us a share in God's life**
- **Relates us intimately to the Trinity**

Our new relationship to the Trinity makes us:

- **Adopted children of God**
- **Members of Christ's body**
- **Temples of the Spirit**

1 Pick one biblical example involving water and explain how the water acted as a symbol and agent of death and rebirth.

2 Explain why baptism by immersion better symbolizes our participation in Jesus' death and resurrection.

3 Briefly explain (a) how Baptism came to be separated from the other two sacraments of initiation and (b) when and under what circumstances they have now been restored to a single ceremony.

4 List and briefly explain (a) the three stages of the baptismal liturgy; (b) the symbolism of the following: anointing, clothing with a white garment, handing of a lighted candle to the newly baptized; (c) the threefold grace of Baptism.

5 List (a) the three ordinary ministers of Baptism, (b) who may baptize in an emergency, (c) the three minimal requirements that need to be observed by one baptizing in an emergency.

Reflect

1 Fifty-two Americans were held hostage by Iran for 444 days during 1980 and 1981. On Christmas, three American ministers were permitted to enter Iran, hold services, and give the hostages messages from loved ones.

One message to hostage Barry Rosen was especially moving. The minister began by saying to Barry, "I saw your wife, Barbara, and your son, Alexander, in New York. Alexander is a lovely boy; he told me to give you this." Then he kissed Barry on the cheek. Barry had all he could do to fight back the tears.

■ **Why do you think kissing the boy's father was more effective than saying, "Your son sends his love"?**
■ **How was the real kiss (relayed through the minister) somewhat like a sacrament?**
■ **Why do people often become less affectionate (outwardly) as we grow older, and is this good or bad?**

2 Upon entering a church, Catholics frequently dip their hand in holy water and bless themselves. A girl said recently:

I just learned that taking holy water and signing ourselves "In the name of the Father, and of the Son, and of the Holy Spirit" is intended to be a renewal of our Baptism. That makes this practice so much more meaningful. But I'll bet most Catholics don't know the meaning of it.

■ **To test the girl's thesis, ask three Catholics if they know the meaning of taking holy water and blessing themselves upon entering a church. Write out a brief report on the response each of the three gave.**

3 The following is an excerpt from a letter from a Chicago father to his son in college:

I had breakfast with Joe, my friend,
the elderly Jewish doctor.
He was reminiscing
about his days as a young resident
at Alexian Brothers Hospital
on Chicago's southwest side.
He was there in the 30s
when the neighborhood was mostly composed
of immigrants from middle Europe.

Often he would receive a call at an odd hour
and would hurry through a cold winter night
to deliver a baby in some old two-flat.
Most of these buildings
had just a single coal-fired stove in the kitchen.
It provided heat for the entire flat.

And so, more often than not,
the mother would give birth in the kitchen
near the stove.
Joe said about half a dozen times
during those years
the child would be stillborn.
There he would be next to all that heat and pain
holding a dead baby
while trying to comfort a grieving mother.

He said that on each of these occasions
he put the child in the mother's arms,
went to the sink for a cup of water,
dipped his finger into it,
and traced on the child's forehead
the sign of the cross, saying,
"I baptize you in the name of the Father,
the Son, and the Holy Spirit."
He asked me
if I thought these baptisms were valid.
GEORGE PENCE

■ **How would you answer the old Jewish doctor's question?**
■ **What struck you most about the above letter? Explain.**

PRAYER TIME
with the Lord

The following prayer was written by General MacArthur in the Philippines in the opening days of the Pacific War. Made public after the general's death in 1964, it was left as a spiritual legacy to his son.

Build me a son, O Lord,
who will be strong enough
to know when he is weak,
brave enough
to face himself when he is afraid . . .

Build me a son whose wishes
will not take the place of deeds.
Lead him, I pray,
not in the path of ease and comfort,
but under the stress and spur
of difficulties and challenge.
Let him learn to stand up in the storm;
let him learn compassion for those who fall.

Build me a son
whose heart will be clear,
whose goals will be high;
a son who will master himself
before he seeks to master other men;
one who will reach into the future,
yet never forget the past.

And after all these things are his,
add, I pray, enough of a sense of humor
so that he may always be serious
yet never take himself seriously. . . .
Then, I his father, will dare to whisper,
'I have not lived in vain.'

■ **Compose a similar prayer that begins, "Build me into a parent, O Lord. . . ."**

PRAYER Journal

The following prayer is a reflection on the sacraments by a twentieth-century theologian.

Lord, your salvation
is bound up with a visible Church. . . .
Your grace comes to us in ways
that we can see, hear, and feel. . . .
It warms my heart
to know that I can be sure
of your powerful life-giving presence
in the water of Baptism,
in the word of Reconciliation,
and in the bread of the Eucharist.

KARL RAHNER (SLIGHTLY ADAPTED)

■ *Compose a similar prayer to Jesus about one sacrament in particular, explaining how you feel about it; why you don't receive it more often; how you might make the reception of it more meaningful.*

_____

_____

_____

_____

_____

_____

_____

_____

_____

SCRIPTURE Journal

1	Baptism	Acts 8:26–40
2	Baptism mandate	Matthew 28:16–20
3	Baptism into Christ	Romans 6:3–11
4	Baptism is a rebirth	John 3:1–6
5	Baptism unites us all	Galatians 3:26–29

■ *Pick one of the above passages. Read it prayerfully and write a short statement to Jesus expressing your feelings about it.*

_____

_____

_____

_____

_____

_____

Confirmation

*Philip went to the principal city
in Samaria and preached the Messiah
to the people there. . . .*

*The apostles in Jerusalem heard
that the people of Samaria
had received the word of God,
so they sent Peter and John to them.*

*When they arrived,
they prayed for the believers . . .
Then Peter and John
placed their hands on them and
they received the Holy Spirit.*
ACTS 8:5; 14–17

*Confirmation communicates to us
the same fullness of the Spirit
that the disciples received on Pentecost.
It perfects what was begun in Baptism,
deepens our bond
with the Holy Trinity,
strengthens our bond with the Church,
and missions us to witness to Jesus.*

One Tooth

One Tooth was an old woodcutter in New Guinea. He made his living cutting wood for the missionary clinic. He got his name from the fact that he had only one tooth in his upper jaw.

One Tooth had just become a Christian. So he spent time each day reading the Gospel to outpatients in the waiting room of the clinic. Day after day, he shared his faith with these suffering people.

One day he began having trouble reading. He went to a doctor at the clinic. After examining him, the doctor said, "One Tooth, I have something hard to tell you. You're going blind."

The next day, One Tooth didn't show up at the clinic. Nor did he show up the day after that. Then the doctor learned that the old woodcutter was living alone on a deserted part of the island.

So the doctor went to see him. He asked, "Why have you come out here, One Tooth?" The old woodcutter replied:

*Ever since you said I was going blind,
I've been memorizing
the important parts of the Gospel.*

I've already memorized Jesus' birth,
several miracles and parables,
and Jesus' death and resurrection.
Soon I'll be back at the hospital,
telling the outpatients about Jesus.

1 How does this story relate to the sacrament of Confirmation?

Coming of the Spirit

Before ascending to his Father, Jesus told his disciples:

*"In a few days you will be baptized with
the Holy Spirit. . . .
You will be filled with power,
and you will be witnesses for me . . .
to the ends of the earth."* ACTS 1:5, 8

A few days later, while the disciples were gathered in prayer, it happened:

*Suddenly
there was a noise from the sky . . .*

*like a strong wind blowing,
and it filled the whole house. . . .
They were all filled
with the Holy Spirit.* ACTS 2:2, 4

Sharing the Spirit

After receiving the Holy Spirit, the Apostles began the awesome mission of sharing the Spirit with other believers. Thus, we read:

*When the people of Samaria
believed Philip's message
about the good news
of the Kingdom of God,
they were baptized . . .*

*Then Peter and John placed hands on
them and they received the Holy Spirit.*
ACTS 8:4–7, 12, 17

2 Why do you think Philip did not lay hands on the Samaritans and give the Holy Spirit to them himself?

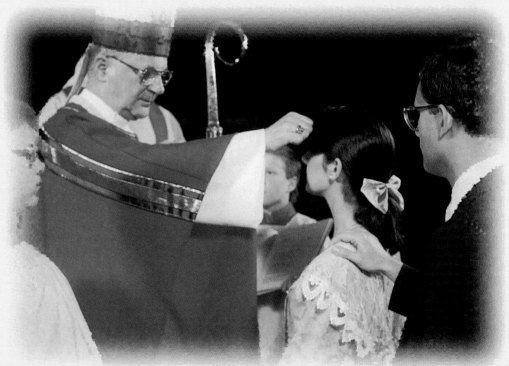

In the last 20 years of her life, Clara Hale has served as foster mother to over 500 babies born of drug-addicted mothers.

These babies enter life with a drug dependency themselves. When a baby is crying from the pain of withdrawal, Clara says:

*All you can do is hold it close
and say to it,
"I love you, and God loves you,
and your mama loves you.
Your mama just needs
more time."*

■ *Give an example of an adult you know who performs some volunteer service.*

■ *What service are you performing or might you perform?*

Sacrament of Confirmation

This brings us to the sacrament of Confirmation. Through it, we receive the same full outpouring of the Holy Spirit that the disciples themselves received when the Holy Spirit descended upon them on Pentecost. CCC 1302

The purpose of the outpouring is to do for us what it did for the disciples: to mission and empower us to assume an active role in the work of the Church by:

■ **Witnessing to the faith**
■ **Spreading the faith**

3 *Where and at what age were you confirmed? What do you remember most about the occasion?*

Liturgy of Confirmation

The sacrament of Confirmation is celebrated for new adult Catholics at the Easter Vigil Service.

It follows immediately after Baptism to underscore the close unity between these two sacraments.

The liturgy of Confirmation involves three stages:

■ **Invitation**
■ **Laying on of hands**
■ **Anointing with Chrism**

Invitation

The presiding minister begins by saying to the candidates and their godparents and sponsors these or similar words:

*Born again in Christ by baptism,
you have become members of Christ
and of his priestly people.*

*Now you are to share in the outpouring
of the Holy Spirit . . .
sent by the Lord upon his apostles . . .*

*It will make you more like Christ,
help you to witness to him,
and take an active role
in building up the Body of Christ.*

The presiding minister then invites the entire congregation to pray, saying:

*Let us pray to God our Father,
that he will pour out the Holy Spirit
on these newly baptized
to strengthen them with his gifts
and anoint them to be more like Christ,
the Son of God.*

Laying on of hands

The second stage of the liturgy begins with the presiding minister extending his hands over the entire group to be confirmed. CCC 1299

The rite of extending hands over another, or laying hands on them, dates back to Old Testament times. Thus, when Moses was old, God instructed him to communicate to Joshua a share in his own authority, saying:

"Take Joshua son of Nun . . .
and place your hands on his head . . ."
Moses did
as the LORD had commanded. . . ."
NUMBERS 27:18, 20, 22

Later, in New Testament times, the Apostles used this same rite to commission the first deacons. "The Apostles prayed and placed their hands on them." ACTS 6:6; CCC 1288

After extending his hands over the candidates to be confirmed, the presiding minister prays:

Michelangelo's *Moses.*

All-powerful God,
Father of our Lord Jesus Christ,
by water and the Holy Spirit
you freed your sons and daughters
from sin and gave them new life.

Send your Holy Spirit upon them
to be their helper and guide.

Give them the spirit of wisdom
and understanding,
the spirit of right judgment
and courage,
the spirit of knowledge and reverence.
Fill them with the spirit of
wonder and awe in your presence.

4 Which of these above "gifts of the Spirit" do you feel is needed most today?

Anointing with Chrism

The "laying on" of hands is followed by the most important rite of the sacrament of Confirmation.

It is conferred through the anointing
with chrism on the forehead,
which is done
by the laying on of the hand,
and through the words: "Be sealed
with the Gift of the Holy Spirit."
CCC 1300

Anointing with oil goes back to biblical times. CCC 695 Moses used it to confer *priesthood* on Aaron. EXODUS 29:7

Samuel used it to confer kingship on David. 1 SAMUEL 16:13

And, finally, Elijah used it to anoint Elisha a *prophet.* 1 KINGS 19:16

Ruddell Norris

Young Ruddell Norris was aware that by our Confirmation, we are called to spread the good news of the Gospel. His problem was that he was shy. How could he preach the Gospel?

Ruddell's solution was ingenious. He spent a percentage of his allowance on Catholic pamphlets and placed them in hospital lobbies and other appropriate places.

One day he heard a new church member say to a member of his family:

I first learned about the Church
in a rather unusual way.
I saw a pamphlet
about the Catholic Church
in a hospital lobby
and began reading it.
And that's how it all started.

THINK
about it

Be careful how you live; you may be the only Bible some person ever reads.

W. J. Toms

Anointing with oil played an important role in Old Testament times in creating *prophets, priests,* and *kings.* Understandably, it plays a similar role in New Testament times. CCC 783–86

This brings us to an important moment in the liturgy of anointing. It is called "sealing." CCC 698 An ancient Christian writing explains it this way:

*The soldier chosen for service . . .
receives on his hand the seal
showing what king he will serve.*

*So it is with you.
You were chosen
to serve the king of heaven,
and will henceforth bear his seal.*

Saint Paul writes:

The Spirit is God's mark of ownership [seal] on you, a guarantee that the day will come when God will set you free.
EPHESIANS 4:30

And so the anointing ends with these words: "Be sealed with the Gift of the Holy Spirit."

Sharing in the missions of Jesus

Confirmation calls, empowers, and perfects in us a share in the three missions of Jesus:

- ■ **Prophet**
- ■ **Priest**
- ■ **King**

The *prophetic* mission commissions us to teach and to witness to the Gospel. CCC 904–907

The *priestly* mission commissions us to offer ourselves with Christ to the Father in the Eucharist. CCC 900–903

The *kingly* mission commissions us to continue Christ's work of building up God's kingdom on earth. CCC 908–913

Four graces of Confirmation

Confirmation communicates to us the same Holy Spirit that the disciples received on Pentecost. Through Confirmation, the Holy Spirit confers on us a fourfold grace.

It *perfects* what was begun in Baptism, *deepens* our union with the Trinity, *strengthens* our bond with the Church, and *missions* us to witness and work for the spread of God's Kingdom.

5 List some situations where young people can be more effective witnesses and workers in God's Kingdom.

The Confirmation liturgy of the Easter Vigil Service ends with the whole community welcoming the new Christians. Then comes a dramatic moment.

Everyone present stands in solidarity with the new Christians. Holding lighted candles, they renew their baptismal commitment, saying "I do" to these questions:

Do you believe in God,
the Father Almighty,
creator of heaven and earth?

Do you believe in Jesus Christ,
his only Son, our Lord,
who was born of the Virgin Mary,
was crucified, died, and was buried,
rose from the dead, and now is seated
at the right hand of the Father?

Do you believe in the Holy Spirit,
the holy Catholic Church,
the communion of saints,
the forgiveness of sins,
the resurrection of the body,
and the life everlasting?

A fitting way to conclude our study of the sacrament of Confirmation is to reflect on these words of Saint Anselm:

Recall that you have received
the spiritual seal . . .
Guard what you have received.

God the Father
has marked you with his sign;
Christ the Lord has confirmed you
and placed his pledge,
the Holy Spirit, in your hearts.

DE MYSTERIIS

Recap

On Pentecost the Spirit came upon the disciples and formed them into one body, with Jesus as head of the body. COLOSSIANS 1:18

From that moment on, the risen Jesus not only became present in the Church but also began to act through it, especially in the sacraments. The first of these seven sacraments is Baptism.

The second sacrament is Confirmation. Its overall purpose is to mission and empower us to assume a more active role in the work of the Church by:

■ **Witnessing to the faith**
■ **Spreading the faith**

Toward this end, it empowers us to share in the threefold mission of Jesus as:

■ **Prophet**
■ **Priest**
■ **King**

The liturgy of Confirmation involves three stages:

■ **Invitation**
■ **Laying on of hands**
■ **Anointing with Chrism**

The fourfold grace of the sacrament of Confirmation includes the following:

perfects what was begun in us in Baptism, *deepens* our relationship with the Trinity, *strengthens* our bond with the Church, and *missions* us to spread the Gospel.

Review

1 What is the name of the day on which we celebrate the Holy Spirit descending upon the disciples?

2 Who (a) converted and baptized many in Samaria, (b) came from Jerusalem to communicate the Holy Spirit to them?

3 List and briefly explain the three stages of the liturgy of Confirmation.

4 Briefly explain how the "laying on of hands" is deeply rooted in the Old Testament.

5 List and briefly explain the three missions of Jesus that Confirmation calls and empowers us to continue.

6 Briefly explain how "anointing" is deeply rooted in the Old Testament.

7 List the four main graces of the sacrament of Confirmation.

Reflect

1 October 23, 1945, was the day Jackie Robinson became baseball's first black athlete. Jackie's entry into baseball was not easy. Racial slurs and insults were a common occurrence.

One day in Boston's Fenway Park, the situation got especially bad. At one point the all-star shortstop, Pee Wee Reese, a Southerner, called time, walked over to second base, put his arm around Jackie, and just stood there looking at the fans.

■ *On a scale of one (low) to ten (high), how strong is prejudice in your school; and how do you account for the amount of prejudice that is there?*
■ *Describe a time when, like Pee Wee Reese, you took a stand against some prejudice (racial or otherwise).*

2 Imagine, for the moment, that you are financially secure and could spend the rest of your life doing whatever you wished for the spreading of the Gospel.

■ *What are one or two things that you would seriously consider doing and why?*

3 Robert was one of Esther Thompson's favorite young people. After her husband died, Robert did all her odd jobs, like mowing the lawn and shoveling snow. A real friendship developed between them.

Thus, Esther faced an embarrassing situation when Robert invited her to his Confirmation. All her life she had mistrusted Catholic "magical" rituals. After agonizing over the invitation, she finally pushed aside her distrust and went. Esther was unprepared for what happened. She wrote later:

The Confirmation service dissolved
my years of ignorant distrust. . . .
The Catholic faith was beautiful.
Three years have passed and
I'm a Catholic now.
I thank God every day that Robert invited me
to attend the sacrament of Confirmation.

■ *That beautiful story raises a question. If someone like Esther asks you, "What are these magical rituals that you Catholics have?" how would you go about answering the question in a way they might understand and find helpful?*

PRAYER TIME
with the Lord

One of the problems people encounter in praying is distractions. Here's one person's prayer about the problem:

God, help my thoughts!
They stray from me,
setting off on the wildest journeys.
When I am at prayer, they run off
like naughty children, making trouble. . . .

My thoughts can cross an ocean
with a single leap.
They can fly from earth to heaven,
and back again, in a single second.

They come to me for a fleeting moment,
and then away they flee.
No chains, no locks can hold them back. . . .

They slip from my grasp like tails of eels;
they swoop hither and thither
like swallows in flight. . . .

Christ, who can see into every heart, and
read every mind,
take hold of my thoughts.
Bring my thoughts back to me,
and clasp me to yourself. AUTHOR UNKNOWN

■ **One spiritual writer suggests that God may actually speak to us in prayer through our distractions. How might God do this?**
■ **Compose a prayer to Jesus, similar to the one above, about the distractions you encounter in praying.**

PRAYER Journal

A simple way to pray is called "meditative reading." You take a prayer, read a line at a time, apply it to your life, and speak to Jesus about it. Take Saint Ignatius' "Prayer for Generosity":

Lord, teach me to be generous.
Teach me to serve you as you deserve;
to give and not to count the cost;
to fight and not to heed the wounds;
to toil and not to seek for rest;
to labor and not to ask for reward,
except to know that I am doing your will.

Here's how you might pray the first line:

Jesus, it's no use trying to fool you.
You know that I'm a pretty selfish person.
Work one of your miracles on me.
Teach how me to change. Please! Please!

■ *Now pray one of the next six lines.*

_____

_____

_____

_____

_____

_____

_____

_____

_____

_____

SCRIPTURE Journal

1 **Confirmation**   Acts 8:14–17
2 **One Spirit, many gifts** 1 Cor. 12:1–11
3 **One body, many gifts**   1 Cor. 12:27–31
4 **Live in the light**   Ephesians 5:1–11
5 **Taught by the Spirit**   1 Cor. 2:10–16

■ *Pick one of the above passages. Read it prayerfully and write a short statement to Jesus expressing your feelings about it.*

_____

_____

_____

_____

_____

_____

_____

Eucharist

When the hour came, Jesus took his place at table with his apostles. . . .

*Then he took a piece of bread,
gave thanks to God, broke it,
and gave it to them, saying,
"This is my body, which is given for you.
Do this in memory of me."*

*In the same way,
he gave them the cup after supper,
saying,
"This cup is God's new covenant
sealed with my blood,
which is poured out for you.
Take this and share it among yourselves."*
LUKE 22:14, 19–20

**In the Mass, the entire Church,
through the Spirit,
unites itself with Jesus
in offering its sacrifice
of praise and thanksgiving
to the Father.**

Call to worship

Father Walter Ciszek studied Russian with the hope of doing missionary work in that country. After ordination, he went to Poland. When the Nazis invaded it, he disguised himself as a Polish laborer and joined prisoners being sent to labor camps in Russia.

Two years later, the Soviet secret police accused him of being a Vatican spy and sentenced him to 23 years hard labor in Siberia. Upon his release in 1963, he wrote a book entitled *He Leadeth Me.* One passage in it reads:

*I have seen . . . prisoners
deprive their bodies of needed sleep
in order to get up before the rising bell
for a secret Mass. . . .
We would be severely
punished if we were discovered. . . .*

The Masses were held in "drafty storage shacks" and sometimes outside "huddled in mud or slush. In these primitive conditions, the Mass brought us closer to God than anyone might conceivably imagine."

In those days Catholics did not eat or drink after midnight when receiving the "Body of the Lord" the next morning.

Some prisoners could not attend these secret Masses, so Father Ciszek consecrated extra hosts and distributed them when he could. That meant that some prisoners had to wait until night. Ciszek writes:

*Yet these men would actually
fast all day long
and do exhausting physical labor
without a bite to eat . . .
just to be able to receive
the Holy Eucharist.*

1 Why doesn't the Eucharist seem to mean as much to people today as it did to people in previous decades?

Last Supper

The Eucharist completes the sacraments of initiation. CCC 1322 The Eucharist lies at the very heart of our Catholic faith and worship. It is at the focus of everything we believe, everything we do, everything we hope for. CCC 1324

When we celebrate the Eucharist, we carry out the command that Jesus gave us at the Last Supper, "Do this in memory of me."

Two movements

To understand the movement or flow of the Eucharist (Mass), it helps to recall that ancient Jews worshiped in two different places: the synagogue LUKE 4:16 and the Temple LUKE 2:41.

There was a synagogue in each town; but there was only one Temple—in Jerusalem.

Synagogues were mainly places of prayer and instruction. People went there to read and reflect on the Word of God.

The Temple was mainly a place of prayer and sacrifice. People went there to make offerings to God. LUKE 2:24

The eucharistic celebration is made up of two movements that echo the synagogue and the Temple services. These two movements are called:

■ **Liturgy of the Word**
■ **Liturgy of the Eucharist**

Each one follows a similar threefold format:

■ **Introductory rite**
■ **Reading rite**
■ **Concluding rite**

■ **Introductory rite**
■ **Eucharistic rite**
■ **Concluding rite**

2 On a scale of one (not very) to ten (very), how closely would you say the synagogue and temple services fit what we do at Mass today? Explain.

Liturgy of the Word

In his book, *What the Jews Believe,* Philip Bernstein recounts this story:

*When the synagogue
of which this writer is now the minister
burned down, an Irish policeman
dashed to the ark and seized the Torah.
He handed it to the rabbi
who was rushing into the building.*

*"Here," he said,
"I have saved your crucifix."
Well, the Jews have no crucifix,
but the policeman had the right idea:
the scrolls are the most sacred
symbol of Judaism.*

Ancient Jews kept the scrolls of God's Word in a sacred place, called the Ark. It is akin to the tabernacle in Catholic churches. Before each service, they took the scroll from the ark and carried it in procession around the synagogue.

3 Have you ever visited a Jewish synagogue or a Protestant service? What struck you most about it? Explain.

Introductory rite

The celebration of the Liturgy of the Word begins similar to the way the Jewish synagogue service does.

The congregation stands and sings. As they do, the ministers march in procession to the sanctuary. The focal point of the procession is the book of God's Word, held high by the lector.

When the procession reaches the sanctuary, the book is placed on the lectern. The priest, "acting in the person of Christ," presides over the assembly. CCC 1348

After greeting the people, he invites all to carry out the command that Jesus gave us in his Sermon on the Mount. Jesus said that if we gather for worship and have not forgiven someone, we should do that first. Only then should we begin our worship. MATTHEW 5:23–24

So, the presider invites all present to pause and ask forgiveness of God and one another for any sins against them.

THINK
about it

If God were to appear to starving people, he would not dare appear in any form other than food.

Mohandas K. Gandhi

4 What do you do when you find it hard to forgive someone for something they've done to you?

At some celebrations, this "penitential rite" is followed by a hymn of thanks and adoration (praise). Called the *Gloria*, it begins:

Glory to God in the highest,
and peace to his people on earth.
Lord God, heavenly King,
almighty God and Father,
we worship you, we give you thanks,
we praise you for your glory. . . .

The presider then leads the assembly in prayer. Here is a typical prayer:

Almighty God, ever-loving Father,
your care extends
beyond the boundaries of race and nation
to the hearts of all who live.
May the walls,
which prejudice raises between us,
crumble beneath the shadow
of your outstretched arm.
We ask this through Christ our Lord.
TWENTIETH SUNDAY OF THE YEAR

And so the Introductory Rite prepares us for the heart of the Liturgy of the Word, which now follows.

Reading rite

Saint Luke gives us a beautiful description of how the reading of God's Word was celebrated in ancient synagogues. He writes:

Jesus went to Nazareth,
where he was brought up,
and on the Sabbath,
he went as usual to the synagogue.

He stood up to read the Scriptures and
was handed the book
of the prophet Isaiah.
He unrolled the scroll
and found the place where it is written,

"The Spirit of the Lord is upon me,
because he has chosen me
to bring good news to the poor.

"He has sent me
to proclaim liberty to the captives
and recovery of sight to the blind,
to set free the oppressed and
announce that the time has come
when the Lord will save his people."

Jesus rolled up the scroll,
gave it back to the attendant,
and sat down.
All the people in the synagogue
had their eyes fixed on him,
as he said to them,

"This passage of scripture
has come true today,
as you heard it being read."
They were all well impressed with him
and marveled at the eloquent words
that he spoke. LUKE 4:16–22

At Sunday celebrations of the Eucharist, the proclamation of the Word consists of three readings.

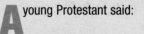

A Broadway play, *The Royal Hunt of the Sun,* dealt with Spain's conquest of Peru. In one scene a Spaniard gives an Inca leader a Bible, saying that it is God's Word.

Filled with curiosity, the leader raises the Bible to his ear and listens. When he hears nothing, he slams the Bible to the ground, feeling that he has been deceived.

This raises the question: How do we go about listening to God's word?

First we listen with our *body;* that is, we listen with reverent attention.

Second, we listen with our *mind;* that is, we try to make the passage come alive in our imagination. We try to visualize the scene and feel the excitement Jesus' disciples felt as they watched and listened to it unfold.

Third, we listen with our *heart;* that is, we "take it to heart."

Finally, we listen with our soul. This means that we listen with faith. We believe God's Word has the power to touch us and transform us. So we listen with confidence, knowing that if we persevere, the day will come when it will touch us profoundly.

■ *Which of the four ways to listen do you find most difficult: body, mind, heart, or soul? Explain.*

First reading

This reading is usually from the Old Testament, the same collection of readings from which Jesus read in the synagogue at Nazareth.

5 *During what season of the year is the first reading taken not from the Old Testament, but from the Acts of the Apostles? Why the Acts?*

Responsorial psalm

The first reading is followed by a *Responsorial Psalm.* Selected from the Book of Psalms, it serves as a prayerful meditation on the first reading.

Second reading

The next reading is taken from the New Testament, usually one of Paul's letters. These letters deal with early Christian problems. Surprisingly, they often deal with problems that are similar to our own problems.

Third reading

The final reading is the most important one. It is taken from one of the four Gospels. Normally, we show the importance of this reading in a fourfold way:

■ **Introducing it with an acclamation**
■ **Standing for the reading of it**
■ **Signing ourselves when it begins**
■ **Having it read by presider or deacon**

The "signing" of ourselves goes back to early Christian times. It consists in tracing a small cross on the forehead, lips, and heart. While doing so, many people pray silently:

May God's Word be in my mind, on my lips, and in my heart that I may worthily proclaim it by word and by example.

After the reading of the Gospel, the presider usually kisses the text, elevates the book, and says, "The Gospel of the Lord." All respond, "Praise to you, Lord Jesus Christ."

Homily

The Gospel reading is followed by the homily. It is given either by the presider or a deacon. The homilist does what Jesus did in the synagogue in Nazareth. He explains and applies the Word to the congregation.

Homilists have a difficult assignment. First, most congregations are made up of people of different ages and backgrounds. This makes it hard to appeal to everyone. Second, not all homilists are gifted communicators.

And so the homily may not always be as inspiring as we'd like it to be. But we should not forget Jesus' words to his disciples: "Whoever listens to you listens to me." LUKE 10:16

6 Describe a recent homily that you found to be better than ordinary.

Concluding rite

The Liturgy of the Word concludes in a twofold way: with the Creed and the General Intercessions.

The Creed is a summary of what we Catholics believe. The General Intercessions are an expression to God of our needs and the needs of our world.

And so the first movement of the Mass sets the *mood of faith* in which we can celebrate the *mystery of faith*. This brings us to the second movement of the Mass.

A pastor began his homily by holding up a huge triangle. He said:

*My homily is like this triangle.
It has three points.
The first point is
that millions of people
are starving and homeless.*

*The second point is
that most people
don't give a damn.*

*The third point is
that some of you
are probably more disturbed
by the fact that
I just said "damn"
than you are by the fact
that millions are starving
and homeless.*

■ *How would you evaluate the pastor's homily and why?*
■ *If you could preach one homily on national TV, what would you preach about? Why?*
■ *What visual aid/aids might you use?*

Skeeter

Young Skeeter Rayburn could not speak or use his limbs. He lay on his back 24 hours a day. His only means of communication was an electric typewriter, which he pressed one key at a time by means of a stylus attached to his head. Using this method, he wrote an article on what the Eucharist meant to him. He writes:

*One of my crosses . . .
is cerebral palsy's jerkiness. . . .
My muscles have spasms and
my arms and legs jerk wildly
until I think I will go mad.
At these moments,
I remember Jesus' torturous
writhings on the cross . . .
But he endured it silently.
Can I do less with my little
contortions with Jesus
living in me?*

*Another cross is
waiting for things.
I have to wait
to go to the bathroom;
wait to have my nose
cleaned out
when I can hardly breathe;
wait to be covered
when I am cold. . . .
In these periods I recall, again,
what Jesus did for me
on the cross.
Can I do less for him?*

Eucharist magazine

Liturgy of the Eucharist

Charles Butler went to visit his son, who was working in the Amazon Basin in Brazil. When he arrived in Brazil, he took a small plane to a tiny town in the Basin. There, he and the pilot went to a local cafe for a meal.

An old-timer in the cafe began talking to the pilot. They soon discovered that they were both from the same province of Brazil. Next they discovered they were both from the same small town.

When Charles and the pilot finished their meal, the old-timer said to the pilot jokingly, "You know, if we keep talking, we might discover that we are from the same family."

That story makes a good bridge to the second movement of the Mass, the Liturgy of the Eucharist. Through it, we discover, in a special way, that we are family. We are much more. We are members of Christ's Body. Saint Paul says of the Eucharistic meal:

*Because there is one loaf of bread,
all of us, though many, are one body,
for we all share the same loaf.*
1 CORINTHIANS 10:17

To understand the Liturgy of the Eucharist, we need to go back to the Jewish Passover meal.

In eating this meal together, Jews did far more than *remember* and celebrate the event that freed their ancestors from Egyptian slavery.

They believed that, through faith, they brought that event into present, so that they could participate in it as truly as if they had been present at the original event.

It was with this understanding that Jesus sat down with his disciples to eat the Passover meal. And it was during this meal that he instituted the Eucharist.

*Jesus took his place at the table
with his apostles. . . .
Then he took a piece of bread,
gave thanks to God,
broke it, and gave it to them, saying:
"This is my body
which is given up for you.
Do this in memory of me."*
LUKE 22:14, 19

When Jesus said, "Do this in *memory* of me," he did more than give us a command to remember and reenact what he did. He gave us a way to be present, in faith, to this great mystery just as truly as his apostles were 2000 years ago. CCC 1341, 1363

7 Why was it fitting for Jesus to choose the Jewish passover meal as the setting and the occasion for instituting the Eucharist?

Introductory rite

Just as the Liturgy of the Word began with a procession, so the Liturgy of the Eucharist begins with a procession. It begins with members of the congregation bringing the gifts of bread and wine to the Lord's Table (altar).

The presider takes them and prepares them. When he is finished preparing them, he invites the assembly to pray that they "may be acceptable to God, the almighty Father." The introductory rite ends with the presider praying in words like this:

Lord our God, may the bread and wine you give us for our nourishment on earth become the sacrament of our eternal life.
Fifth Sunday of the Year

We are now ready for the most sacred moment of the entire eucharistic celebration.

Eucharistic prayer

This sacred prayer begins with a "dialogue" in which the presider exhorts the assembly: "Lift up your hearts" and "give thanks to the Lord."

The brief dialogue is followed by the preface. It begins with the presider giving thanks to God:

Father,
all-powerful and ever-living God,
we do well always and everywhere
to give you thanks.

The Preface concludes with the entire assembly saying or singing:

Holy, holy, holy Lord,
God of power and might.
Heaven and earth
are full of your glory.

Hosanna in the highest.
Blessed is he who comes
in the name of the Lord.
Hosanna in the highest.

The words "Holy, holy, holy" recall Isaiah's vision of heaven. The Lord was seated on a throne. "Around him flaming creatures . . . were calling out: 'Holy, holy, holy!' " Isaiah 6:2–3

The words "Hosanna . . . Blessed is he who comes in the name of the Lord" recall the first Palm Sunday. The crowds called out to Jesus: "Hosanna . . . blessed is he who comes in the name of the Lord." Matthew 21:9 NAB

8 Why are the references to Isaiah and the Palm Sunday crowd appropriate at this point in the Mass?

Invocation of the Spirit

The Eucharistic Prayer continues with the presider asking the Father to send the Holy Spirit to make present the Body and Blood of Jesus under the signs of bread and wine. CCC 1353

Institution narrative

Next, the presider recalls the words of Jesus at the Last Supper, saying:

He took a piece of bread,
gave thanks to God, broke it,
and gave it to them, saying:

"This is my body,
which is given up for you.
Do this in memory of me."

These words recall the day when, on a hillside outside Capernaum, Jesus made this awesome promise to his followers:

"I am the living bread
that came down from heaven.
If anyone eats this bread,
he will live forever.
The bread that I will give . . .
is my flesh . . .
that the world may live." JOHN 6:51

Then the presider does what Jesus did at the end of the Passover meal, saying:

In the same way
he gave them the cup after supper,
saying, "This cup is God's new covenant
sealed with my blood,
which is poured out for you."
LUKE 22:19–20

Two points need to be stressed here. The *first point* is Jesus' words:

"This is my body,
which is given for you. . . .
This cup is . . . my blood
which is poured out for you"

They speak of *sacrifice* and indicate that the Last Supper is closely linked with Jesus' sacrifice on the cross. By sharing in the Eucharist we are sharing, also, in Jesus' sacrifice on the cross. Saint Paul writes:

The cup we use in the Lord's Supper . . .
when we drink from it,
we are sharing in the blood of Christ.
And the bread we break: when we eat it,
we are sharing in the body of Christ.
1 CORINTHIANS 10:16

The *second point* is Jesus' words: "This cup is God's new covenant sealed with my blood." They recall the "new covenant" promised in Jeremiah 31:31 and indicate that it is being inaugurated by Jesus. The words "sealed with my blood" recall God's

Memorial prayer

The Eucharistic Prayer continues with what is called the Memorial Prayer. The presider recalls Jesus' death and resurrection and offers them to the Father, in words like this:

In memory of his death and resurrection,
we offer you, Father,
this life-giving bread and this saving cup.

And so every Eucharist makes "sacramentally present under the species of bread and wine, Christ's body and blood, his sacrifice offered on the cross once for all." CCC 1353 In other words, "the sacrifice of Christ and the sacrifice of the Eucharist are one single sacrifice." CCC 1367

Moreover, the whole Church is united in the offering of the Mass: those still on earth, those already in heaven, and the faithful departed who have died in Christ. CCC 1370–71

Intercessions

The Memorial Prayer is followed by a series of intercessions, asking the Father's help in and through Jesus:

Grant that we, who are nourished
by his body and blood,
may be filled with the Holy Spirit,
and become one body,
one spirit in Christ.

May he make us an everlasting gift
to you and enable us to share
in the inheritance of the saints. . . .

We hope to enjoy forever
the visions of your glory
through Christ our Lord,
from whom all good things come.

covenant with Israel at Mount Sinai, when Moses splashed blood on the people and said:

This is the blood that seals the covenant which the LORD *made with you.*
EXODUS 24:8

Memorial acclamation

The "Institutional narrative" is followed by the entire assembly proclaiming together the "mystery of faith," in words like this:

Christ has died,
Christ is risen,
Christ will come again.

9 *Why is this particular acclamation appropriate for this moment in the Mass?*

Saint Justin was born around A.D. 100. In a letter to the pagan Roman emperor, Antoninus Pius, he described the Mass, as it was celebrated in his day:

*On the day of the sun,
all who dwell
in the city or country
gather in the same place.*

*The memoirs of the apostles
and the writings of the prophets
are read. . . .*

*Then someone brings
bread and a cup of water
and wine mixed together
to him who presides. . . .
He takes them
and offers praise and glory
to the Father of the universe,
through the name of the Son
and of the Holy Spirit
and for a considerable time
he gives thanks. . . .*

*When he. . . .
has given thanks
and the people have responded,
those whom we call deacons
give to those present
the "eucharisted" [consecrated]
bread, wine, and water
and take them
to those who are absent.*

Concluding doxology

The Eucharistic Prayer concludes with the presider saying or singing:

*Through him, with him, and in him
in the unity of the Holy spirit,
all glory and honor
is yours almighty Father,
forever and ever.* CCC 1354

The community responds with a resounding "Amen." From earliest times, this response has been called the "Great Amen." In some churches, it explodes to the accompaniment of musical instruments.

Communion rite

The presider then begins the communion rite. He introduces it by inviting everyone to pray in the words Jesus taught us.

Lord's Prayer

The words "give us this day our daily bread" take on special meaning at this moment. For in a few moments, we will receive the body of Christ, who is the "Bread of Life." JOHN 6:35

Sign of peace

The communion rite continues with the presider inviting the community to share a "sign of peace." This usually takes the form of a handshake or hug, with the words "The peace of Christ be with you."

The word "peace" translates the Hebrew word *shalom*, which has no English equivalent. Roughly, it means we wish one another the fullness of every good thing that Jesus came to bring: forgiveness, love, joy.

Communion

The eucharistic meal follows. It is a special moment for the entire community. A priest writes in his Journal:

People come up, hundreds of them. . . .
Suddenly, in the midst of it all,
a wave of gladness comes over me.
I'm so very glad to be here today. . . .
For a few moments I choke and can't say
the simplest words: "The Body of Christ."
JOHN EAGAN, S.J., *A TRAVELLER TOWARD THE DAWN*

Saint Paul said, "Because the loaf of bread is one, we, though many, are one body, for we all partake of the one loaf." 1 CORINTHIANS 10:17

Paul's words remind us that what we eat in ordinary meals becomes a part of us. In the eucharistic meal, however, we become a part of what we eat—the Body of Christ.

10 How do I spend the moments in line walking up to receive Holy Communion? Walking back after receiving it? How might I use them in the best possible way?

Concluding rite

The presider brings to a close the communion rite, praying in words like this:

Lord, you have nourished us
with bread from heaven.
Fill us with your Spirit and
make us one in peace and love.
We ask this through Christ our Lord.
SECOND SUNDAY OF THE YEAR

The Mass ends with the "dismissal rite." The presider blesses the assembly and charges all to "go in peace and love to serve the Lord."

Commenting on the dismissal rite someone said:

The holiest moment
in the church service
is the moment when God's people—
strengthened by preaching
and sacrament—
go out of the church door into the world
to be Church.
ERNEST SOUTHCOURT

11 How would you explain what he had in mind?

PRAYER hotline

Lord Jesus,
you are to me
medicine
when I am sick;
strength
when I need help;
life itself
when I fear death.

You are
the way
when I long for heaven;
light
when all is dark;
nourishment
when I need food.

Glory be to you
for ever and ever.

Saint Anselm

Recap
Review

When we celebrate the Eucharist, we carry out the Lord's Last Supper command: "Do this in memory of me." It consists of "one single act of worship" with a twofold moment:

- **Liturgy of the Word**
- **Liturgy of the Eucharist**

Each begins with an Introductory Rite and ends with a Concluding Rite: CCC 1346

- **Introductory Rite**
- **Liturgy of the Word**
- **Concluding Rite**

- **Introductory Rite**
- **Liturgy of the Eucharist**
- **Concluding Rite**

The Liturgy of the Eucharist is the heart of celebration. In it, the presider calls upon the Father to send the Holy Spirit to transform the bread and wine into Jesus' body and blood.

The liturgy continues with the entire Church offering itself with Jesus in "his sacrifice of praise and thanksgiving offered once and for all on the cross to his Father." CCC 1407

It ends with the eucharistic meal, which proclaims the Lord's death until he comes in glory.

It transforms the members of the Church more fully into what they receive: the Body of Christ.

1 List (a) the two worship places in Israel in Jesus' time, (b) the kind of service held in each, (c) to what movement of the Eucharist each service is related.

2 List (a) the source from which each of the three Sunday readings is usually taken, (b) what follows the first reading and the purpose it serves, (c) what follows the the third reading and it's purpose.

3 List and briefly explain (a) two reasons why the homily is a difficult assignment, (b) what we should keep in mind as we listen to it, (c) the four ways we should listen to God's Word, as it is proclaimed and explained, (d) the twofold way the Liturgy of the Word ends.

4 List (a) the Jewish meal during which Jesus instituted the Eucharist, (b) what this Jewish meal celebrated, (c) in what sense are Jesus' words, "Do this in memory of me," more than an invitation to remember some event that took place 2,000 years ago.

5 Explain how the words Jesus used to institute the Eucharist recall (a) God's old covenant with Israel, (b) God's promise to Jeremiah, (c) Jesus' promise to his followers on a hillside outside Capernaum.

6 List and briefly explain the two points in the "institutional narrative" that need to be stressed.

7 List and briefly explain (a) how the sacrifice of Christ on Calvary is related to the sacrifice of the Eucharist, (b) how the sacrifice of the Christ on Calvary is made present in the Eucharist (Mass).

8 Explain briefly (a) what the words "Holy, holy, holy" recall, (b) what event the word "Hosanna" recalls, (c) the meaning of the Hebrew word *shalom*, (d) how the effect of the food we eat at ordinary meals has a totally different effect from the food we eat in the eucharistic meal.

Reflect

1 Neil Armstrong and Ed Aldrin landed on the moon July 20, 1969. Aldrin writes:

I was able to serve myself communion
on the moon . . . My pastor gave me
a miniature chalice . . .
with a small amount of bread and wine.

Just after Mike Collins passed over
us one revolution after our landing . . .

I unstowed these elements . . . during my
requested air-to-ground silence.
I then read some passages from the Bible . . .
celebrated communion . . .
and offered some private prayers.
LIFE MAGAZINE 8/22/69

■ *Why do/don't you think it was appropriate for Aldrin to perform such a personal act of worship on the moon?*
■ *What private prayers do you offer before and after Communion? Explain.*

2 As a young man, Scott ripped apart a rosary, and gave out anti-Catholic literature. Later as a Protestant minister, he questioned what he'd been taught about the Eucharist, namely that it was a symbol. To make a long story short, he began to read up on Catholic belief in the Eucharist. The more he read, the more he was drawn to Catholicism. One day, he went to a Catholic church to see what went on at the celebration of the Eucharist. Deeply moved, he wrote:

After pronouncing the words of consecration,
the priest held up the Host. I felt as if the last drop
of doubt had been drained from me.
With all my heart, I whispered,
"My Lord and my God.". . .

I left the chapel not telling a soul
where I had been . . .
But the next day I was back,
and the next, and the next. . . .
I had fallen . . . in love
with our Lord in the Eucharist.
His presence to me . . .
was powerful and personal.
SCOTT HAHN: ONE COMES HOME TO ROME

■ *Why do "convert" Catholics often have a greater appreciation of the Mass than "cradle" Catholics do?*

3 Regina Riley prayed for years that her two sons would return to the practice of their faith. One Sunday she saw them across the aisle. Later she asked them what brought them back.

They said that while vacationing in Colorado, they picked up an old man one Sunday. It was pouring rain, and he was getting soaked. He said he was on his way to Mass three miles up the mountain road.

When they got to the church, they decided to attend the Mass and take the man home afterward. "You know," the younger brother told his mother, "it felt so right—like returning home after a long trip."

■ *What are some reasons young people stop practicing their faith? What are some of the reasons they begin again?*

PRAYER TIME
with the Lord

A priest wrote in his spiritual journal:

*At the "Our Father," holding hands . . .
and singing . . .
suddenly the beauty of it all struck me, and
I almost lost it with a rush of emotion.*

*And then at Communion time,
as I broke and folded over the host
and then held it up: insight! . . .
This is Jesus, God's own Son,
the one who stands before each human being
and invites himself in—
the great God of the stars and the sky . . .*

*The people came up, hundreds of them:
grandmas and grandpas with canes . . .
mothers and fathers holding their children,
careworn faces and happy faces—
and suddenly in the midst of it all
a wave of gladness comes over me.*

*I'm so very glad to be here today. . . .
For a few moments
I choke and can't say the simplest words:
"The Body of Christ."*

JOHN EAGEN, S.J., *A TRAVELLER TOWARD THE DAWN*

■ *Can I recall a memorable Communion moment of my own? When? Where? With whom?*

PRAYER Journal

The Sunday after his child was born, Steve Garwood brought Communion home to his wife. He saw that friends had dropped in to see the baby. So he placed it on a shelf in the living room.

Visitors kept coming all day. By the time the last one left, he hadn't had time to be alone with his wife, who had just fallen asleep, As he passed through the living room, he knelt. He was overwhelmed by a sense of God's presence. He wrote later:

Blood pounded in my ears
and all the hairs of my body stood on end.
"Lord Jesus," I said,
"have mercy on me, an ungrateful sinner.
You are here before me, in my house,
and you have blessed me so much."

■ *Compose a prayer that you could put in your wallet and pray to prepare for Communion; another to pray after receiving Communion.*

SCRIPTURE Journal

1	**Synagogue worship**	**Acts 10:34–43**
2	**Temple worship**	**Leviticus 16:1–28**
3	**Liturgy of the Word**	**Luke 4:14–21**
4	**Liturgy of Eucharist**	**Luke 22:14–20**
5	**Eucharist and Paul**	**1 Cor. 11:17–29**

■ *Pick one of the above passages. Read it prayerfully and write a short statement to Jesus expressing your feelings about it.*

Reconciliation

Be merciful to me, O God . . .
wipe away my sins! . . .

*Create a pure heart in me . . .
and put a new and loyal spirit in me.
Do not banish me from your presence;
do not take your spirit away from me.*

*Give me again the joy
that comes from your salvation. . . .
Spare my life, O God, and save me.*
PSALM 51:1–2, 10–12

**Like the father of the prodigal son,
God runs out to greet us, hug us,
and welcome us back,
when he sees us returning
after we have foolishly left home
and sinned against him.**

Call to conversion

Saint Augustine was born in Africa in the year A.D. 354. His youth was a stormy period. In his twenties, he moved to Milan. There he became a professor of rhetoric; but his personal life remained stormy. One day, while pondering his life, he burst into tears and called to God:

*How long will you be angry with me?
Forever? Why not at this very hour
put an end to my evil life?*

He was crying out like this when, suddenly, he heard the voice of a child. The voice seemed to say, "Take and read!" He writes:

I stood up . . . got a Bible, and opened it. The first words my eyes fell upon were from the letter to the Romans:

"Throw off the words of darkness . . .
put on the Lord Jesus Christ,
and make no provision
for the desires of the flesh."
ROMANS 13:12–14

My heart was suddenly flooded
with a light that erased all my doubts.
My soul was filled with a deep peace.
THE CONFESSIONS OF SAINT AUGUSTINE, BOOK 8

1 Why do you think it took Augustine so many years and so much spiritual pain before he was able to turn his life around?

Augustine experienced what all of us must go through to some extent: conversion. By conversion we mean, with the help of God's grace, to turn away from sin and to turn back to God.

The first step in the conversion process is to admit that we have sinned. Commenting on the inability of many people to admit they have sinned, someone said: "The worst sin is not to sin, but to deny it." Scripture adds:

If we say that we have no sin,
we deceive ourselves, and . . .
make a liar out of God. 1 JOHN 1:8, 10

2 How do you account for the inability of a growing number of people today to admit they have sinned?

Sacraments of healing

Each of us has been incorporated into Christ's Body, the Church, by the "sacraments of Initiation." This transformed us into new beings. Saint Paul writes:

Anyone who is joined to Christ
is a new being;
the old is gone, the new has come.
1 CORINTHIANS 5:17

But even after our incorporation into Christ, we still remain fragile human beings both physically and spiritually. This brings us to the sacraments of healing: Reconciliation and Anointing of the Sick.

Reconciliation restores or repairs our divine life when it has been weakened or lost through sin. CCC 1420–21

The Anointing of the Sick strengthens our divine life against vulnerabilities linked with illness or old age. CCC 1511, 1527

Let us now take a closer look at the first of these two "healing" sacraments.

Sacrament of Reconciliation

Jesus, the Son of God . . .
is not one who cannot feel sympathy
for our weaknesses.

On the contrary . . .
[Jesus] was tempted in every way
that we are, but did not sin.

Let us have confidence, then,
and approach God's throne,
where there is grace.

There we will receive mercy
and find grace to to help us
just when we need it. HEBREWS 4:14–16

Jesus forgave sinners

A beautiful illustration of Jesus' power over sin occurs in Luke's Gospel. One day, some religious leaders were listening to Jesus teach. Suddenly, a group of people came forward carrying a paralyzed man.

When Jesus saw the man, he was moved with pity and said, "Your sins are forgiven." When the religious leaders heard this, they grew angry.

NARRATOR *Jesus knew their thoughts and said to them:*

JESUS *Why do you think such things? Is it easier to say, "Your sins are forgiven you," or to say, "Get up and walk"? I will prove to you, then, that the Son of Man has authority on earth to forgive sins.*

NARRATOR *So he said to the paralyzed man . . .*

JESUS *Get up, pick up your bed, and go home!*

NARRATOR *At once the man got up in front of them all, took the bed he had been lying on, and went home, praising God.*

They were all completely amazed! Full of fear, they praised God, saying, "What marvelous things we have seen today!" LUKE 5:22–25

4 *Had friends not brought the paralytic to Jesus, he may never have been healed physically and spiritually. Describe some way we bring others to Jesus.*

Jesus knew human nature and how fragile and vulnerable it is. This is why he instituted the sacrament of Reconciliation. It was to invite us to open our hearts to forgiveness "just when we need it." Novelist Somerset Maugham spoke for many when he wrote:

I have committed follies.
I have a sensitive conscience and
I have done certain things in my life
that I am unable to entirely forget.

If I had been fortunate enough
to be a Catholic, I could have delivered
myself of them at confession and
after performing the penance imposed,
received absolution
and put them out of my mind forever.

To get a better understanding of the sacrament of Reconciliation, we need to recall two important truths. Jesus:

■ **Had the power to forgive sins**
■ **Shared this power with his Church**

3 *Can you recall how Jesus showed that he had the power to forgive? Can you recall when and how he shared this power with his Church?*

Jesus shared his power

Jesus did more than forgive people. He shared with his Church his power to forgive sins. He did this in two stages. First, he shared his power, in a general way. CCC 551–53

NARRATOR   *Jesus went to the territory near the town of Caesarea Philippi, where he asked his disciples:*

JESUS   *Who do people say the Son of Man is?*

DISCIPLES   *Some say John the Baptist. Others say Elijah, while others say Jeremiah or some other prophet.*

JESUS   *What about you? Who do you say I am?*

PETER   *You are the Messiah, the Son of the living God.*

JESUS   *Good for you, Simon son of Jonah! For this truth did not come to you from any human being, but it was given to you directly by my Father in heaven.*

And so I tell you, Peter: you are a rock, and on this rock foundation I will build my church. . . .

I will give you the keys to the Kingdom of heaven; what you prohibit on earth will be prohibited in heaven, and what you permit on earth will be permitted in heaven.
MATTHEW 16:13–19

And so Jesus shared his power, *in general*, with his Church. He made Peter the rock of his Church and gave him the "keys of the Kingdom of heaven." CCC 1443–44

This brings us to the second stage, sharing with his Church in a specific way the power *to forgive sins*. It took place on Easter Sunday night, when the Apostles were gathered together in prayer. Suddenly, Jesus appeared to them. They were overjoyed. After greeting them, Jesus said:

"Peace be with you. As the Father sent me, so I send you." Then he breathed on them and said,

"Receive the Holy Spirit. If you forgive people's sins, they are forgiven; if you do not forgive them, they are not forgiven." JOHN 20:21–22

That first Easter night, Jesus shared with his Church, in an explicit way, the power to forgive.

At first, the power to forgive sins, sounds like a strange Easter gift. But a little thought shows that it is not. Rather, it is the perfect Easter gift. This is why Jesus came into the world: to free people from the tyranny of sin and to reconcile them with God and one another. CCC 1440–45, 1485

Thus, Jesus' Easter gift empowers his Apostles to communicate his saving power to all peoples of all times. CCC 1447

5 Scripture describes God "breathing" life into Adam. Why do you think Jesus chose to use this same "breathing" image to share his power with his Apostles?

The Man Who Lost Himself concerns a hero who trails a suspect to a Paris hotel. To learn the suspect's room number without arousing suspicion, the hero gives the clerk his own name and asks if a man by that name is registered.

While the clerk checks the room list, the hero plans to watch for the suspect's number.

To the hero's surprise, the clerk doesn't check the list. He simply says, "He's in room 40; he's expecting you." The hero follows the bellhop to room 40.

When the door opens, he sees a man who is his double, except that he's heavier and older. It is the hero himself, twenty years in the future.

The story is science fiction, but it contains an important truth: There's a person in everyone's future. It is the person we are becoming.

■ *What kind of person am I becoming?*
■ *How sure am I of this?*

The Church forgives sins

The Apostles exercised the power to forgive sins. They did this, first of all, through Baptism. Thus, we find Peter exhorting the crowd that had gathered for Pentecost:

Each one of you must turn away from your sins and be baptized in the name of Jesus Christ, so that your sins will be forgiven; and you will receive God's gift, the Holy Spirit. ACTS 2:38

A second way the Church exercises its power to forgive sins is through the sacrament of Reconciliation. It is the chief way by which sins committed after Baptism are forgiven.

6 Can you recall another sacrament besides Baptism and Reconciliation, which forgives sin? Is there any other way sin is forgiven?

Liturgy of Reconciliation

Perhaps the best way to understand the celebration of the sacrament of Reconciliation is to view it against the background of the parable of the prodigal son. Recall the parable.

A father had two sons. One day, the younger one decided to leave home. So he demanded his share of the inheritance.

When the son received it, he left home and squandered it foolishly.

NARRATOR *Then a severe famine spread across that country, and he was left without a thing. So he went to work for one of the citizens of that country, who sent him out to his farm to take care of the pigs. . . .*

At last he came to his senses and said,

SON *"All my father's hired workers have more than they can eat, and here I am about to starve! I will get up and go to my father and say,*

" 'Father, I have sinned against God and against you. I am no longer fit to be called your son; treat me as one of your hired workers.' "

NARRATOR So he got up
and started back to his father.
He was still a long way from
home when his father saw
him; his heart was filled with
pity, and he ran, threw his
arms around his son, and
kissed him.

SON Father, I have sinned against
God and against you. . . .

FATHER Hurry! Bring the best robe
and put it on him.
Put a ring on his finger
and shoes on his feet.
Then go and get the prize calf
and kill it, and let us celebrate
with a feast!

NARRATOR And so the feasting began.
In the meantime, the older son
was out in the field.
On his way back when he
came close to the house, he
heard the music and dancing.
So he called out to one of the
servants and asked him,

BROTHER What's going on?

SERVANT Your brother has come back
home, and your father has
killed the prize calf, because
he got him back safe and
sound.

NARRATOR The older brother was so
angry that he would not go
into the house; so his father
came out and begged him to
come in. . . .

BROTHER Look, all these years I have
worked for you like a slave,
and I have never disobeyed
your orders. What have you
given me?

But this son of yours wasted
all your property on
prostitutes, and when he
comes back home, you kill the
prize calf for him!

FATHER My son,
you are always here with me,
and everything I have is yours.
But we had to celebrate . . .
because your brother was dead,
but now he is alive; he was lost,
but now he has been found.
LUKE 15:11–32

A closer reading of the parable shows that when the younger son came to his senses, he did the following four things:

■ **Examined his conscience**
■ **Repented his sin**
■ **Confessed his sin**
■ **Amended his life**

7 *Identify where the younger son does the above four things in the parable.*

Here are four steps involved in confessing our sins:

1. We introduce ourselves.
   Father, I am a 15-year-old high school student.

2. We state when we last celebrated the sacrament.
   It's been a year since my last confession.

3. We explain any long absence from the sacrament.
   The reason for my absence is fear or shame (or whatever).

4. We confess our sins.
   I don't think I committed any mortal sins. I did steal a $10 item from a large department store. I unintentionally drank too much one time. I had sinful thoughts frequently, but I tried to put them out of my mind as best I could. I'd appreciate any suggestions you might have on this latter problem. This is all, Father.

9 *Explain why the information under each step is important.*

Penitent's role

The parable of the prodigal son is a beautiful illustration of what we do in the sacrament of Reconciliation. CCC, 1439, 1480–84 It is the same four things that the son did. We:

- ■ **Examine our conscience**
- ■ **Repent our sins (contrition)**
- ■ **Confess our sins**
- ■ **Amend our life (satisfaction)**

8 *Which one of the above four things do you find most difficult in the sacrament of Reconciliation? Explain.*

Let us now look at each one of these four points more closely.

Examination

In our daily lives, we sometimes fail, through our own fault, to live and love as Jesus taught us to do. We call these moral failures *sin.* We prepare for the sacrament of Reconciliation by examining our conscience. Catholic tradition distinguishes two kinds of sin: *mortal* (very serious) and *venial* (less serious). 1 JOHN 5:16–17

For a sin to be mortal, three conditions must be present: CCC 1857

- ■ **Grave matter**
- ■ **Full knowledge**
- ■ **Full consent of the will**

Grave matter means that what we do is objectively grave; e.g., adultery. CCC 1858

Full knowledge means we are fully aware of the graveness of an act. In spite of this, we choose to do it anyway. CCC 1859

Full consent of the will means we act freely. We are not influenced or pressured in a way that diminishes our free will. CCC 1859

For a sin to be *venial*, we do something that does not involve serious matter (stealing a small article); or we do something without our full knowledge or consent (vandalize someone's property while intoxicated). CCC 1862–63

Contrition

Contrition consists of being sorry for our sins, along with the resolve—with the help of God's grace—not to sin again. Depending on whether our sorrow stems from a love of God or from a lesser motive, such as fear of punishment, it is:

- **Perfect**   **Love of God**
- **Imperfect**   **Lesser motive**

Perfect contrition forgives venial sins and mortal sins, providing it includes the resolve to celebrate the sacrament as soon as reasonable. CCC 1451–52

Imperfect contrition, of itself, does not forgive mortal sin, but prepares us to receive forgiveness in the sacrament of Reconciliation. CCC 1453

It is well to make our act of contrition before entering the confessional.

Confession

Mortal sins must be confessed according to kind (what we did) and number (how often we did it).

Strictly speaking, venial sins need not be confessed. Nevertheless, it is highly advisable, at least, in a general way. For example, we may say, "I am not always as patient as I should be, especially with my younger brothers and sisters."

Here is a thumbnail review of some sins of *commission* (doing something we shouldn't do) and *omission* (not doing something we should do):

Commission:
- **Damaging what is another's**
- **Misusing alcohol, drugs, or sex**
- **Stealing**
- **Other (jealousy, lying, cheating)**

10 *Pick one of the above sins under "commission" and decide what would make it a mortal sin. Do the same with one of the sins listed under "omission."*

Omission: failing in:
- **Love of family or others**
- **Prayer or worship of God**
- **Kindness toward family or others**

Satisfaction

Many sins wrong others. So we must do what is reasonably possible to repair any harm. Sin, also, harms ourself, as well as our relationship with God and our brothers and sisters. CCC 1459

Satisfaction has to do with "making up for" or "making satisfaction for" the harmful effects of our sins, both to ourselves and to others.

John Eagen

John Eagen was a student at Campion High School in Wisconsin. One weekend he made a closed retreat. During the retreat, he made a decision to do something he'd been putting off. He decided to celebrate the sacrament of Reconciliation. He writes:

*To my surprise the priest said
nothing about my sins.
He spoke only
of God's love for me.
I left the chapel and
walked out into the beauty
of the afternoon.
Joy began to well up
and run in my heart
different from anything I'd ever
experienced. I don't think I'd
ever been happier in my life.*

*At length, I found myself
out on the golf course.
I remember lying down
out of sheer joy
on a bunker with my eyes
to the blue sky
and my arms wide open
to the Lord. . . .
How long I lay there
I don't remember.
All I do remember
is that I felt
enormously close to God.*

John Eagen: *A Traveler Toward the Dawn*
(slightly adapted)

To help us begin our journey back to spiritual health, the priest assigns a penance. For example, he assigns prayers designed to help open our hearts to God's healing grace. CCC 1460

If a priest assigns a penance that would prove difficult to do, we should feel free to ask him to change it to something else.

Priest's role

The priest's role in the celebration of the sacrament follows the pattern of the father in the Parable of the Prodigal Son. CCC 1461–67

First, the father threw his arms around his son and kissed him. In other words, he welcomed him back as if he had never left home.

Next, he put shoes on his son's feet. This symbolized that he was forgiving him totally. In ancient times, slaves went barefoot; sons wore shoes. The shoes took away the sign that said the boy was somebody's slave and gave the sign that he was somebody's son.

Then the father gave his son a ring, symbolizing that he was restoring the son to the full status he had before he left home. Undoubtedly, the ring was a signet ring, containing the family seal. To possess it was to possess the power to act in the family's name.

Finally, the father held a feast in his son's honor. This celebration recalls Jesus' words:

*"There will be more joy in heaven
over one sinner who repents
than over ninety-nine respectable people
who do not need to repent."* LUKE 15:7

Thus, in the sacrament of Reconciliation, the priest does what the father in the parable did:

- **Welcomes us back**
- **Forgives us**
- **Restores us to full life**
- **Rejoices with us**

Grace of Reconciliation

British violinist Peter Cropper was invited to Finland for a special concert. As a personal favor, the Royal Academy of Music lent Peter their priceless 285-year-old Stradivarius violin. That violin was known the world over for its incredible sound.

At the concert, a nightmare happened. Going on stage, Peter tripped and fell. The violin broke into several pieces. Peter flew home to England in a state of shock.

The Royal Academy of Music hired a master craftsperson, Charles Beare, to try to repair the priceless violin. He spent countless, tedious hours repairing the violin.

Then came the moment of truth. How would the violin sound? Those present couldn't believe their ears. The violin's sound was better than before.

This story makes a beautiful conclusion to our study of the sacrament of Reconciliation. Many people, including Saint Augustine, have personally experienced that the celebration of the sacrament often leaves them stronger and more committed to God than they were before they sinned.

We may summarize the graces of the sacrament as follows:

- **Reconciliation with God and Church**
- **Remission of punishment due to sin**
- **Healing to better follow Jesus**
- **Serenity of conscience** CCC 1496

PRACTICAL Connection

People ask, "How often should we celebrate Reconciliation?" The obvious answer is, "As often as the Spirit moves us to do so." Certainly, we will want to celebrate it after a serious break with God and God's family (mortal sin).

Normally, during certain periods of our life we will experience the need or desire to celebrate more often. CCC 1425–39 There are, however, spiritual benefits from celebrating it regularly (say every few months). It sharpens spiritual sensitivity, combats spiritual laziness, heals spiritual weakness, and deepens spiritual unity with God and God's people.

Recap

Jesus forgave sin and shared this power and ministry with his Church. The Church exercises this power and ministry in a special way in the sacrament of Reconciliation.

To understand Reconciliation it helps to view it against the backdrop of the parable of the prodigal son. What the son does in the parable, we do in Reconciliation:

- **Examine our conscience**
- **Repent our sins (contrition)**
- **Confess our sins**
- **Amend our lives (satisfaction)**

And what the father of the prodigal son does, the priest does:

- **Welcomes us back**
- **Forgives us our sins**
- **Restores us to full life**
- **Rejoices with us**

Sin divides into two groups: commission and omission. It also divides into:

- **Mortal**   grave
- **Venial**   less grave

For a sin to be mortal three conditions must be present:

- **Grave matter**
- **Full knowledge**
- **Full consent of the will**

Review

1 Explain (a) what we mean by conversion and (b) what is the first step in the conversion process.

2 Explain when and how Jesus (a) showed he had the power to forgive sins, (b) shared this power in a general way, (c) shared it in a specific way.

3 Why was the power to forgive sins a perfect Easter gift?

4 List and explain (a) the four things the prodigal son did when he came to his senses and (b) how the four things relate to what we do in the sacrament of Reconciliation.

5 List and briefly explain (a) the two kinds of sin and how each affects our relationship with God, (b) the three conditions that must be present for the most serious of these two sins, (c) what we mean by contrition, (d) the two kinds of contrition.

6 List and briefly explain (a) the four steps involved in confessing our sins, (b) what we mean by satisfaction, and (c) why the priest assigns a penance.

7 List and briefly explain (a) the four things the father of the prodigal son did upon his son's return, and how they relate to Reconciliation, (b) the symbolism of the kiss, shoes, ring, feast, (c) how often we should celebrate reconciliation, (d) the graces of the sacrament of Reconciliation.

Reflect

1 In 1984 Velma Barfield became the first woman in 22 years to be executed in the United States. Convicted of killing four people in 1978, the Velma of 1984 was totally different from the Velma of 1978. She had undergone a deep conversion. A high point in her conversion came when she wrote on the flyleaf of her Bible:

*Sin is being called all kinds
of fancy names nowadays
but it's time we came to grips with ourselves and
call sin what it really is—SIN.*

*It's the ancient enemy of the soul.
It has never changed.
Tonight . . . I'm going to start . . .
naming my sins before the Lord
and trust him for deliverance.*

Velma Barfield: Woman on Death Row

■ **Why don't people today "call sin what it really is—SIN"?**
■ **When was the last time you named your sins "before the Lord" in the sacrament of Reconciliation, and what led you celebrate it then?**
■ **What are several things that tend to keep you from celebrating it more often?**

2 Lee Iacocca has been called an "American legend." He rescued the Chrysler corporation from bankruptcy. In his autobiography, he says of the sacrament of Reconciliation:

*In my teens I began to appreciate
the importance of the most misunderstood rite
in the Catholic Church.
I not only had to think out
my transgressions . . .
I had to speak them . . .*

*The necessity of weighing right from wrong
on a regular basis
turned out to be the best therapy I ever had.*

Iacocca: An Autobiography

■ **Why do you think Iacocca "began to appreciate the importance" of the sacrament in his teens?**
■ **Why would/wouldn't you agree that it's the Church's "most misunderstood rite"?**
■ **What are some of the reasons you think "weighing right from wrong on a regular basis turned out to be the best therapy" Iacocca ever had?**

3 Greek Orthodox Catholics celebrate the sacrament of Reconciliation facing an icon of the risen Christ.

■ **Why do you think they stand, rather than kneel or sit?**
■ **Why do you think they face an icon, rather than face each other?**

PRAYER TIME
with the Lord

A man once said that one of the best things he ever did was to memorize the "Act of Contrition."

Sin came into his life in later years, he said. It was the one prayer that gave him peace of mind and eventually changed his life.

The following "Act of Contrition" is one every Catholic should take time to memorize:

Merciful God,
like the prodigal son,
I come home in sorrow.
I have sinned against you
and your people.

With the help of your grace,
I promise to try to walk
in the light of your presence
and avoid whatever might lead me
back into the darkness. M.L.

■ **Compose a similar "Act of Contrition." Make it come from the heart.**

PRAYER Journal

A Broadway play concerned a young drug addict who quit school and left home. In an unforgettable scene, the young person looks up to heaven and cries out in deep anguish:

How I wish life was like a notebook,
so I could tear out the pages where
I made mistakes and throw them away!

Thanks to Jesus, life is like a notebook. We can tear out the pages with the mistakes and throw them away.

■ *What is one page I'd like to tear out and throw away? Write a brief prayer to Jesus about it.*

SCRIPTURE Journal

1	**Jesus came for sinners**	**Luke 5:27–32**
2	**Jesus visits a sinner**	**Luke 19:1–10**
3	**Jesus defends a sinner**	**Luke 7:36–50**
4	**Jesus forgives a sinner**	**Luke 5:17–26**
5	**Jesus says, "Forgive"**	**Matthew 18:21–35**

■ *Pick one of the above passages. Read it prayerfully and write out a brief statement to Jesus expressing your feelings about it.*

Anointing of the Sick

M y friends, remember the prophets
who spoke in the name of the Lord.
Take them as examples
of patient endurance under suffering. . . .

Are any among you sick?
They should send for the church elders,
who will pray for them
and rub olive oil on them in the name
of the Lord. JAMES 5:10, 14

**The sacrament of
the Anointing of the Sick
restores us to spiritual health
and often to physical health;
unites us with Jesus' suffering on the
cross, enabling us to participate
in a special way in his saving work;
prepares us for entry into eternal life,
should our illness become terminal.**

Call to heal

E ighty-eight-year-old John lives
alone. On Sunday mornings his
rocking chair moves a little faster as he
anticipates seeing a special person.
That person is Marie.

Marie is a college student and a
eucharistic minister in her parish. A
dimension of the ministry is to bring
Communion to the sick.

When Marie arrives at John's
apartment around eleven o'clock, she
begins by reading the Sunday Gospel.
Then she summarizes the homily that
she has just listened to at the ten
o'clock Mass. Finally, she and John join
hands and pray the Lord's Prayer in
preparation for Communion.

After John receives Communion, Marie pauses briefly to give John a little time to pray silently. Then she reads slowly to John from a prayerbook. His favorite prayer is:

Lord, free your servant
from sickness, and restore him to health . . .
strengthen him by your power,
protect him by your might, and
give him all that is needed for his welfare.

Following the prayer, John and Marie spend a few minutes visiting with each other. Then she disappears down the steps, as John stands at the window and waves good-bye.

Marie leaves with the realization that she has not only brought John Communion but also assurance that the Christian community is concerned about his physical and spiritual well-being and healing.

1 *What are some ways I might reach out to the elderly and the very sick to make their lives less lonely and more pleasant?*

Sacraments of healing

Each of us has been incorporated into Christ's Body, the Church, by the "sacraments of initiation." This transformed us into new beings.

But even after our incorporation into Christ, we still remain fragile human beings, both physically and spiritually.

When our physical well-being is threatened, the second "healing" sacrament comes to our aid. Let's take a closer look at how it does this.

Anointing of the Sick

The true story of John and Marie dramatizes the Church's special concern for the elderly and the very sick. One of the reasons for this concern is that illness and old age—

especially when prolonged—tend to adversely affect not only the body but, more importantly, the spirit.

For example, they can create in us a feeling of isolation and deep loneliness. They can plunge us into a state of mental depression that can threaten our very life of faith. CCC 1500–1501

It is for reasons like this that Jesus himself reached out in a special way, during his life on earth, to the sick and the infirm.

Jesus healed people

The Church's special concern for sick and infirm people, therefore, is an extension of Jesus' own concern for them. Consider this example of Jesus' concern:

*Jesus and his disciples . . .
left the synagogue and went straight to
the home of Simon and Andrew.*

*Simon's mother-in-law
was sick in bed with fever. . . .
Jesus took her by the hand,
and helped her up. The fever left her,
and she began to wait on them.*

*After the sun had set and evening had
come, people brought to Jesus all the sick
and those who had demons.*

*All the people of the town
gathered in front of the house.
Jesus healed many who were sick . . .
and drove out many demons.*
MARK 1:29–34

From the beginning of his ministry, Jesus showed a special concern for people suffering from serious ailments. It led him to heal people, especially those whose ailments were long-standing. MATTHEW 9:2, 20, 27; JOHN 5:5

2 *If Jesus had the power to heal people, why didn't he heal all people, and not just a few?*

Jesus shared his power

Jesus did more than heal seriously ailing people. He also shared with his followers the power to heal them. CCC 1506–9

*Jesus called the twelve disciples together
and gave them power and authority
to drive out demons and to cure diseases.
Then he sent them out to preach the
Kingdom of God and to heal diseases. . . .*

*The disciples
left and traveled through all the villages,
preaching the Good News
and healing people everywhere.*
LUKE 9:1–2, 6

The impact that the healing of people had on the disciples made them acutely aware of the new power that Jesus had given them.

The Church heals people

The awareness of their healing power led the disciples to alert the Christian community to make use of this great gift. CCC 1510–11 Thus, we read in the Letter from James:

Are any among you sick?
They should send for the church elders,
who will pray for them
and rub olive oil on them
in the name of the Lord.

This prayer made in faith
will heal the sick . . .
and the sins they have committed
will be forgiven. JAMES 5:14–15

3 Why didn't early Christians simply rub olive oil on the sick themselves, rather than call church elders?

Sacramental healing

We saw how Jesus healed people by touching them, anointing them, and praying over them. In other words, he healed them through the *bodily* actions of his *earthly* body.

Today, Jesus continues to heal people by touching them, anointing them, and praying over them. Only now he does this through the *sacramental* (liturgical) actions of his *mystical* body. CCC 1070 Consider an example:

A Vietnam veteran was recuperating in Walter Reed Hospital in Washington, D.C. In a letter to a friend, he described his experience of the sacrament of the Anointing of the Sick. It took place shortly after he was hit by mortar fire in battle. He writes:

From the split second I was hit,
I was completely alone.
I've heard it said, but never realized it—
when you're dying there's no one but you.
You're all alone.

I was hurt bad, real bad;
a 4.2 mortar shell landed
about six feet behind me and took off my
left leg, badly ripped up my left arm,
hit me in the back, head, hip, and ankle.

Shock was instantaneous, but I fought it—
knowing that if I went out
I'd never wake up again.

There were three or four medics
hovering over me, all shook up,
trying to help me. . . .
I tried to pray but couldn't. . . .
Well, with a hell of a lot of stubbornness
and luck (providence),
I lived to make it to the chopper
two hours after being hit.

After they carried me
into the first aid station,
I felt four or five people scrubbing my body
in different places.
This brought me to open my eyes,
and I could see about a foot
in front of me—
not too well at that.

Anyway,
someone bent over me and began to pray.
I wasn't sure who it was, but I thought
it looked like our batallion chaplain;
his nose was practically on mine.

After I saw him place his hands
on my head,
I started to go out—
I figured for the last time.
When I talked I could only whisper,
and this took all I had.

As I was going out, my eyes closed
and I heard Father say,
"Are you sorry for your sins?"
With my last breath
and all I had, I whispered, "Hell, yes!"

Then a split second before I went out,
I felt oil on my forehead,
and something happened
which I'll never forget—something which
I never experienced before in my life!

All of a sudden,
I stopped gasping for every inch of life;
I just burst with joy. . . . I felt like
I had just got a million cc's of morphine.
I was on cloud nine.
I felt free of body and mind.

After this,
I was conscious about three or four times
during the next ten-day period;
I never worried about dying.
In fact, I was waiting for it.

**4 What part of the soldier's account
did I find most inspiring and personally
meaningful? Explain**

Celebrating the sacrament

The sacrament may be celebrated anywhere: on a battlefield, at home, or in a hospital. An ideal place and time—whenever possible—is during the celebration of the "Mass of the Anointing of the Sick."

It is ideal because it stresses that the celebration is not a private action involving only the priest and the sick person. It is a communal action involving the whole Body of Christ.

In other words, Christ's Body, the Church, is like a human body. If one member is spiritually sick, the entire body is affected. So it is fitting that other members of Christ's Body (especially family and friends) be present.

In many cases, however, the condition of ailing people is such that they are unable to be anointed during Mass.

When this is the case, the anointing takes place in a hospital room or in a home at the bedside of the sick person.

If the sick person is physically able and wishes to celebrate the sacrament of Reconciliation, this takes place before the sacrament. If the person is not physically able to do so, then the sacrament follows this basic format:

- **Preparation**   **Prayerful instruction**
- **Celebration**   **Anointing**
- **Conclusion**   **Prayer and blessing**

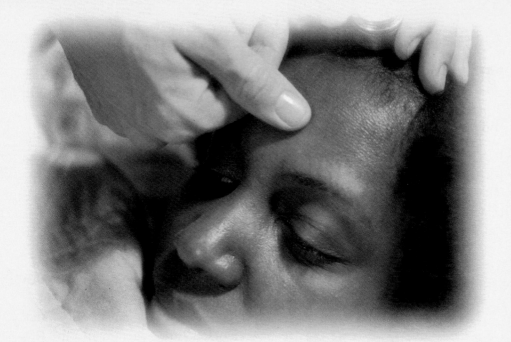

Preparation

The liturgy begins with a greeting similar to the one used at Mass. The Instruction consists of recalling the words of the Letter from James (cited on p.184) followed by a brief prayer for the sick person.

The liturgy continues with the priest laying his hands on the ailing person, as Jesus often did when healing people. MARK 6:5, CCC 1513

If it is fitting, the priest may invite those present to lay hands on the sick person also. This reinforces the fact that the sacrament is an action of the whole Body of Christ. CCC 1516

Anointing

Next, the priest follows the instruction of Jesus to his disciples and the instruction of the Letter of James.

He anoints the sick person with oil. MARK 6:13, JAMES 5:14–15 He begins with the forehead, praying:

*Through this holy anointing,
may the Lord in love and mercy help you
with the grace of the Holy Spirit. Amen.*

Then the priest anoints the hands, praying:

*May the Lord who frees you from sin
save you and raise you up. Amen.*

Actress Ann Jillian found a growth on her body; she feared the worst. Before going to the doctor, she went to St. Francis de Sales Church. Over its entrance is an inscription she had often seen, but never read until now. It said:

*The same everlasting Father
who cares for you today
will take care of you tomorrow
and every day.
Either he will shield you
from suffering, or he will give you
unfailing strength to bear it.
Be at peace then and put aside
all anxious thoughts and
imaginations.*

Those words gave Ann hope just when she needed it most. Two weeks later, she successfully underwent a double mastectomy (removal of both breasts).

■ *What keeps me from greater trust in God?*

Conclusion

The liturgy ends with everyone present reciting the Lord's Prayer. It is followed by a brief closing prayer and a blessing.

If the person is physically able and wishes to receive communion, that takes place at this point. If not, the celebration ends with a blessing similar to the one used at Mass.

Who should be anointed?

A priest was called to a Los Angeles hospital to anoint an elderly woman named Gladys. She was not Catholic, but had asked to receive the sacrament. Just before the chaplain arrived, Gladys lapsed into a coma. He anointed her and she went on to recover.

It surprises some Catholics that the chaplain gave the sacrament to a person who was not Catholic. The Church permits this if the person has been baptized, believes Jesus acts through the sacrament, and requests to receive it.

It also surprises some Catholics that the sacrament was celebrated while Gladys was in a coma. The Church celebrates the sacrament in this situation (and similar situations such as unconsciousness or sedated patients) if they have requested it or would probably request it if they could.

Generally speaking, the sacrament of the Anointing of the Sick is for people who are seriously ill, or seriously weakened from advanced age.

It is important to note here that serious illness does not mean terminal illness. Nor does it mean an illness that puts a person in immediate danger of death. It simply means any illness that seriously impairs the health of a person. It also means the sacrament should be received before a serious operation. CCC 1514–15

If during the same illness the person's condition takes a turn for the worse or develops a new illness (e.g., pneumonia), the sacrament may be repeated. This holds true, also, for the elderly whose frailty becomes more pronounced.

In brief, then, the sacrament of the Anointing of the Sick may and should be celebrated by those who are:

- **Seriously ill**
- **Seriously weakened by advanced age**
- **Scheduled for serious surgery**
- **Suffering a relapse or new illness**

Grace of Anointing

People suffering from serious illness often suffer from anxiety. They may even be tempted to lose their trust in God. To these people the sacrament of the Anointing of the Sick is the occasion for special grace. We may sum this grace up as follows.

It restores us to health, if this be for our good. If not, it gives us the strength and the serenity to bear suffering, as Jesus did. CCC 1520, 1532

It forgives our sins if, for any reason, we are unable to celebrate the sacrament of Reconciliation. CCC 1532

It unites us with the suffering of Jesus on the cross, enabling us to participate in a special way in his saving work. CCC 1521

Finally, if our illness, in God's providence, is destined to become terminal, the sacrament of the Anointing of the Sick prepares us for entry into eternal life. CCC 1523

5 *Reread the Vietnam soldier's account of his experience of the sacrament of the Anointing of the Sick and indicate where he seems to be alluding to one or several of the above graces.*

Viaticum

With the sacrament of Anointing of the Sick, the Church offers those who are about to leave this life the Eucharist as *viaticum* (spiritual nourishment for the journey). CCC 1517, 1524

Received at this moment, the Eucharist acts as a kind of preparation for *eternal life* and the *resurrection*. Jesus said: "Those who eat my flesh and drink my blood have *eternal life*, and I will *raise them to life* on the last day." JOHN 6:54

So the sacraments of Baptism, Confirmation, and the Eucharist form a spiritual unity. They *begin* our earthly pilgrimage and serve as *sacraments of initiation*. CCC 1525

The sacraments of Reconciliation, Anointing of the Sick, and the Eucharist form a similar spiritual unity. They *end* our earthly pilgrimage and serve as *sacraments of completion*. CCC 1525

Recap

The Church has a special ministry to the sick and the elderly. It is a continuation of Jesus' earthly healing ministry through the members of his Church body (mystical body).

The focus of the ministry is the sacrament of the Anointing of the Sick. Four groups should receive this sacrament, those who are:

■ **Seriously ill**
■ **Seriously weakened by advanced age**
■ **Scheduled for serious surgery**
■ **Experiencing a relapse or new sickness**

The liturgy of the sacrament follows a simple, prayerful format:

■ **Preparation**   **Prayerful instruction**
■ **Celebration**   **Anointing**
■ **Conclusion**   **Prayer and blessing**

The special graces of the sacrament are:

■ **Restoration to spiritual health**
■ **Frequent restoration to physical health**
■ **Special union with the suffering of Jesus**
■ **Preparation for entry into eternal life**

Review

1 Explain why the infirm elderly and the very sick often need the special love and concern.

2 List and briefly explain (a) one specific example of Jesus' concern for the sick infirm, (b) when and how Jesus shared his healing power with his disciples, (c) what letter in the New Testament exhorts early Christians to celebrate the sacrament, (d) the difference between how Jesus healed people in gospel times and today.

3 Explain (a) why Mass is an ideal setting for celebrating the sacrament of the Anointing of the Sick, (b) the three steps by which the sacrament is celebrated in a hospital setting.

4 When a person wants to celebrate the sacrament of Reconciliation and receive Communion along with the sacrament of Anointing, when should these sacraments be celebrated?

5 Under what conditions may the sacrament of Anointing be given to (a) non-Catholics, (b) adults in a coma or in a sedated state?

6 List (a) four groups of ailing people who should request the sacrament of the Anointing of the Sick, (b) the four graces of the sacrament, and explain (c) the connection between the Baptism, Confirmation, and Eucharist, and Reconciliation, the Anointing of the Sick, and the Eucharist *as viaticum.*

Reflect

1 Advanced age can make people feel that they are useless and even a burden to others. This is tragic, because they can often give to others (especially the young) something no one else can give them. To illustrate, consider this excerpt from an essay by a third grader:

Grandmothers don't have to be smart,
only answer questions like,
"Why isn't God married?"
and "How come dogs chase cats?"
A grandmother is a lady
with no children of her own. . . .
She likes other people's little girls and boys.
Everyone should have a grandmother, especially if
they don't have TV. QUOTED BY DR. JAMES DOBSON

■ **Describe an experience that made you realize the important role (a) older people can play in the lives of younger people, (b) younger people can play in the lives of older people.**

2 Brother Mike Newman ministers to the sick, not only bodily but also spiritually. One day he prayed over a patient named Alice, who was in a coma. Three days later, she came out of the coma. She recalled his prayer and told him how much it meant to her. He gives these suggestions for dealing with people when they appear completely unconscious:

(a) Talk to them, because there is a good chance they can still hear you.
(b) Talk to them by name and in an adult way.
(c) Pray out loud and slowly, using familiar prayers like the Lord's Prayer.
(d) Suggest they pray with you in their minds.

■ **Describe a time when you prayed for (or with) a very sick person. Did you feel comfortable doing this? Why would or wouldn't you like someone to do this for you when you were seriously sick?**

3 *The American Journal of Nursing* describes an experiment at a New York hospital, in which nurses placed hands on patients with the intention to heal them. The patients improved dramatically over a similar group not treated in this way. Francis MacNutt says:

These studies provide evidence
to show that, simply in the natural order,
the patients' power to recover
improves when the nurses lay on hands. . . .
The way they understand it is
that there is a natural power of life
in loving people
which is communicated in a special way through the power of touch.

■ **If "loving hands" can heal naturally, why do we need a sacrament for this?**
■ **Can you think of an everyday example in which placing loving hands on someone can help them immensely?**
■ **Describe a time when someone's love and concern produced an emotional or spiritual healing in you.**

PRAYER TIME
with the Lord

A high school student wrote: "When my mother died, I was bewildered and lost. I missed her immensely. Everything she ever touched became precious. Then, one day, I noticed a card under the glass top of my dresser. I recalled seeing it there for the first time after my mother went to the hospital. But I did not bother to read it. Now I pulled it out and read it:

For ev'ry pain we must bear,
For ev'ry burden, ev'ry care,
there's a reason.

For ev'ry grief that bows the head,
for ev'ry teardrop that is shed,
there's a reason.

For ev'ry hurt, for ev'ry plight,
For ev'ry lonely, pain-racked night,
there's a reason.

But if we trust God, as we should,
It will work out for our good.
He knows the reason. AUTHOR UNKNOWN

After reading the prayer the student said, "I could picture my mother coming into my room and slipping the card beneath the glass, as if to say, 'It's all right, God knows the reason.' From that moment on I was able to accept my mother's death."

JON CACCITORE

■ *Recall an episode that gave you an insight into the faith of one or both of your parents.*

PRAYER Journal

In the movie *Little Big Man*, Old Lodgeskin made a final prayer to God before dying:

I thank you for making me a human being.
I thank you for my defeats.
I thank you for my sight.
And I thank you for my blindness
which has helped me see even further.

■ **Reflect on the final sentence of the prayer and recall an example (preferably from your own life) to illustrate it.**

■ **Imagine you are alone and have only minutes to live. Compose a prayer you would like to make to God at that critical moment of your life.**

_____
_____
_____
_____
_____
_____
_____
_____
_____

SCRIPTURE Journal

1	Jesus heals the sick	Luke 7:1–10
2	Jesus shares his power	Luke 10:1–9
3	Disciples heal the sick	Luke 10:17–24
4	Church heals the sick	Acts 5:12–16
5	Church urges healing	James 5:13–20

■ **Pick one of the above passages. Read it prayerfully and write out a brief statement to Jesus expressing your feelings about it.**

_____
_____
_____
_____
_____

Marriage

T*hen God said,*
"And now we will make human beings;
they will be like us and resemble us. . . .
God . . . created them male and female . . .
blessed them, and said, 'Have many
children' . . . and it was done."
GENESIS 1:26–28, 30

That is why a man leaves his father and
mother and is united with his wife,
and they become one. GENESIS 2:24

The story of the human race
is a love story.
It begins with God's decision to create
man and woman in the divine image.
It continues with God's decision to
join man and woman
in a union of love
so intimate that they "become one."

The vocation of marriage was written
in the very nature of man and woman
as they came from the hand of God.

Call to love

In the movie *Shadow of the Hawk*, a young couple and a native American guide are slogging up a mountainside. At one point, the young woman slumps to the ground and says, "I can't take another step."

The young man lifts her to her feet and says, "But, darling, we must go on. We have no choice." She shakes her head and says, "I can't."

Then the guide says to the young man, "Hold her close to your heart. Let your love and strength flow from your body into her body." The young man does this, and in a few minutes the woman smiles and says, "Let's get started again."

We can all relate to that episode. There are times when we, too, don't think we can go on. Then someone holds us close and lets their love and strength flow into our body. And that gives us the strength to go on.

Love is the vocation of every human being. Our life on earth will not be judged by the fame we achieved or the fortune we acquired. Rather, it will be judged by the love we showed. Mother Teresa put it this way:

At the hour of death
when we come face to face with God,
we are going to be judged on love;
not how much we have done, but
how much love we have put into the doing.

There are many relationships of love between human beings. For example, there is the love of a parent for a child, a child for a parent, a spouse for a spouse, a brother for a sister, a sister for a brother.

There's the love for a friend of the same sex, for a friend of the opposite sex. You can go on and on. Only one of these love relationships, however, was raised to the level of a sacrament by Jesus.

1 *Of all the love relationships that are possible between human beings, which do you think is capable of producing the deepest and strongest bond?*

Sacraments of service

Through the seven sacraments, Jesus continues the work of salvation, which he began during his earthly life.

These sacraments are usually grouped under the following three headings:

- **Sacraments of Initiation**
- **Sacraments of Healing**
- **Sacraments of Service**

The "Sacraments of Initiation" incorporate us into the Body of Christ and give us a share in the Trinity's own divine life.

The "Sacraments of Healing" restore, repair, and fortify divine life when it is threatened.

This brings us to the "Sacraments of Service": Marriage and Holy Orders. They are directed toward the welfare of the Body of Christ.

Marriage unites husband and wife and graces them to build up the Body of Christ. Holy Orders consecrates special members of Christ's Body to teach, guide, and lead the other members.

Marriage is one of the most important steps we will ever take. Therefore, we should prepare for it spiritually and psychologically. Under normal conditions, most dioceses require up to six months' preparation. This includes:

Interviews with a priest or deacon; presentation of recent certificates of Baptism, Communion, and Confirmation; and personal and liturgical preparation.

A baptismal certificate affirms one's Catholic identity. It may be obtained by contacting the parish where the baptism took place.

Most dioceses provide a variety of preparation options, such as Pre-Cana conferences and Engagement Encounters.

Sacrament of marriage

Of all the love relationships among people, the marriage between husband and wife is special. It has its origin in the God who created them.

The vocation of marriage was written in the nature of man and woman as they came from God's hand. CCC 1603

With the coming of Jesus, God raises married love to the dignity of a sacrament. And through the sacrament God blesses the lives of married people so profoundly that their love has the potential of mirroring God's own love for the human race.

Mirror of God's love

God's love for the human race has two distinguishing characteristics that stand out like the sun and the moon in the sky. God's love is:

- **Creative**   **Life-giving**
- **Redemptive**   **Forgiving**

It is *creative* or *life-giving* in the sense that God's love gave birth to the human family. It is *redemptive* or *forgiving* in the sense that when the human family sinned, God forgave and redeemed it. CCC 1602–11

Married love mirrors God's creative and redemptive love. It, too, is life-giving and forgiving.

It is *life-giving* in the sense that the love of husband and wife brings forth life, just as God's love did. CCC 2366–70 It is also life-giving in the sense that it provides a climate of love in which this life can grow and mature, into adulthood. CCC 1652–55

Married love is *forgiving* in the sense that husband and wife forgive the hurts they cause one another, either intentionally or unintentionally. CCC 1644 They do not stop loving.

Mirror of Christ's love

Paul carries the image of married love a step further. He compares it to Christ's love for the Church, saying, "Husbands, love your wives just as Christ loved the church and gave his life for it." EPHESIANS 5:25

We pray to God in the liturgy of the Wedding Mass:

All-powerful and ever-living God . . .
the love of husband and wife . . .
bears the imprint
of your own divine love.

In brief, God elevated married love to the dignity of a sacrament, mirroring:

- **God's love for the human family**
- **Christ's love for the Church**

2 If married love is so richly blessed, why do so many marriages fall short of what God intended a marriage to be?

Commitment of marriage

There is an ancient story about a young man who knocked at the door of a house. A voice from inside said, "Who is it?"

The young man said, "It is I. I've come to ask permission to marry your daughter."

The voice from inside said, "You're not ready; come back in a year."

3 What made the "voice" say, "You're not ready yet"?

A year later, the young man returned and knocked again.

The voice from within said, "Who is it?" The young man said, "It is your daughter and I. We've come to ask your permission to marry."

The voice from within said, "You are now ready. Please come in."

This story illustrates how important it is that both marriage partners are ready. This readiness can be achieved only by:

- **Extended courtship**
- **Serious reflection**
- **Honest discussion**
- **Mutual prayer**

Marriage covenant

Today, much is said about "marriage contracts." But this is not what marriage is all about—each partner protecting her or his material possessions, time, career, and so on. Marriage is a covenant.

A *contract* protects the parties in advance. It spells out what is expected of each party. A *covenant* does not.

A *covenant* is an unconditional, mutual pledge to love and serve the other forever: in good times and in bad times, in sickness and in health, for better or for worse.

4 Why do you think it is essential that the marriage covenant be "unconditional" and "forever"?

The *challenge* of this phase is to keep the four levels of attraction in harmony and balance. The danger is to let one level roam out of control and overwhelm the others.

5 *Can I give a concrete example of what is meant by letting "one level roam out of control and overwhelm the other"?*

If a couple meets the challenge and survives the danger, their attraction will flower into a commitment to marry.

Integration

Second, is the *integration* phase. Once a couple marry, they begin the important process of integrating the excitement of love with the ordinariness of everyday life.

6 *What do I understand by the statement "integrating the excitement of love with the ordinariness of everyday life"?*

The *challenge* of this phase is to retain love as the couple's top priority. It is to keep love from becoming routine. The *danger* is to begin to take love for granted and subordinate it to other things.

Dynamic of marriage

Most marriages go through a four-phase cycle. An understanding of this cycle can spell the difference between a happy marriage or a painful one. The four phases are:

■ **Attraction**
■ **Integration**
■ **Conflict**
■ **Maturation**

Attraction

First, there is the *attraction* phase. It is the thrilling experience of being drawn to one another in a way that makes life pulsate with excitement. This phase takes place at four human levels: physical, emotional, intellectual, and spiritual.

Conflict

Third, there is the *conflict* phase. It begins when marriage partners fail the *challenge* or fall into the danger of the second phase. When this happens—and it does to *some degree* in most marriages—the relationship enters a critical stage. Faults that were once overlooked now ignite sharp conflict. The "adoring spouse" becomes a "nagging adversary."

7 *How would I counsel a couple to handle problems that arise in this stage"?*

The *challenge* of this phase is to steer conflict into constructive directions. The *danger* is to avoid or suppress conflict rather than deal with it. If it is suppressed, communication breaks down and resentment builds.

Maturation

The fourth phase is the *maturation* phase. It begins when the partners resolve to deal constructively with conflict and rediscover love. It can be the most beautiful period in a marriage.

To understand how this phase works, think of human intimacy as having a "rubber band dimension." Father Andrew Greeley explains it this way:

The two lovers drift apart. . . . but the residual power of their affection (pair bonding) is often,

indeed usually, sufficiently strong to impel them back to one another.

Awkwardly, clumsily, blunderingly, they stumble into one another's arms, forgive each other, and begin again in a new burst of romantic love.
THE BOTTOM LINE CATECHISM

The *challenge* of this phase is to forgive the other's faults and to rediscover his or her goodness. The danger is to give up and let love die, rather than let it be reborn.

If marriage partners meet the challenge and avoid the *danger*, the residual power of their affection will launch them into a new dimension of married love. And it will be more beautiful and more romantic than the love they first shared.

8 *Why will it be more beautiful and more romantic than the love they first shared?*

This brings us to a question of which we are all too painfully aware of in our modern world.

Marriage bond

From earliest times, the Church has taught that the marriage bond cannot be broken or dissolved. It bases its teaching on Jesus' words: We "must not separate, then, what God has joined together." MARK 10:9

In other words, by divine law, the marriage bond is "perpetual and exclusive." CCC 1606–08

9 *What is meant by "perpetual and exclusive"?*

Tom rented a seaside cottage for a two-week vacation with his wife. He resolved that for two weeks he'd be the ideal husband: caring and thoughtful.

Everything went well, until the last day. Then Tom caught his wife staring at him through tear-filled eyes:

"Tom," she said,
"Do you know something I don't?"
"What ever do you mean?"
he replied.
"Well," she said,
"just before our vacation,
I went to the doctor
for my checkup.
Ever since then,
you've been so kind to me.
Did the doctor tell you
something about me?
Do I have cancer?
Am I going to die?
Is that why you're so kind to me?"

It took a minute
for her words to sink in.
Then Tom broke into a laugh,
threw his arms around her,
and said,
"No dear, you're not going to die.
I'm just beginning to live."

Retold from *Guideposts* magazine

I n ancient times, a town fort in Weinsberg, Germany, was surrounded by an enemy. The enemy commander, who prided himself on being honest and noble, agreed to let all the women and children leave the fort.

He also agreed to let the women take with them their most precious possession.

When the moment of evacuation came, the commander couldn't believe what he saw: a long line of children and women leaving the fort. On the back of each woman was her most precious possession: her husband.

Retold from Ruth Youngdahl Nelson:
A Grandma's Letters to God

■ *Why do difficulties bring some couples closer together, but have just the opposite effect on other couples?*

The Church recognizes, however, that living out the lofty vocation of marriage involves "good times and bad." And sometimes the "bad times" overpower the "good times." Marriage partners begin to admit things they denied before being married. Problems that they hoped marriage would solve grow even worse. CCC 1606–08

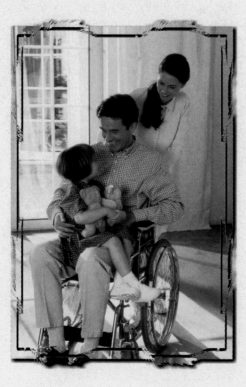

When harsh realities like this set in, the couple can best express genuine marital love in two ways, especially by:

■ **Praying together for God's help**
■ **Consulting a professional counselor**

Often this twofold expression of love bears remarkable fruit, leading to a deeper, more mature love for one another.

But sometimes it doesn't. And so the Church recognizes the reality of failed marriages:

There are some situations in which living together becomes practically impossible for a variety of reasons.

In such cases the Church permits the physical separation of the couple and their living apart. CCC 1649

Remarriage, however, is possible only when one's spouse dies or an *annulment* is granted.

An annulment is a judgment by the Church that what seemed a marriage, was not. CCC 1625–29 Therefore, it is *not* a divorce or separation.

10 *In what sense is an annulment totally different from a divorce or separation?*

Some grounds for the annulment of a marriage are the following. One or both parties:

■ **Lack maturity to marry**
■ **Lack the freedom to marry**
■ **Feign consent**
■ **Hide a defect to gain consent**

11 *Give one concrete example of each of the above.*

Catholics who remarry, when they are *not* free to do so, should continue to worship with the community and seek its support, even though they may not receive Communion. CCC 1648–51

12 *Why are they not free to receive Communion?*

Interfaith marriage

All religions recognize that a marriage between persons of different faiths is a serious step. Some religions discourage it on principle.

13 *What are some of the problems connected with an interfaith marriage?*

An interfaith marriage should be entered into only after profound reflection, frank communication, and mutual prayer for guidance.

There are many issues that need to be faced honestly in advance.

Catholic partners in an interfaith marriage must affirm commitment to their own faith and to sharing it with their children.

Their partners, in return, must respect this twofold commitment.

An interfaith marriage may take place in either a Catholic church or the place of worship of the other partner.

Since marriage partners confer marriage on each other (their mutual consent is the basis of their marriage), a priest, deacon, rabbi, or minister (with the Church's approval) may perform the ceremony.

One final point.

A Catholic who married outside of the Church and wants to be reunited with the Church should consult a priest about the possibility of validating the marriage (marrying within the Church) in a private ceremony.

Event of grace

The sacrament of marriage is an "event of grace." But it is not a "one-time event" that takes place on a couple's wedding day and ends there.

Rather, it is an "ongoing event" that continues throughout the couple's entire life. It is something the couple must never stop working at.

A fitting conclusion to our reflection on the marriage vocation is Paul's beautiful description of mature love:

Love is patient and kind;
it is not jealous or conceited or proud;
love is not ill-mannered
or selfish or irritable;
love does not keep a record of wrongs;
love is not happy with evil,
but happy with truth.
Love never gives up . . .
Love is eternal. 1 CORINTHIANS 13:4–8

14 *Why do you think couples fail to work hard at their marriage? What suggestion would you have for them?*

THINK
about it

Making the decision to have a child— it's momentous. It is to decide forever to have your heart walk around outside your body.

Elizabeth Stone

Recap

Of all the loves two people can enjoy, only one was raised by Jesus to the level of a sacrament: married love. It mirrors:

- **God's love for the human family**
- **Christ's love for the Church**

Married love mirrors God's love in that it, too, is both:

- **Creative**   **Life-giving**
- **Redemptive**   **Forgiving**

The dynamic of most marriages involves four critical stages:

- **Attraction**
- **Integration**
- **Conflict**
- **Maturation**

Because marriage is such an important step in life, it should be preceded by:

- **Extended courtship**
- **Serious reflection**
- **Honest discussion**
- **Mutual prayer**

Review

1 List (a) four love relationships people can enjoy, and (b) the only one Jesus elevated to the dignity of a sacrament.

2 List, and briefly explain, how married love mirrors God's love for the human family.

3 Upon what words of Jesus does the Church base its teaching that there can be no remarriage after a divorce while both parties are alive?

4 List the four steps that should precede the commitment that marriage involves on the part of both people.

5 List and briefly describe (a) the four phases through which most marriages pass, and (b) the challenge and the danger that each phase presents.

6 What is an annulment? Give three examples of "grounds for an annulment."

7 What does the Church teach about (a) separation, (b) divorce without remarriage?

8 What is (a) the attitude of all religions toward interfaith marriages, and (b) what do they recommend for those considering such a marriage?

9 What is the obligation of a Catholic partner concerning interfaith marriage?

10 Where may an interfaith marriage take place, and who may perform it?

Reflect

1 Barbara Walters was interviewing a famous couple on *60 Minutes*. She asked them:

"How have you managed
to keep your love alive
across 35 years of married life?"
When they didn't answer right away,
she tried to help them, saying,
"Was it because both of you
were so willing to give and take
on a 50–50 basis?"

The wife broke into a gentle laugh
and said, "Oh my!
Married life never breaks that evenly.
Sometimes it's more like 90–10."

That was a high point of the interview, because it made such an important point: When it comes to love, you can't keep score. The day a husband and wife begin to do so is the day the marriage begins to die.

■ **Explain the statement, "When it comes to love, we can't keep score."**
■ **To what extent does the statement apply to (a) brothers and sisters, (b) two friends?**

2 In his book *You Are the Light of the World*, John Catoir writes:

Studies conducted over a seven-year period
at the University of Virginia
found that within one year of their divorce,
60 percent of the husbands
and 73 percent of the wives
felt that they might have made a mistake.

Even those who thought
their marriages
were destructive relationships
said that maybe they could have
worked out their marital problems
if they had tried harder.

■ **From your own family experience, make a list of four or five reasons why husbands and wives run into marriage problems.**
■ **Show your list to a married friend or to one or both of your parents and ask them to critique the reasons. What reasons would they delete or modify? What reasons would they add?**

3 In his book *Born Again*, Charles Colson said of himself and his wife: "In the ten years we've been married, I realized we'd never discussed . . . the living God, the faith deep down inside each one of us."

■ **To what extent does your family discuss such things at home? Recall a good discussion you had in your home recently. What did you find especially good about it?**

PRAYER TIME
with the Lord

L ord, enter our house.
Bless it and make it a home.

Bless our roof
that it may shelter us
on good days and bad days.

Bless our doors
that they may stand open
to friend and foe alike.

Bless our rooms
that they may be places
of love and peace.

Above all, bless our family.
Bless us one and all.

Bless our minds
that they may be open to your Word—
and to the words of each other.

Bless our arms
that they may reach out to the needy—
and to the needs of each other.

Bless our hearts
that they will be filled with love for you—
and with love for each other. M.L.

■ *Write a similar blessing of your own.*

PRAYER *Journal*

Bitterness paralyzes life;
  Love empowers it.
Bitterness sours life;
Love sweetens life.

Bitterness sickens life;
Love heals life.
Bitterness blesses life;
Love anoints its eyes.

HARRY EMERSON FOSDICK

■ *Compose two verses of your own. Replace* **bitterness, love** *and* **life** *with one of the following sets (or a set of your own).*

1 *Criticism*   *Praise*   *Self-esteem*
2 *Suspicion*   *Trust*   *Friendship*
3 *Cheating*   *Honesty*   *Character*

Thus, one of your verses might read:

Criticism bombs self-esteem;
Praise builds self-esteem;
Criticism shipwrecks relationships;
praise keeps them afloat.

_____
_____
_____
_____
_____
_____
_____
_____
_____
_____
_____
_____

SCRIPTURE *Journal*

1 **Love story**   **Ruth 1:1–4:22**
2 **Love song**   **Song of Songs 1:1–8:14**
3 **Loving wife**   **Proverbs 31:10–31**
4 **Gift of love**   **John 2:1–12**
5 **Perfect love**   **1 John 4:7–12**

■ *Pick one of the above passages. Read it prayerfully and write a short statement to Jesus expressing your feelings about it.*

_____
_____
_____
_____
_____
_____

Holy Orders

E*very high priest
is chosen from his fellow men
and appointed to serve God on their behalf,
to offer sacrifices and offerings for sins.*

*Since he himself is weak in many ways,
he is able to be gentle with those
who are ignorant and make mistakes.
And because he is himself weak,
he must offer sacrifices
not only for the sins of the people
but also for his own sins.* HEBREWS 5:1–3

**Baptism makes
every Christian a sharer,
to some extent,
in the priesthood of Christ.
Besides sharing
in this common** *priesthood,*
**some Christians are also called
to share in Christ's
ministerial priesthood:
to preach the Gospel,
preside at worship,
and pastor members of Christ's Body.**

Call to service

Television's Phil Donahue once observed that people who commit themselves to service usually pass through three stages.

First, there is the *fun* stage. That's when they say, "I love doing this. Why did I wait so long to get involved?"

Next, there's the *intolerant* stage. That's when they say, "Anyone who isn't involved isn't really a Christian."

Finally, there's the *reality* stage. That's when they suddenly realize that their involvement is going to make only a small dent in the world's problems. At this stage, saints are made.

1 *How do you understand the statement, "At this stage saints are made"?*

Sacraments of service

By the "sacraments of initiation" every Christian has been incorporated into the Body of Christ and called to service. For this reason, Jesus instituted two special "sacraments of service": Marriage and Holy Orders.

Marriage serves the Body of Christ by building it up in membership and holiness. Holy Orders serves the Body of Christ by pastoral leadership.

Common priesthood

When we think of Holy Orders, we think immediately of the *priesthood,* and rightly so.

On the other hand, we must keep in mind that by our baptism we all participate in the priesthood of Christ. Peter writes to the Christians of his day:

You are the chosen race,
the King's priests, a holy nation,
God's own people, chosen
to proclaim the wonderful acts of God,
who called you out of darkness
into his own marvelous light.
1 PETER 2:9

Every baptized Christian, therefore, participates in the priesthood of Christ.

We call this participation the *common* priesthood of the faithful to distinguish it from the *ordained* priesthood.

Ordained priesthood

The *ordained* priesthood differs in an essential way from the *common* priesthood. It is not something that you choose, in the sense that it is an option for all Christians. CCC 1591–2

Rather, it is something that you are "called" to by God. Thus, we frequently speak of someone having a *vocation* ("calling") to the priesthood.

Whereas the common priesthood is conferred by the sacrament of Baptism, the *ordained* priesthood is conferred by the sacrament of Holy Orders.

The *ordained* priesthood is also called the *ministerial* priesthood. This title stressed its special ministry to the Church.

Let us take a closer look at the "call" to the ordained priesthood and the service or "ministry" it performs.

John Catoir

As a young man
I felt a strong attraction
for the priesthood, but I held back.
I was afraid to assume
the many burdens;
afraid of all the alligators
in the swamp of life;
afraid of failing. . . .

It took me about seven years
of inner turmoil,
from high school
through college and
military service,
before I had the courage
to say 'yes' to God's call.
I never regretted my decision.

John Catoir: *That Your Joy May Be Full*

THINK about it

**Blessed are they
who place themselves
in the hands of Jesus.
He will place himself
in their hands.**

Anonymous

Sacrament of Holy Orders

Father John Eagen writes in his inspiring spiritual autobiography:

*There's a marvelous line
in Alan Paton's book
Cry, the Beloved Country:*

*When someone tries to thank
the old black preacher for his kindness
and tells him, "You are a good man,"
the old man says simply:
"No. I'm just a weak sinful man,
but the Lord has laid his hands on me
and that is all."*

*To me that says it exactly.
The Lord has laid his hands on me.
When I was a freshman at Campion
in the first closed retreat of my life,
unexpectedly God . . .
touched my life deeply . . .
and that is all.*

A TRAVELLER TOWARD THE DAWN (condensed)

**2 What is a "closed retreat"? Have you
ever made one? How do you think God
decides on whom to "lay hands"?**

Besides participation in the *common* priesthood, to which all Christians are called, some Christians are called to special service within the Church. This call is to the *ministerial* or *ordained* priesthood. CCC 1547

The special call to the *ordained* priesthood is rooted in the Old Testament.

There God chose the twelve tribes of Israel to be a *priestly* people. EXODUS 19:3 But within the twelve tribes, God chose one tribe, Levi, for liturgical service to the other tribes. NUMBERS 47:53, JOSHUA 13:33

This special call of the tribe of Levi helps us to understand the special call of the *ordained* priesthood in the New Testament. It is at the service of the *common* priesthood. CCC 1547

The *ordained* priesthood is conferred by the sacrament of Holy Orders and exercised in three different degrees:

- **Bishops**   CCC 1593–94
- **Priests**   CCC 1595
- **Deacons**   CCC 1596

Bishops

As successor of the Apostles, the bishop receives the "fullness" of the sacrament. CCC 1555–61

This "fullness" gives him both the authority and the responsibility to carry out the threefold, apostolic mission. CCC 939 It involves:

- **Teaching**   **Preaching the Gospel**
- **Sanctifying**   **Presiding at worship**
- **Leading**   **Pastoring spiritually**

The "fullness" of Holy Orders unites the bishops into a "college of bishops," under the leadership of the bishop of Rome.

Just as Peter held a special leadership role among the Apostles, so his successor, the "Bishop of Rome," holds a special leadership role among the "college of bishops." CCC 880–82

Scripture gives a number of examples that reflect Peter's leadership role. For example, he:

- **Heads list of Apostles**   Lk 6:14
- **Speaks for Apostles**   Acts 2–5
- **Holds keys**   Mt 16:19
- **Instructs leaders**   Gal 1:18

This special leadership role of the "Bishop of Rome" prompted eleventh-century Christians to give him a special title: *Pope,* which means "Father of the fathers."

Christians continue to call him by this title.

Priests

As the early Church grew in numbers, the bishop could no longer serve all the people entrusted to his care. He therefore ordained co-workers. CCC 1562–68

Given the name "presbyters" (priests), they were put in charge of smaller units (parishes) of the bishop's assigned territory (diocese). They exercised their ministry only with permission of the bishop and in communion with him.

3 *What do I look for most in a priest?*

Deacons

Deacons are single or married men who have felt God's call to ordained ministry. CCC 1569–71 They serve the Catholic community in a variety of ways. CCC 1569–71 For example, they:

- **Baptize new members**
- **Assist at and bless marriages**
- **Preside over funerals**
- **Perform ministries of charity**

4 *Why would/wouldn't I consider a call from God to Church ministry as a deacon?*

To a young man who wishes to be a Jesuit, I would say:

Stay at home if this idea makes you unsettled or nervous. Do not come to us if you love the Church like a stepmother, rather than a mother; Do not come if you think that in so doing you will be doing the Society of Jesus a favor.

Come if serving Christ is at the very center of your life. Come if you have an open spirit, a reasonably open mind and a heart larger than the world. Come if you know how to tell a joke and can laugh with others and . . . on occasions you can laugh at yourself.

Pedro Arrupe, General of the Society of Jesus

■ **Why would this statement make you more/less attracted to the priesthood?**

"I will go! Send me!"

Isaiah 6:8

Celebration of Holy Orders

The celebration of the sacrament of Holy Orders follows the same liturgical movement for all three degrees. CCC 1597 It consists of two essential elements:

■ **Imposing hands**
■ **Prayer of consecration**

The prayer of consecration asks God to give to the ordinand (one being ordained) the graces of the Holy Spirit needed to carry out his ministry.

Exercise of Holy Orders

Let us now take a closer look at how the "college of bishops," under the leadership of the pope, the bishop of Rome, carry out the ministry conferred upon them by Holy Orders.

One day, Jesus was instructing his disciples. In the course of the instruction, he turned to Peter and said to him:

"You are a rock,
and on this rock foundation
I will build my church. . . .
I will give you
the keys of the Kingdom of heaven;
what you prohibit on earth
will be prohibited in heaven,
and what you permit on earth
will be permitted in heaven."
MATTHEW 16:18–19

And just before ascending to his Father, Jesus commissioned Peter and the Apostles to teach all nations, saying, "I will be with you always to the end of the age." MATTHEW 28:20

To assist the Apostles and their successors in this awesome task, Jesus promised them the help of the Holy Spirit:

I will ask the Father,
and he will give you another Helper,
who will stay with you forever.
He is the Spirit. . . .
whom the Father will send in my name,
will teach you everything
and make you remember
all that I have told you. JOHN 14:16–17, 26

It is against this background that we must consider the teaching office of the bishops, under the leadership of the pope.

We sometimes refer to this teaching office as the *magisterium* of the Church. A much misunderstood dimension of this teaching office is *infallibility*. CCC 888–92

Infallibility

Simply put, infallibility means that God will not allow his Church to depart from the teachings of Jesus in matters of faith and morals.

Somewhat as the Holy Spirit guided the authors of Scripture in matters relating to salvation, so the Holy Spirit guides the teachers of the Church in matters relating to faith and morals.

Consider two ways infallibility is exercised.

First, the pope, as head of the college of bishops, teaches infallibility when, by virtue of his office as supreme pastor and teacher of the faithful, he proclaims, by a definitive act, a doctrine relating to faith and morals to be infallible.

Second, it is also present when the "college of bishops," acting together with the pope, exercise their official teaching office (magisterium), especially in an ecumenical council.

Therefore, when the Church, in one of these two situations, proposes a doctrine "for belief as being divinely revealed" and as the teaching of Christ, the doctrine "must be adhered to with the obedience of faith. CCC 891

In brief, then, the charism of infallibility is simply the carrying out of Jesus' promise to his Apostles.

5 *Why is the charism of infallibility so essential when it comes to interpreting Scripture and truths relating to matters of faith and morals?*

Commenting on the need for some way of settling disputes, such as those regarding biblical interpretation, one Protestant writer candidly observes:

*The conference of Luther and Zwingli . . .
to unify the German and Swiss
Reformation, broke down . . .
over the failure of the two leaders
to agree on the interpretation
of a single Biblical text:
"This is my Body."*

From that day on the misuse of the Bible has vitiated the spirit of Protestantism . . . and divided it into sects.
CHARLES CLAYTON MORRISON:
PROTESTANT MISUSE OF THE BIBLE

PRACTICAL
Connection

Saint Ignatius of Antioch writes about A.D. 110:

*Let everyone revere. . . .
the bishop as the image
of the Father and
the presbyters [priests]
as the senate of God.*

AD TRALL 3,1

Bishops of the world gathered in Rome.

Recap

By our Baptism into the Body of Christ we become a priestly people. This priesthood is called the "common priesthood of the faithful." Besides this priesthood, some are called to special service within the Church. This call is to the "ordained priesthood." Conferred by Holy Orders, it is exercised in three degrees: bishops, priests, deacons.

The bishops, successors of the Apostles, receive the fullness of the sacrament, empowering them to:

- **Teach**
- **Sanctify**
- **Lead**
- **Preach the Gospel**
- **Preside at worship**
- **Pastoral guidance**

The sacrament of Holy Orders is conferred by the:

- **Imposition of hands**
- **Prayer of Consecration**

Peter held a special leadership role among the apostles. For example, he:

- **Heads all lists of Apostles**
- **Speaks for the Apostles**
- **Holds the "Keys of the Kingdom"**
- **Instructs others in leadership**

The bishop of Rome is the successor of Peter and holds a special leadership role within the "college of bishops."

Jesus commissioned the Apostles and their successors to "hand on the faith," promising them the guidance of the Holy Spirit. A part of that promise is the "charism of infallibility." Simply put, it means that God will not allow his Church to err in matters relating to salvation.

Review

1 Briefly explain (a) "common priesthood of the faithful," (b) *ordained* priesthood.

2 List (a) the three degrees of the ordained priesthood, (b) the four ways, mentioned in the text, by which deacons serve the Catholic community.

3 List (a) four examples from Scripture that reflect Peter's leadership role among the Apostles, (b) the biblical reference and words by which Jesus conferred the leadership authority of his Church upon Peter, (c) the name we give Peter's successor.

4 Cite biblical passages that show that Jesus (a) commanded the Apostles to teach in his name, (b) promised them that the Holy Spirit would guide them in this task.

5 Briefly explain (a) infallibility, (b) two ways infallibility is exercised, (c) what is required of us when it is exercised concerning some doctrine, (d) what we mean by "magisterium."

6 How did the conference between Luther and Zwingli illustrate the practical need for the charism of infallibility?

7 Briefly explain (a) what is meant by "celibacy," (b) when the practice became universal in the Roman Catholic Church, (c) two reasons for it.

Reflect

1 John Eagan, S.J., writes in his spiritual journal, *A Traveller Toward the Dawn*:

At the Our Father, holding hands and singing,
suddenly the beauty of it all struck me,
and I almost lost it with a rush of emotion.

And then at Communion time
as I broke and folded over the host
and then held it up: insight.
This is Jesus, God's own Son,
the one who stands before each human being
the Great God of the stars and skies.

The people come up, hundreds of them,
and suddenly in the midst of it all
a wave of gladness comes over me.
I'm so glad to be here today.
For a moment I choke and can't say
the simple words: "The Body of Christ." (CONDENSED)

■ *Interview (in person or by phone) a priest, sister, brother, or deacon about their calling:*
(a) When they first experienced the call.
(b) What their first response to it was.
(c) What moved them to say "Yes."
(d) If they have ever regretted their decision.
(e) What do they think is the best age for a decision of this type and why.

2 Imagine that you have been hired by a team of professional advertising consultants. The team has been commissioned to design a one-minute television commercial to run just before half-time of the Super Bowl. Its purpose is to invite young people to consider the religious ministry.

■ *What "gimmick" would you suggest the team use to get the attention of the young viewers they want to reach? What would you suggest they say to them once they had their attention?*

3 Saint Francis Xavier was a talented athlete at the University of Paris. There he felt the call to the priesthood, responded to it, and became a missionary to India. He wrote to a friend:

The native Christians here have no priests.
There is nobody to say Mass for them,
nobody to teach them. . . .

Many people are not becoming Christian
for one reason only: there is nobody
to make them Christians.

Again and again,
I have thought of going around to
the universities of Europe and crying out
like a madman [for young people
to come to help me].

■ *List some reasons why you think there is an even greater shortage of vocations to the priesthood, sisterhood, brotherhood, and deaconate in our day.*

PRAYER TIME
with the Lord

Jane Austen was an acclaimed eighteenth-century British novelist. One of her most popular novels, *Pride and Prejudice*, was made into a Hollywood film. She also wrote a prayer that needs to be repeated again and again. It reads:

Grant us grace, Almighty Father,
so to pray as to deserve to be heard.

Pray the following "Prayer for Priests" in a way "as to deserve to be heard":

O Jesus, I pray
for your faithful and fervent priests;
for your unfaithful and tepid priests;
for your priests laboring at home
or abroad in distant mission fields.

for your tempted priests . . .
for your young priests . . .
for your dying priests. . . .

But above all I recommend to you
the priests dearest to me;
the priest who baptized me;
the priests who absolved me from my sins;
the priests at whose Masses I assisted. . . .

O Jesus, keep them all close to your heart,
and bless them abundantly in time and
in eternity. AUTHOR UNKNOWN

■ **Identify a priest who influenced or impacted your life in some way and what it was that he did or said.**

PRAYER Journal

Jean Baptiste Lacordaire was born in France. He began studying law, but changed the course of his life and became a priest. Eulogizing the vocation of a priest, he wrote:

To live in the midst of the world
Without wishing its pleasures,
To be a member of each family . . .
To share all sufferings,
To penetrate all secrets,
To heal all wounds . . .
To bring pardon and hope.
My God, what a life, and it is yours
O priest of Jesus Christ.

■ *Compose a prayer for someone who has played an important role in your life: a priest, a teacher, a parent, a friend.*

SCRIPTURE Journal

1 **Jesus the priest**   Hebrews 4:14–5:10
2 **Peter the leader**   Acts 1:15–26
3 **Church leaders**   1 Timothy 3:1–13
4 **Ordination**   1 Timothy 4:6–16
5 **Paul and celibacy** 1 Corinthians 7:32–35

■ *Pick one of the above passages. Read it prayerfully and write a short statement to Jesus expressing your feelings about it.*

WITNESS
We journey together

One night,
John Ruskin was seated by a window,
staring into the distance,
watching a lamplighter
ignite street lamp after street lamp.

Because it was dark,
he couldn't see the lamplighter—
only the trail of lights he lit.
Turning to a friend, John said,

"That's my image of a Christian.
You may not have seen him,
but you know he passed by
from the trail of light
he left behind."

LOOKING Back

One period in my life when I felt good about the way I was living out my faith was _____

_____

One reason why I felt good about the way I was living it was

_____

LOOKING Ahead

Recall that our faith journey is divided into the following three stages:

- **WORD** — God reaches out to us. (Revelation)
- **WORSHIP** — We reach out to God. (Sacraments)
- **WITNESS** — We journey together. (Commandments)

In the first two stages, we saw how God reached out to us and invited us to journey with him through life. In this final stage, we take a look at what God's invitation involves.

17

Praying

*Very early . . . long before daylight,
Jesus got up and left the house.
He went out of town to a lonely place,
where he prayed.* Mark 1:35

*Jesus went up a hill to pray
and spent the whole night there
praying to God.* Luke 6:12

*Jesus left the city and went,
as he usually did,
to the Mount of Olives. . . .
When he arrived at the place . . .
he went off a stone's throw
and knelt down and prayed.*
LUKE 22:39–41

**Prayer takes place in a variety of
settings and in a variety of ways.
What counts is not so much
what we think or say, but the love
that energizes our thinking or our
saying.**

Sadhu and the boy

A boy was watching a sadhu (an Indian holy man) praying on the bank of a river. When the sadhu finished, the boy walked over to him at the water's edge and said, "Teach me to pray!"

The sadhu looked directly into the boy's eyes for a minute. Then he took the boy's head, plunged it under water, and held it there. When the boy finally broke loose and got his breath back, he sputtered, "What did you do that for?" The sadhu said:

*I just gave you your first lesson in prayer.
When you want to pray
as badly as you wanted to breathe
when you were under water,
only then will I be able to teach you.*

The sadhu's point is an important one. Prayer is more a thing of the heart than of the head. The first condition for learning to pray, therefore, is a longing in the heart—a deep-down desire to learn to pray.

This brings us to an important point when it comes to prayer: why we pray.

1 *What do you think is the primary reason we should pray to God?*

Prayer purpose

If we asked people walking out of a church on Sunday morning why they pray, they would probably give us a menu of reasons. Prayer gives us:

- **Peace that the world can't give**
- **Wisdom that no education can give**
- **Strength to live as we ought**
- **Forgiveness for something we did**
- **Help that only God can give**

2 *For what reason do you find yourself praying mostly? Explain.*

Expression of love

The above reasons are excellent ones for praying; but they cannot be the *primary* reasons for praying. Why? It's because they all deal with the usefulness of prayer.

Prayer is a lot like friendship. A friendship can serve many useful purposes. For example, our friend is always ready to help us. But usefulness can never be the primary reason for the friendship. Why not?

If that is the primary reason for befriending someone, then there is no true friendship. We don't "use" a friend. The same is true of God. We don't use God.

But there is another reason usefulness can't be the primary reason for praying. It is this. The day may come when the prayer may no longer seem useful.

For example, the time may come when, for some reason or another, it seems that God no longer answers our prayers. If this is our main reason for praying, we may be tempted to give it up.

What, then, is the *primary* reason for praying? Prayer is an *expression of love to God*, who is love. It is an expression of love to God, who created us, redeemed us, and continually graces us.

Expression of our needs

Does this mean that we shouldn't pray to God for useful things, such as peace, wisdom, or help in an exam? Of course not! Jesus himself taught us to pray for such things, saying:

Ask, and you will receive;
seek, and you will find;
knock, and the door will be
opened to you. Luke 11:9

Not only did Jesus teach us to pray for things, he did it himself. For example, he prayed in the garden of Gethsemane:

James Murdoch spent three weeks in the White House as the guest of President Abraham Lincoln. One night, before the Battle of Bull Run, Murdoch couldn't sleep. Suddenly, he heard moaning. He went to see what it was. He writes:

I saw the President
kneeling beside an open window.
His back was toward me. . . .
Then he cried out
in tones so pleading
and sorrowful:

"O thou God that heard Solomon
on the night when he prayed
for wisdom, hear me;
I cannot lead this people,
I cannot guide the affairs
of this nation without thy help.
I am poor, and weak, and sinful.
O God! . . .
hear me and save this nation."

Lincoln Talks: A Biography in Anecdote:,
Emanuel Hertz, ed.

Father, if you will
take this cup of suffering from me.
Not my will, however,
but your will be done. LUKE 22:42

Our reason for praying is twofold. It is the way we express to God our:

- **Personal love**
- **Personal needs**

This brings us to the question of how to pray.

Prayer procedure

Henry David Thoreau was a nineteenth-century naturalist. He lived a part of his life in a tiny hut on Walden Pond outside of Concord, Massachusetts. Describing its simple furnishings, he wrote in his book *Walden*:

I had three chairs in my small hut:
one for solitude, two for friendship,
and three for society.

Thoreau's description points to an important psychological fact about our human nature. It has three dimensions:

- **Personal**   Solitude
- **Interpersonal**   Friendship
- **Social**   Community

In other words, there are times when we need to be alone. There are times when we need the support of family and close friends. And there are times when we need the support of the total community.

What is true of our psychological makeup is true also of our spiritual makeup.

Sometimes we need to pray alone, sometimes we need to pray with family and friends CCC 2685, 2689, and sometimes we need the support of the community.

3 *Give a concrete example to illustrate a time when we might feel the need to pray in each of these three settings.*

The Gospel portrays Jesus praying in all three of these settings:

- **Alone**   MARK 1:35
- **With friends**   LUKE 9:28
- **With the community** LUKE 4:16

Praying daily to God alone is as important as eating and sleeping. We need spiritual food as much as we need physical food.

Furthermore, unless we learn to relate to God in solitude, we will find it next to impossible to relate to God in small group or community prayer. Praying in private is the key that unlocks the door to praying with others.

4 *Why do you think praying in solitude is the key to praying with meaning in a small group or community setting?*

Four preparatory steps

When we want to get to know someone better, we agree on places and times to meet. We don't leave these things to chance. Getting to know each other is too important for that.

It is the same with getting to know God better through prayer. Four steps are involved in preparing for serious prayer:

- **Finding a place**
- **Scheduling a time**
- **Choosing a posture**
- **Entering God's presence**

The first step is finding a place to pray. CCC 2691 Some people can pray anywhere. But it usually helps to have

privacy or solitude. Jesus sought solitude. For example, he "went up a hill to pray" LUKE 6:12 and "out of town to a lonely place" MARK 1:35.

The important thing about a prayer place is that we feel comfortable there, for example, a "prayer chair" in our own room.

5 *Where do you usually pray? Explain.*

The second step in serious prayer is scheduling a *time* to meet God on a brief daily basis. Some people pray best in the morning; others pray best at night. Jesus prayed at both times. The Gospel says, "Very early the next morning Jesus prayed" and "Jesus spent the whole night praying." MARK 1:35; LUKE 6:12.

Finding a time for prayer is important. It might be that we will have to experiment for a week or so to find the time that fits us best.

6 *When do you usually pray and how do you pray?*

The third step is taking a posture for praying. Some people prefer sitting, some kneeling, others lying down. Jesus used different postures. For example, he "knelt down" LUKE 22:41 and prayed "face downward on the ground" MATTHEW 26:39.

The best posture for prayer is the one that helps you to pray. Again, this often requires experimentation.

7 *What posture do you usually use when you pray?*

The fourth and final step for serious prayer is entering into God's *presence*. One method people have found helpful for doing this is the following:

After taking our prayer posture—for example, sitting in a chair—we spend a minute or so becoming aware of our clothes gripping our legs, our shoes gripping our feet, and the chair gripping our body.

When we are ready, we recall how present God is to us. We pray in words like this:

*Lord, you embrace me
infinitely more firmly
than the clothes on my body,
the shoes on my feet,
and the chair in which I sit.
May my awareness of their embrace
deepen my awareness of your embrace.*

Here it is important to realize that a sensible awareness of God's presence is a gift. God gives us this awareness from time to time.

When this happens, we simply remain in God's presence, savoring it.

An awareness of God's presence is a profound prayer in itself. Any effort, however, to try to feel it is usually wrong.

8 *Why do you think trying to feel God's presence will usually be wrong?*

Four points of focus

Our prayer can take different points of focus. Four widespread ones are:

- **Adoration**   CCC 2626–28, 2639–43
- **Contrition**   CCC 2629–31
- **Thanksgiving** CCC 2637–38
- **Supplication** CCC 2629–36

The focus of *adoration* is the mystery of God's glory. An example of this form of prayer is the Apostle Thomas. He falls on his knees before the risen Jesus and prays, "My Lord and my God!" JOHN 20:28

The focus of *contrition* is the mystery of God's mercy. An example of this form of prayer is the tax collector in Jesus' Parable of the Pharisee and the Tax Collector. Jesus says of the tax collector:

He stood at a distance and
would not ever raise his face to heaven,
but beat on his breast and said,
"God, have pity on me, a sinner!"
Luke 18:13

The focus of *thanksgiving* is the mystery of God's goodness to us. An example is Jesus himself. One day his disciples returned all excited about preaching and healing people. Upon seeing this, Jesus thanked his Father in heaven, saying:

Father, Lord of heaven and earth!
I thank you because
you have shown to the unlearned
what you have hidden from the wise
and learned. Luke 10:21

Finally, the focus of *supplication* (petition) is the mystery of God's loving concern for us. Jesus told his disciples:

Ask, and you will receive;
seek, and you will find;
knock, and the door will be
opened to you." Luke 11:9

Jesus referred to the "prayer of petition" frequently in the Gospels. He himself used this prayer in the garden, praying, "Father, if you will, take this cup of suffering away from me."

9 Which prayer form do you find yourself using most frequently?

Prayer of petition

The prayer of petition is probably the most popular focus of people's prayers. It is important, therefore, to make a few special comments about it. Two points deserve special mention.

First, it presumes that what we ask for is for our greater spiritual welfare and in harmony with God's will.

Second, it presumes that God often answers our prayers in ways different from what we expect or in ways that we may not recognize until much later in our life. An anonymous poet refers to this latter point when he writes:

I asked for health,
that I might do greater things;
I was given infirmity,
that I might do better things. . . .

I asked for riches,
that I might be happy;
I was given poverty,
that I might be wise.

I asked for power,
that I might have the praise of men;
I was given weakness,
that I might feel the need of God. . . .

I asked for all things,
that I might enjoy life;
I was given life,
that I might enjoy all things. . . .

I got nothing I asked for,
but everything I hoped for.
Almost despite myself,
my unspoken prayers were answered.

I am among all men
most richly blessed.

Piri Thomas

Piri Thomas was a convict, a drug pusher, and an attempted killer. He was sharing a prison cell with the "thin kid." One night he was moved to repentance for his sinful life.

He waited until the thin kid was asleep. Then he knelt down and prayed out loud. He writes in *Down These Mean Streets:*

I told God
what was in my heart. . . .
I talked to him plain. . . .
I talked to him of my wants
and lacks, of my hopes
and disappointments.

After Piri finished praying, a voice said, "Amen." It was the thin kid. Thomas writes:

No one spoke for a long time.
Then the kid whispered,
"I believe in Dios also."

The two young men talked a long time. Finally, Piri climbed back into his bunk, saying:

"Good night, Chico, I'm thinking
that God is always with us.
It's just that we aren't
always with him."

I fell asleep thinking that
I heard the kid crying softly.
Cry kid, I thought.
I hear even Christ cried.

In his book *God Calling,* A. J. Russell has God say some-thing like this:

*Have you ever thought
what it means
to be able to visit me
any time you wish?*

*Even important people
can't visit heads of state
like that.
They must make an
appointment months in advance.*

*But I invite you
to visit with me
any time you wish.*

*I do more, I will visit
with you at any hour
of the day or night,
should you invite me.*

■ **Why don't I invite God into
my life more often?**

Three forms of prayer

A high school student wrote the following reflection in a home-work assignment. It is a beautiful illustration of the three forms prayer ordinarily takes.

*One day after playing in the park,
I went to a nearby fountain for some water.
The cool water tasted good,
and I felt refreshment enter my tired body.*

*Then, I lay down and began to think.
"We need water to drink.
But where does water come from?"
"Clouds!" I thought, "but where do clouds
come from?" "Vaporized moisture."
This went on until I was left
with just one answer: God!*

*Then I kind of talked to God
for a little bit in my own words.*

*For the next couple of minutes,
I just lay on the grass,
looking up at the sky,
in awe of what God must be like.*
SLIGHTLY ADAPTED

This student's beautiful experience illustrates the three forms of prayer.

■ **Meditation**   **Thinking about God**
■ **Conversation**   **Conversing with God**
■ **Contemplation**   **Resting in God**

10 *Recall a time when you had an experience somewhat like the student above.*

Often, the above three forms of prayer are so closely interwoven in one and the same prayer that it is hard to say where one stops and the other begins.

Let's take a closer look at each.

First, *meditation.* CCC 2705–8 Its focus is the *mind.* It involves a prayerful probing of the idea of God—or some other spiritual truth. In other words, it is doing what the student did:

*Then, I lay down and began to think.
"We need water to drink.
But where does water come from? . . ."
This went on until I was left
with just one answer: God!*

Second, *conversation.* CCC 2700–2704, 2607–10 Its focus is the *heart.* It involves talking to God from the heart, as the student did, "Then I talked to God . . . in my own words."

Third, *contemplation.* CCC 2709–19 Its focus is the *soul.* It involves resting quietly in God's presence, open to whatever God may wish to say to me in the depths of my being. The student said:

*For the next couple of minutes,
I just lay on the grass, looking up at the sky, in awe of what God must be like.*

11 *Which of these three prayer forms do you normally find yourself using most? Explain.*

Two prayers

Jesus told two parables to illustrate two important attitudes that we should have when we pray. CCC 2613 The first one reads:

*Once there were two men
who went up to the Temple to pray:
one was a Pharisee,
the other a tax collector.*

*The Pharisee . . . prayed,
"I thank you, God . . .
that I am not like that
tax collector over there.
I fast two days a week and give you
one tenth of all my income."*

*But the tax collector stood at a distance
and wouldn't even raise his face to heaven,
but beat on his breast and said,
"God have mercy on me a sinner!"*

*"I tell you," said Jesus,
"the tax collector, and not the Pharisee,
was in the right with God
when he went home.*

*For those who make themselves great
will be humbled,
and those who humble themselves
will be made great."* LUKE 18:10–14

Night visitor

A second prayer attitude that Jesus said we should strive to have in prayer is referred to in his Parable of the Night Visitor. It reads:

*Suppose one of you should go
to a friend's house at midnight and say,*

*"Friend,
let me borrow three loaves of bread.
A friend of mine who is on a trip
has just come to my house,
and I don't have any food for him!"*

*And suppose
your friend should answer from inside . . .
"The door is already locked,
and my children and I are in bed.
I can't get up and give you anything."
Well, what then?*

*"I tell you
that even if he will not get up
and give you the bread
because you are his friend,
yet he will get up
and give you everything you need
because you are not ashamed
to keep asking.*

*"And so I say to you:
Ask, and you will receive;
seek and you will find;
knock, and the door
will be opened to you."* LUKE 11:5–9

12 *Why do you think so many people begin a prayer program, but fail to persevere in it?*

At this moment, millions of invisible TV signals swirl around us in living color and sound. But the only way we can prove this fact is to tune them in on a TV set.

Just as a TV world swirls about us invisibly, so does the faith world in which God lives. And just as we need a TV set to get in touch with the TV world, so we need prayer to get in touch with the faith world.

■ *What is one reason, right now in your life, why you'd really like to get in touch with the faith world and God?*

THINK
about it

Turn to the LORD and pray now that he is near.

Isaiah 55:6

Recap

The first condition for learning to pray is the desire to pray. Prayer is, above all, an expression of love to God, who is love. Prayer takes place in one of three settings:

- **Alone**
- **Family or friends**
- **Large community**

Four preparatory steps to any serious prayer program involve:

- **Finding a place**
- **Scheduling a time**
- **Choosing a posture**
- **Entering God's presence**

Four points of focus that are commonly found in people's prayers are:

- **Adoration**   **Focus on God's glory**
- **Contrition**   **Focus on God's mercy**
- **Thanksgiving**   **Focus on God's goodness**
- **Supplication**   **Focus on God's concern**

Prayer normally follows the following three styles or forms:

- **Meditation**   **Thinking about God**
- **Conversation**   **Conversing with God**
- **Contemplation**   **Resting in God**

Two attitudes we should have in praying are:

- **Humility**
- **Perseverance**

Review

1 Explain (a) the first condition for learning to pray, (b) two reasons the useful benefits of prayer can't be the primary reason we pray, (c) the primary reason we pray.

2 List and briefly explain (a) the three settings of prayer, (b) the four preparatory steps of prayer.

3 List and briefly explain (a) the four points of focus common in most people's prayer, (b) two points to keep in mind when it comes to asking God for things.

4 List and briefly explain (a) the three forms that prayer normally takes, and (b) how these forms normally appear in most prayers.

5 List and briefly explain the two prayer attitudes that we should have and what parable Jesus used to teach and illustrate each.

Reflect

1 A lay minister headed for Room 201. A nurse told her a patient was there from her hometown. When she got to the room, however, the expected patient was not there. The lay minister apologized to the occupant, saying she probably got her numbers mixed up. But the patient said, "Please stay! It's no mistake that you came here today. I've been praying for the courage to talk with someone like you, but I couldn't bring myself to do it."

■ *On a scale of one (little) to ten (lots), how much confidence do you have that God answers prayers?*
■ *How do you explain the fact that some prayers do not seem to be answered?*

2 Charlie Rumbaugh grew up in reform schools, jails, and hospital wards. At the age of seventeen, he escaped from a manic depressive ward, found a gun, and held up a jewelry store. A scuffle followed and the jeweler was killed.

A Texas judge sentenced Charlie to death. During his stay on death row, guards treated Charlie badly on several occasions. Shortly before being executed, Charlie asked a friend to pray that he'd be able to forgive the guards before he died. Moments before he received the lethal injection, Charlie said to all involved, "You may not forgive me, but I forgive you." Then he said to the warden, "I'm ready."

■ *How did Charlie's final moments resemble Jesus' final moments?*
■ *Describe a time when you found it hard to forgive someone.*

3 One winter night a high school student and her friend were driving down an icy road. They noticed something on the side of the road. It turned out to be an old man who had fallen on the ice. They put the man in the car.

While her friend ran to a nearby house to call the paramedics, the other student asked the man, "Do you believe in God?" The injured man nodded. With that, the student prayed the Our Father a sentence at a time, pausing to let the old man repeat the words after her.

Later, the student said, "That Our Father was the most meaningful prayer of my life."

■ *Describe a time when you and a friend helped someone as the two friends did.*
■ *Recall one of the most meaningful prayers you ever prayed.*

4 Bryon Dell grew up on a farm in Nebraska. One morning when Bryon was herding the cows, his pony, Frisky, became frightened and bolted off at breakneck speed. Bryon held on for dear life and remained unhurt. That night his father knelt with him to thank God that he was not hurt. That incident took place over 50 years ago, and Bryon has never forgotten it. It inspired him to make prayer a regular part of his daily life.

■ *Describe a happening from your childhood that continues to have an impact on you.*
■ *Did any of your parents ever pray with you? Explain.*

PRAYER TIME
with the Lord

Mike Valentino, a junior in a Chicago high school, describes his first sky dive:

The plane door opens.
The spotter pats my back. I jump!

I strive for stability—the poetic arch.
I have it! I have it! I'm poetry in motion.
It's great! It's great!
I feel a jolt. My chute has opened up.
Tears blur my eyes. I thank God out loud!

Wow! What a beautiful place the sky is!
It's like a giant cathedral! It's God's place!
And more beautiful than I ever dreamed of!

It's a heaven here. Yes, a heaven!
I feel I'm dreaming.
But no dream has ever been so real.

I look down—to prepare for landing.
I ride the wind. I'm holding—facing the wind.
My landing is great!

Joy and pride well up inside me.
I'm a sky diver;
and I'll never again be the same.

■ *Would you say Mike's prayerful experience during his sky dive is an example of contemplation, meditation, or conversation? Explain.*

PRAYER Journal

Prayer often occurs after we experience a "natural high." Here are seven "natural highs" that one girl said "raise my mind and heart to God and move me to want to give thanks."

- *Having my last class canceled on a spring day*
- *Listening to my headphones as I jog along on a sunny fall afternoon*
- *Watching my baby brother do something for the first time after I taught him*
- *Seeing a falling star on a clear night*
- *Enjoying a hot shower after a strenuous workout on a winter day*
- *Skiing or sledding down a hill while big snowflakes are falling*
- *Watching my dog jump around because he's so glad to see me*

■ *List seven "natural highs" that "raise your mind and heart to God and move you to want to give thanks."*

_____

_____

_____

_____

_____

_____

_____

_____

_____

_____

_____

_____

_____

SCRIPTURE Journal

1	Pray with humility	Luke 18:9–14
2	Pray with generosity	2 Chron. 1:7–12
3	Pray with simplicity	Matthew 6:5–13
4	Pray with vigor	Luke 11:5–13
5	Pray with perseverance	Luke 18:1–8

■ *Pick one of the above passages. Read it prayerfully and write a short statement to Jesus expressing your feelings about it.*

_____

_____

_____

_____

_____

_____

18 Choosing Love

*T*he command I am giving you today . . .
is not up in the sky. . . .
You do not have to ask,
"Who will go up and
bring it down for us,
so that we can hear it and obey it?"

*No, it is here with you.
You know it and can quote it,
so now obey it. . . .
Choose life. Love the LORD your God.*
DEUTERONOMY 30:11–15, 19–20

**Christian morality
may be described as "choosing life."
It is choosing to live
my human life on earth
in such a way as to make the leap
to divine life in heaven.**

Big Bang?

*T*he Bible teaches *that* God created the world and all that is in it. But it does not explain *how* God created it.

In other words, the biblical writer did not intend the creation story to be an eyewitness account of what actually happened.

Nor did he intend it to be a scientific explanation of how the various things on earth came about.

For example, the Bible does not say how the following first appeared on earth:

- **Water, soil, minerals**
- **Countless varieties of plants**
- **Myriad insects, birds, animals**
- **Different races of people**

To what extent were these things created individually by God?

Did God simply create the basic form from which the myriad variations gradually emerged?

Or is it possible—as Saint Augustine suggested centuries ago—that God created a "seed" or "seeds" from which everything emerged gradually over eons of centuries?

1 *How do you feel about such suggested scenarios?*

Big question?

If you asked most scientists *how* creation took place, they'd probably say, "At this point in time and human understanding, the *big bang theory* seems like a reasonable scenario.

It holds that a giant "fireball" in space exploded millions of years ago. From that explosion, the universe emerged by a series of *quantum leaps*. For example, the leaps conceivably went from:

- **Nonlife to vegetative life**
- **Vegetative life to animal life**
- **Animal life to human life**

If you telescoped into a single year the three major quantum leaps, the timetable might look like this:

Jan 1	**Big Bang occurs**
Sep 1	**Earth appears**
Dec 1	**Animal life appears**
Dec 31	**Human life appears**

The leap to the *human* life was the critical one. It gave birth to human beings, made in the image of God. Capable of pondering the past and raising questions about the future, human beings could now ask the critical question:

Is human life the last quantum leap in God's plan? Or is there another leap ahead?

2 *How would you be inclined to answer this question?*

Jesus' response

It is against this exciting background that the teachings of Jesus take on fascinating, new significance concerning the "human life stage."

First of all, Jesus taught that the "human life stage" is not the last stage in God's plan. A "leap" to a more remarkable "last stage" lies ahead.

Leap to divine life

*I have come
in order that you might have life—
life in all its fullness. . . .*

*For what my Father wants is that all
who see the Son and believe in him
should have eternal life.
And I will raise them to life
on the last day.* JOHN 10:10; 6:40

Jesus teaches that another "leap" lies ahead. It is the leap to *eternal, divine* life. Or to put it another way, it is the leap from a human life to a share in the very life of the Holy Trinity.

We explicitly affirm our faith in this final stage of our destiny in every Mass. When the priest pours a few drops of water into the wine, he prays silently:

*By the mystery of this water and wine
may we come to share
in the divinity of Christ
who humbled himself to share
in our humanity.*

This brings us to a second thing that Jesus makes clear about the human life stage of creation.

Freedom to choose

Prior to human life, all leaps to a new life took place randomly and blindly.

In other words, prior to the human stage, no other stage of development possessed the ability or the freedom to choose to leap to the next stage.

With the arrival of human life, all this changed. God gave to human beings the awesome responsibility of taking control of their destiny.

God gave them the power and the freedom to choose to make the leap to eternal, divine life or not.

So the teaching of Jesus makes two points clear about human beings. God:

- **Invites us to share in the divine life**
- **Leaves us free to accept or reject it**

3 *Why do you think God gives to each human the awesome choice to accept or reject the invitation to divine life?*

Christian morality

Imagine that the deterioration of planet earth made it impossible for human life to survive beyond ten more years. What would happen?

Scientists would begin a frantic search for another planet that would be capable of supporting human life. Suppose they found one. What then? We would be ecstatic!

But there is *bad* news and *good* news. The bad news is that life on the new planet is significantly different from life on planet Earth. The *good* news is that human beings have the ability to adapt to life on the new planet. It is not easy; but it is possible.

What do you think would happen at this point? Scientists would learn everything they could about life on the new planet. Then they would build centers on earth reproducing the exact conditions of the new planet.

At these centers, they would conduct programs to teach people how to adapt to the new life. Obviously, only people who persevered in adapting to the new life would be shuttled to the new planet.

This parable gives us an insight into what Christian morality is all about. Think of it this way.

Old age and illness make it impossible for human beings to live indefinitely on planet Earth. Jesus has revealed, however, that there is another planet, so to speak, beyond this one: heaven. But life in heaven is totally different from life on earth.

But there is *good* news. Jesus taught us how to live in this life in a way that will adapt us and prepare us for life in heaven.

Viewed this way, Christian morality is simply choosing to live in this life in a way that prepares us for the leap to divine life.

4 To what extent does this view of Christian morality differ from the one you have had up to this point in your life?

Sheila Cassidy

England's Doctor Sheila Cassidy spent four years working among the very poor in Chile. One day she was arrested for treating a political enemy of the state. For four days she was tortured and questioned. She wrote later:

For the first time in my life
I thought I was going to die. . . .
I was experiencing
in some slight way
what Christ had suffered. . . .

I suddenly felt
enormously loved . . .
because I felt I had in a way
participated in his suffering. . . .
I remembered the prayer
Dietrich Bonhoeffer wrote
while he was waiting execution:

"In me there is darkness,
but in Thee there is light. . . .
Lord, whatsoever this day
may bring
Thy name be praised."

"Prayer Under Duress"

After three weeks in solitary and five weeks in a detention camp, she was expelled from Chile and returned safely to England.

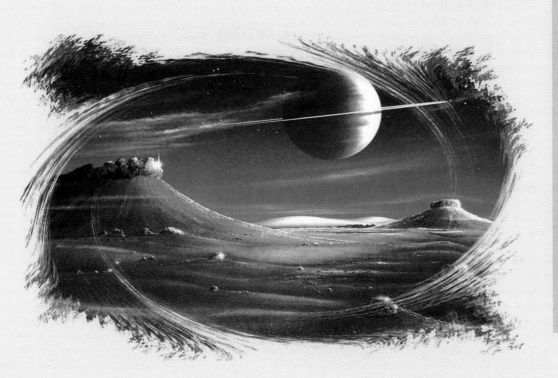

Choosing life

The choice that Moses set before each Israelite is the same choice that God sets before each human being:

*I am now giving you
the choice between life and death . . .
and I call heaven and earth
to witness the choice you make.
Choose life.* DEUTERONOMY 30:19

Our Christian calling in this life is to choose to live in a way that prepares us to make the leap to *divine* life in the next.

Or, to put it in biblical imagery, it is to "plant the seeds" in this life that will produce a "harvest of eternal life" in the next life. Paul puts it this way:

*You will reap exactly what you plant.
If you plant
in the field of your natural desires,
from it you will gather
the harvest of death.*

*If you plant in the field of the Spirit,
from the Spirit you will gather
the harvest of eternal life.*
GALATIANS 6:7–8

*What I say is this:
let the Spirit direct your lives. . . .
The Spirit has given us life . . .
[and] must also control our lives.*
GALATIANS 5:16, 25

Here we should point out what "planting in the field of the Spirit" involves. It involves letting the Spirit make us instruments of God's love. The "Peace Prayer" of Saint Francis expresses it in these memorable words:

*Lord,
make me an instrument of your peace.*

*Where there is hatred, let me sow love;
where there is injury, pardon;
where there is doubt, faith;
where there is despair, hope;
where there is darkness, light;
where there is sadness, joy.*

*Grant that I may not so much
seek to be consoled as to console;
to be understood as to understand;
to be loved as to love;
for it is in giving that we receive;
it is in pardoning that we are pardoned;
and it is in dying
that we are born to eternal life.*

5 *Explain how the average person might attempt to sow (a) love where there is hatred, (b) pardon where there is injury, (c) faith where there is doubt, (d) hope where there is despair.*

Living as Jesus lived

This brings us to yet an even more personal way of describing Christian morality.

At the Last Supper Jesus washed the feet of his Apostles. When he finished, he sat down at table again and said to them:

*I have set an example for you,
so that you will do
just what I have done for you. . . .
Love one another, just as I love you.*
JOHN 13:15, 15:12

A more personal way of describing Christian morality is as follows: It is saying "yes" to Jesus' invitation to live and love as he did, that we may be raised to life by Jesus on the last day.

Living and loving as Jesus did is not easy. This is because original sin has flawed the human intellect and will. As a result, we are not always able to do what we would like to do.

Paul speaks for all of us when he writes:

*Even though the desire to do good
is in me,
I am not able to do it.
I don't do the good I want to do; instead,
I do the evil that I do not want to do. . . .*

*Who will rescue me from this body
that is taking me to death?*

*Thanks be to God,
who does this
through our Lord Jesus Christ.*
ROMANS 7:18–19, 24–25

Christian morality is a challenge. We can meet it only by remaining united with Jesus, who said:

*A branch cannot bear fruit of itself;
it can do so only if it remains in the vine.
In the same way you cannot bear fruit
unless you remain in me.*

*I am the vine,
and you are the branches. . . .
You can do nothing without me.*
JOHN 15:4–5

6 What is meant by "union with Christ"? What is there about modern life that makes it difficult to remain in union with Christ?

PRAYER
hotline

When the world
has you down,
and you feel rotten as—
you know what,
and you're mad at everybody,
including yourself,
and you're too d_ _ _ tired
to pray,
SCREAM the following prayer
three times
at the top of your voice:

HELP!!!

The butterfly was happy because it was her birthday. So she called over to the caterpillar.

"It's my birthday. Ask me anything and if I can, I will grant it.

The caterpillar thought and thought until his head hurt. Then he said, "Tell me how to become a butterfly."

The butterfly said, "That's very difficult. There is only one way to do it. You must want to fly so badly that you're willing to stop crawling." The same is true of love.

■ **What point does the above story make?**

■ **How do you see it applying to your life?**

Moral growth

Learning to live and love as Jesus did is a growth process that continues all of our life. It involves three stages or "levels of growth."

■ **Self-centered**
■ **Other-centered**
■ **God-centered**

Let's take a closer look at each of these three levels of moral growth.

Self-centered level

During this first level, we live largely by our senses and emotions. Our main concern is our own needs and enjoyment.

At this level we are basically selfish. We want to be free to do whatever we want. We don't realize it, but we are anything but free.

We are slaves of our prejudices and passions. We pursue one fleeting pleasure after another.

We see Jesus' teaching as a *restriction* (to our freedom). It forbids us to do what we want to do. It is something that cramps our style. At this level, we see *sin* merely as *violation* (of a restriction).

As long as we remain at this level, we are doomed to unhappiness.

Other-centered level

We advance to the next level when we begin to shift our focus from ourselves to others.

We do this by assuming social obligations, such as friendships and commitments. By accepting these responsibilities, we take a giant step toward personal freedom.

At this stage, we see Jesus' teaching not as a restriction and as something negative. Rather, we see it as something freeing and positive.

Only in this light can we appreciate the psalmist when he prays to God: "How I love your law!" PSALM 119:97

The psalmist saw God's law as "freeing us from" our own ignorance and passion and "freeing us for" happiness and service to God and neighbor.

At this level, we see Jesus' teaching as a *guide* (to growth and happiness). And we see *sin* as *infidelity* (to growth). It is living irresponsibly and stupidly.

God-centered level

We advance to the final level when we discover our personal relationship with God. This discovery develops out of an awareness of our true *identity* (we are God's children) and our true *destiny* (we are called to eternal life).

At this level, we see Jesus' teaching as concrete signs of God's love for us. God wants us to be happy. God wants to share his own divine life with us.

At this level, we also discover Jesus and why he came into the world: to "free us from sin" and to "free us to love God and neighbor." To put it another way, Jesus came to bring us the "fullness" of life: eternal, divine life.

Finally, at this level, we discover the true relationship between Jesus' teaching and love. *Jesus' teaching* is an invitation (to love). Jesus said:

*Those who accept
my commandments and obey them
are the ones who love me.* JOHN 14:21

And so, at the God-centered level we see Jesus' teaching as an *invitation* (to love). We see sin as a *refusal* (to love).

Sin is saying "no" to Jesus' invitation to live and love as he did.

Viewed this way, Christian morality is choosing to live as Jesus modeled and taught: in a way that prepares us to make the leap to divine life with him in the world to come.

FAITH Connection

We may sum up the way that people at each level of moral growth view Jesus' teaching and sin as follows:

Jesus' teaching

Self	Restriction to freedom
Other	Guide to growth
God	Invitation to love

Sin

Self	Violation of restriction
Other	Infidelity to growth
God	Refusal to love

Recap

If you asked most scientists how creation took place, they'd probably say, "The *big bang theory is a reasonable scenario.*" In any event, the leap to the *human* life was the critical one. It gave birth to human beings, who could now ask the critical question: *Is human life the last quantum leap in God's plan? Or is there another leap ahead?*

Jesus taught that another "leap" lies ahead. It is the leap from human life to a share in the divine life of the Trinity. Jesus also taught that we are free to accept or reject God's invitation to divine life.

In this context, Christian morality is accepting God's invitation to live life on earth in such a way as to make the leap to this awesome life.

Christian morality involves a journey of growth that begins in childhood and never ends. It moves forward gradually through three levels:

- **Self-centered**
- **Other-centered**
- **God-centered**

Our view of *law* and *sin* is conditioned by the growth level at which we find ourselves.

Review

1 Explain briefly (a) the "big bang" theory, (b) the "critical leap" in this theory and why, (c) the "critical question" human beings could now ask.

2 Explain Jesus' twofold teaching about whether or not the "human life stage" is the final stage in God's plan.

3 Describe (a) our Christian calling in this life, (b) what "planting in the field of the Spirit" involves, (c) a *personal* way of describing Christian morality.

4 Explain (a) why Christian morality is a difficult challenge, (b) the image Jesus used to teach us how we can successfully meet this difficult challenge.

5 List and briefly describe (a) the three levels of moral growth, (b) how people in each level view Jesus' teaching, (c) how people in each level view sin.

Reflect

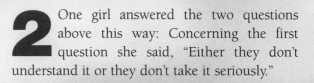

1 In his novel *The Source*, James Michener recreates a time in history when people worshiped many gods.

In one scene, he portrays the people of Makor sacrificing infants and young children to their new god, Melak. Then Michener explains why the people threw out their old gods and adopted a new god.

It was partly because
his demands on them were severe
and partly because
they had grown somewhat contemptuous
of their local gods
precisely because
they were not demanding enough.

A Gallup poll shows that many modern Christians are like the people of Makor. They do not think their religion is very demanding. That poll raises a question: Why do many modern Christians think Jesus' teachings are not demanding?

■ **Why do you think many people feel that Jesus' teachings are not very demanding?**
■ **On a scale of one (not very) to ten (very), how demanding do you think Jesus' teachings are?**

2 One girl answered the two questions above this way: Concerning the first question she said, "Either they don't understand it or they don't take it seriously."

She gave this example of a demanding teaching which she feels many people don't take seriously: "Love your enemies, do good to those who hate you." LUKE 6:27

The girl answered the second question by giving Christianity a rating of "seven."

■ **Why do you agree/disagree with her answer to (a) the first question, (b) the second question?**

3 In her book *Pilgrim at Tinker Creek*, Annie Dillard writes:

I read about an Eskimo hunter
who asked the local missionary priest,
"If I did not know about God and sin,
would I go to hell?"
"No," said the priest,
"not if you did not know."
"Then why," asked the Eskimo earnestly,
"did you tell me?"

■ **How would you answer the hunter?**

PRAYER TIME
with the Lord

The following excerpt is from a letter reportedly written on Christmas Eve 1513, by Fra Giovanni to a friend. Some scholars question its attribution; but few readers question its beauty.

The gloom of the world is but a shadow.
Behind it, yet within our reach, is joy.

There is radiance and glory in the darkness,
could we but see. We have only to look. . . .
I beseech you look.

Life is a generous giver,
but we, judging its gifts by their covering,
cast them away as ugly. . . .

Remove the covering,
and you will find beneath it
a living splendor, woven of love. . . .

Welcome it, grasp it,
and you touch the Angel's hand
that brings it to you.

Everything we call a trial,
a sorrow, or a duty:
believe me, the Angel's hand is there;
the gift is there, and
the wonder of an overshadowing presence.

■ *Compose a brief prayer to Jesus explaining what threatens to keep you from having this vision of the world. End by asking Jesus to help you acquire it.*

PRAYER Journal

Christians come in three models: rafts, sailboats, and tugboats.

Rafts follow Jesus only when someone pulls or pushes them.

Sailboats follow Jesus only in good weather. When stormy weather comes, they go with the wind and the waves. In other words, they follow the crowd more than they follow Jesus.

Tugboats follow Jesus in all weather. They don't always travel fast; but they always travel straight.

■ *Compose (a) an e-mail to Jesus explaining your situation and (b) an e-mail that Jesus may send to you in reply.*

_____

_____

_____

_____

_____

_____

_____

_____

_____

SCRIPTURE Journal

1	**I am in the Father**	**John 14:1–14**
2	**Remain in me**	**John 15:1–11**
3	**You are like light**	**Matthew 5:1–16**
4	**Seek heaven**	**Colossians 3:1–17**
5	**Share God's glory**	**Romans 8:18–30**

■ *Pick one of the above passages. Read it prayerfully and write a short statement to Jesus expressing your feelings about it.*

_____

_____

_____

_____

_____

19 Loving God

*I f we obey God's commands,
then we are sure that we know him.
If we say that we know him,
but do not obey his commands . . .
there is no truth in us.*

*But if we obey his word,
we are the ones whose love for God
has been made perfect. . . .
Those who obey God's commands
live in union with God
and God lives in union with them.*
1 JOHN 2:3, 5–6, 3:24

**The first three commandments
invite us to make love of God
the center of our lives;
and they provide us with
concrete guidelines for doing this.**

The Ten Commandments

How might a television news crew file a report from Mount Sinai shortly after Moses received the Ten Commandments from God? Here's one imaginative scenario:

ANCHOR   *This is Joel ben Isaac reporting from Mount Sinai.*

The Hebrew leader Moses just came down the mountain with a lightning bolt: ten commandments from God. Our roving reporter, Rebecca, is at the scene. What's the mood there, Rebecca?

REPORTER   *Ugly, Joel! Really ugly! That lightning bolt has this crowd up in arms. Pro-choicers call it a criminal attack on human freedom.*

ANCHOR   *How are these laws likely to affect the average people, Rebecca?*

REPORTER   *That's hard to say, Joel. But one camel trader put it this way: "It's going to take more than ten rules to reverse habits that have been built up over the centuries."*

ANCHOR	*Rebecca, how is all this likely to affect Moses' leadership of the people?*
REPORTER	*Again that's hard to say. But as you know, Joel, he's been taking his lumps lately. This could be the straw that breaks his back. He could be history.*

ANCHOR	*Thank you, Rebecca. . . . When we return, a look at how today's events could affect your future.*
	INSPIRED BY JEFFREY RUBIN

1 *How do you think the Israelites really reacted to God's Ten Commandments?*

A high school teacher was talking about Christianity. Suddenly, a girl raised her hand and said:

*"I'm confused!
You just quoted Saint Paul as saying,
"No longer do we serve
in the old way of a written law, but in
a new way of the Spirit." ROMANS 7:6*

*Then you said that the new way is love.
Where does that put
the Ten Commandments?
Did Jesus abolish the commandments
and replace them with love?*

2 *How would you answer the girl?*

Jesus and the Ten Commandments

O ne day a young man asked Jesus, "What good thing must I do to receive eternal life?" Jesus said, "Keep the commandments." The young man asked, "What commandments?" Jesus answered:

*Do not commit murder;
do not commit adultery;
do not steal;
Do not accuse anyone falsely;
respect your father and your mother;
And love your neighbor
as you love yourself. MATTHEW 19:18–19*

On another occasion, someone asked Jesus, "Which is the greatest commandment?" Jesus answered:

*"Love the Lord your God
with all your heart, with all your soul,
and with all your mind. . . ."*

*"The second most important
commandment is like it:
Love your neighbor as you love yourself.*

*"The whole Law of Moses
and the teachings of the prophets
depend on these two commandments."*
MATTHEW 22:37, 39–40

O sborne Jera was startled to hear someone singing at the top of his voice in an empty church in the middle of the day. Looking around, he saw a man, hat in hand, eyes closed, facing the altar. When his song ended, the man opened his eyes. Seeing Jera, he said:

I just felt like singing to God— if he's still here.
Such awful things happening' in the world. Felt like a little song might cheer him up.

Then the man flashed empty hands, saying, "I haven't touched anything." Jera thought, "How wondrously wrong he was to say, 'I haven't touched anything!' "

■ *Explain the following two comments:*
(a) "I felt like singing to God— if he's still here";
(b) "How wrong he was to say, 'I haven't touched anything!' "

Jesus fulfills the commandments

J esus did not abolish the commandments. He brought them to fulfillment and redefined them in terms of love:

- ■ **God**   Commandments 1–3
- ■ **Neighbor**   Commandments 4–10

In redefining the Ten Commandments, Jesus gave them an entirely new focus. He transformed them into:

- ■ **Signs of love**
- ■ **Invitations to love**
- ■ **Guides to love**

First, Jesus transforms the commandments into *signs of love*: our love for Jesus, Jesus' love for us, and our love for one another. Jesus said:

If you love me, you will obey my commandments. . . . My commandment is this: love one another just as I have loved you. JOHN 14:15; 15:12

If you have love for one another, then everyone will know that you are my disciples. JOHN 13:35

Second, Jesus transforms the commandments into *invitations to love.*

Because we are Jesus' disciples, and desire to remain so, the commandments become invitations to love. That is, they summon us to love when we forget to do so, or are tempted not to do so.

Finally, Jesus transforms the commandments into *guides to love.* They point out a loving course of action, when it is not clear what love invites us to do in a given situation.

Gift of the commandments

A fter the Israelites escaped from Egypt, Moses led them through the desert to Mount Sinai. At the foot of the mountain, Moses instructed them to pitch camp.

On the morning of the third day, there was thunder and lightning . . . The LORD. . . called Moses to the top of the mountain . . . Moses then went down to the people and told them what the LORD had said. . . .

These were his words: "I am the LORD your God who brought you out of Egypt." EXODUS 19:16; 20:2, 25

1. Worship no god but me. . . .
2. Keep my name. . . .
3. Keep holy the Sabbath. . . .
4. Respect your father and mother. . . .
5. Do not commit murder.
6. Do not commit adultery.
7. Do not steal.
8. Do not accuse anyone falsely.
9. Do not desire another's wife . . .
10. nor anything else that he owns.

DEUTERONOMY 5:7, 11, 16–21

By his gift of the Ten Commandments to them, God entered into a covenant ("sacred agreement") with Israel. By that covenant, they became God's "chosen people," which means they became God's "chosen instrument" for re-creating the world.

Here's how one modern Jew describes what the covenant did for Israel:

Israel is not a "natural" nation; it is, indeed, not a nation at all like the nations of the world.

It is a supernatural community,
called into being by God
to serve his eternal purposes in history.

It is a community
created by God's special act of covenant . . .
Apart from the covenant,
Israel is as nothing and Jewish existence
is a mere delusion.
The covenant is at the very heart
of the Jewish self-understanding
of its own reality.

WILL HERBERG: "JEWISH EXISTENCE AND SURVIVAL:
A THEOLOGICAL VIEW"

Let us now take a closer look at each of
the first three commandments.

First commandment

A reporter asked Cecil B. DeMille,
the director of the film *The Ten
Commandments,* "What commandment
do you think that people today break
most?"

The director answered, "The very first
commandment: 'Worship no God but
me.' It's the one that Israel broke first,
and it's the one that we still break
most."

DeMille hastened to explain that we do
not fashion idols out of metal and
bow before them. "Rather, we make
idols of flesh and money and bow
before them."

Jesus warned people about this very
danger in his Sermon on the Mount.
He explained why they must worship
God alone, saying:

"Your heart
will always be where your riches are. . . .
You cannot be a slave of two masters;
you will hate one and love the other;
you will be loyal to one
and despise the other.
You cannot serve both God and money."

MATTHEW 6:21–24

Thus, the first commandment is an
invitation to make God the focus of all
our energies and desires. It is an
invitation to:

- ■ **Believe in God**   CCC 2087–89
- ■ **Hope in God**   CCC 2090–92
- ■ **Love God**   CCC 2093–94
- ■ **Serve God**   CCC 2095–2109

That brings us to some specific ways
we violate the first commandment.

Spiritism

A third practice that relates to the first commandment is *spiritism.* CCC 2117 It involves such things as seeking to communicate with the dead through mediums and seances. Again, the Bible prohibits such practices. LEVITICUS 20:27. Commenting on spiritism, Thomas Higgins says in *Man As Man:*

*While most spiritistic mediums
may be laughed at as frauds . . .
not all the phenomena of modern spiritism
may be dismissed as hokum.*

*Some truly genuine effects are wrought.
The explanation of some of these effects
may be traced to occult, but natural
causes, whereas others . . .
can be due only to diabolical intervention.*

4 *Why do you think people who claim psychic powers are able to command such a following over television and the Internet?*

Superstition

In an age of science and reason, it is incredible that some airplanes have no row 13, or seat 13. And some hotels skip from the twelfth floor to the fourteenth, all because some people feel uneasy about the number 13.

This is evidence that *superstition* still plays a surprising role in some people's lives.

3 *What are some other examples of superstition today? What do you think accounts for superstition among many people, even in our day?*

Divination

Somewhat related to superstition is *divination,* which seeks to learn the future from palm readers, fortune-tellers, and horoscopes. Such practices are specifically forbidden in both the Old Testament and in the New Testament. DEUTERONOMY 18:10–11, ACTS 16:16, CCC 2116

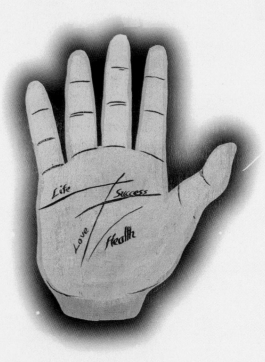

Second commandment

The second commandment reads: "Do not use my name for evil purposes." Commenting on this commandment, someone said, "When I misuse God's name, I don't mean anything by it. It's just a *bad habit* I have."

Try using that excuse when a traffic officer stops you for speeding or when your supervisor catches you arriving late for work.

The second commandment "governs our use of speech in sacred matters." CCC 2142–54 It summons us to keep holy God's name, as Jesus taught us in the Lord's Prayer: "Hallowed be thy name."

Deliberate or careless misuse of God's name offends God, but also our neighbor. Consider two examples.

Cursing

Cursing calls upon God to inflict harm on someone. It dishonors God gravely, because it attempts to make God a partner to evil. CCC 2148

Damning someone in God's name is more often a careless expression of frustration or irritation than a genuine intention to curse.

Misuse of God's name, by one of the above two ways, can lead to scandal, especially where young people are concerned. Scandal is "an attitude or behavior which leads another to do evil." CCC 2284–87 Jesus spoke about it bluntly, saying:

*Things that make people fall into sin
are bound to happen,
but how terrible for the one
who makes them happen!*

*It would be better for him
if he were thrown
into the bottom of the sea
than for him to cause
one of these little ones to sin.
So watch what you do.*
LUKE 17:1–3

5 *List some ways that scandal can be given to "little ones" by (a) adults, especially parents, (b) young people.*

Oaths

A second example of an abuse of God's name is the misuse of *oaths*. Oaths call upon God to witness that we speak the truth. In a society where lying is common, courts require people to swear to their testimony. In grave cases like this, therefore, oaths are permitted.

To lie under oath is a sin of *perjury*. CCC 2149–55 It dishonors God gravely by asking God to witness to a lie.

PRAYER
hotline

**Lord, take my lips
and speak through them;**

**take my mind
and think through it;**

**take my heart
and set it on fire.**

W. H. Aitken

Jacques Braman

One day a young lady asked James Martin, "How can I find God?" This question inspired him to ask people of all ages, religions, and occupations how they found God.

The result was a fascinating book called *How Can I Find God?* One entry in it is by Jacques Braman. It reads:

It was a peaceful evening. My mom and brother and sister and I were on our way to a high school basketball game . . .

It was quiet in the car. . . . I was just looking out the window at the still night, enjoying the stars . . . happy to be on my way to the game.

The happiness that I was feeling grew deeper and . . . I noticed that tears were rolling down my cheeks. This was really weird. . . .

Then I understood. This was how full joy could be . . . a joy that comes only from God.

Third commandment

It is not uncommon to find a pamphlet by some religious sect saying that Christians violate the third commandment. They observe Sunday, and not the Sabbath, as the commandment reads. A few early Jewish converts to Christianity made the same point.

This raises a question. If the third commandment says we should "observe the Sabbath and keep it holy," why did the first followers of Jesus change their observance to Sunday?

Observance of the Lord's Day

There are many reasons. Two major ones are that Jesus rose on Sunday JOHN 20:1 and the Holy Spirit descended upon the followers of Jesus on a Sunday. ACTS 2:1–4

These events gave new significance to this day. They signaled the sunset of the Old Testament era and the sunrise of the New Testament era.

Guided by the Holy Spirit, the followers of Jesus chose Sunday as the day to celebrate the Lord's Supper ACTS 20:7–11 and referred to it as the Lord's Day. REVELATION 1:10

And so, from the very beginning, Sunday was observed in a special manner by the early Church. Modern Church law spells out its observance this way:

On Sundays . . .
the faithful are obliged
to assist at Mass.
They are also to abstain
from such work or business
that inhibit
the worship to be given God,
the joy proper
to the Lord's Day, or
the due relaxation of mind
and body.
CANON LAW 1247

6 *In what sense is this observance of the Lord's Day more sensitive to the differences in people?*

Observance of Holy Days

Besides Sunday, the Church also observes the ancient practice of setting aside holy days for special observance. In the United States, six such days are observed:

- ■ **Mother of God** **January 1**
- ■ **Ascension** **40 days after Easter**
- ■ **Assumption** **August 15**
- ■ **All Saints** **November 1**
- ■ **Immaculate Conception** **December 8**
- ■ **Christmas** **December 25**

By gathering for worship on Sundays and holy days, we proclaim to the world what Jesus proclaimed: that God is our origin and our destiny.

God must therefore be at the heart and center of all human life and activity. CCC 2177–78

Christian responsibility to gather on Sundays and holy days for worship binds us gravely, unless we are excused for a serious reason.

This means that when we are otherwise faithful in our Mass attendance, we need not worry or feel guilty when something comes up that would make it really difficult for us to assist at Mass. CCC 2180–88

THINK
about it

God says . . .
Let's meet at my house
on Sunday before the game.

Billboard sign

Recap

Review

Jesus did not abolish the commandments. Rather, he brought them to fulfillment and redefined them in terms of love:

■ **Commandments 1–3**   **Love of God**
■ **Commandments 4–10**   **Love of neighbor**

In redefining the Ten Commandments, Jesus gave them an entirely new focus. He transforms them into:

■ **Signs of love**
■ **Invitations to love**
■ **Guides to love**

The first three commandments that God gave Moses and the Israelites at the foot of Mount Sinai invite them to make God the focus of all their energies and desires.

Violations of the first three commandments may be summed up as follows:

■ **First**   **Superstition, divination, spiritism**
■ **Second**   **Curses and rash oaths**
■ **Third**   **Failure in Sunday worship**

1 List the Ten Commandments that God gave gave to Moses at the foot of Mount Sinai.

2 Briefly explain how Jesus redefined (a) the first three commandments, (b) the last seven commandments.

3 List and briefly describe the new threefold focus that Jesus gave the commandments.

4 Briefly explain what God's gift of the covenant did for Israel.

5 Identify (a) superstition, (b) divination, (c) spiritism.

6 Briefly explain what we mean by (a) curses, (b) oaths, (c) why oaths are permissible in grave situations, (d) perjury, (e) scandal.

7 List two major reasons why Christians, guided by the Holy Spirit, observe Sunday rather than the Sabbath.

8 List the six holy days and when they are observed by Catholics in the United States.

Reflect

1 Ann Landers received a letter from a young woman who had gone to a fortune-teller. The fortune-teller told her that she would never have a child of her own. The young woman was devastated. She said, "I cried all the way home."

Then to the young woman's great joy, she became pregnant. But her joy soon turned to fear when she recalled what the fortune-teller had said. But the baby arrived on schedule and healthy.

■ *You may have heard the statement, "Something is not bad because it's a sin; it's a sin because it's bad." Explain how the woman's experience illustrates the point of the statement.*
■ *What are two concerns that you have about the future? Explain.*

2 Eugene O'Neill was one of America's great playwrights. He won both the Pulitzer prize and the Nobel prize. The last play he wrote was entitled *Long Day's Journey into Night.*

In it, he has the leading character describe a mystical experience he has. Actually, it was an experience O'Neill himself had in connection with the sea.

It occurred one night when he was lying on the bow of a small boat. The water was spraying and foaming under him and the the white sails of the boat were shining in the moonlight, beautiful and bright above him. He writes:

*For a moment, I lost myself. . . .
I became the white sails and flying spray,
became the beauty and rhythm,
became the moonlight and the ship and
the dim-starred sky!
I belonged . . . within something
greater than my own life.*

■ *How do you interpret O'Neill's words, "I belonged within something greater than my own life"?*
■ *Can you think of a time when you felt the way O'Neill did? Explain.*

3 Marion Bond West lost her father when she was about four years old. This made it necessary for her mother to take a job to support her.

So her mother arranged to have a neighbor baby-sit Marion. Each lunch hour Marion's mother hurried home to eat with her. But when she left after lunch, Marion grew hysterical.

One day Marion's mother stopped coming. Years later, Marion learned why.

Her mother still came each noon, sat at the window, watched her play, and longed to hold her close—especially when she fell and cried. But for Marion's own good, she didn't.

"CLOSE BY," *GUIDEPOSTS,* JUNE 1979

■ *How does this true story have application to God's personal, loving relationship to you?*

PRAYER TIME
with the Lord

I pray because I am a Christian,
and to do what a Christian must do,
I need strength.

I pray because there's confusion in my life,
and to know what is right,
I need light.

I pray because I have questions,
and to keep growing in the faith,
I need help.

I pray because I must make decisions,
and the choices are not always clear,
so I need guidance.

I pray because most of what I have
has been given to me,
and I ought to give thanks.

I pray because Jesus prayed,
and if he considered it important,
so should I. M.L.

■ *After studying the above six reasons,
number them from one to six, in the order that
best describes why you pray.*
■ *Briefly explain your "first" choice.*

PRAYER Journal

Daniel Harrington, S.J., is a biblical scholar. When asked where he finds God, he said:

"I stutter. . . .
As a young boy I read in a newspaper
that Moses stuttered.
I looked it up in the Bible, and sure enough
in Exodus 4:10 Moses says to God:
'I am slow of speech and slow of tongue.'"

But Harrington found much more than this. He found the story of God's self-revelation to Moses and of God's missioning of Moses to speak that self-revelation to the world.

Harrington ended, "I found God in the Bible, and I have continued to do so ever since."

■ **Describe briefly where you find God.**

_____
_____
_____
_____
_____
_____
_____
_____
_____
_____
_____
_____
_____

SCRIPTURE Journal

1	Worship God only	Deuteronomy 4:15–20
2	Keep the Sabbath	Nehemiah 13:15–22
3	Keep Temple holy	Matthew 21:12–16
4	Prayer in the Temple	1 Kings 8:22–30
5	Praise God	Psalm 150

■ *Pick one of the above passages. Read it prayerfully and write a short statement to Jesus expressing your feelings about it.*

_____
_____
_____
_____
_____
_____
_____
_____
_____

Jesus said:
"I love you just as the Father loves me;
remain in my love.

"If you obey my commands,
you will remain in my love,
just as I have obeyed
my Father's commands and
remain in his love. . . .

"My commandment is this:
love one another, just as I love you."
JOHN 15:9–12

Jesus redefined and gave new focus to the Ten Commandments. He transformed them into *signs*, *invitations*, and *guides* of love.

Steve

Sal Lazzarotti boarded a subway for work. Inside the car, a boy of about 18 was holding the center post. Across from him sat a young woman.

At 50th Street the train slowed to a stop. The young woman headed for the door. Suddenly, she began hitting the boy and screaming.

The astonished boy threw up his arms in self-defense. As he did, he must have hit her face, because her lip began bleeding. She shouted, "Police! Police!" Panic-stricken, the boy ran from the car. The young woman ran after him, shouting: "Police! Police!"

Lazzarotti sat stunned. He'd seen the whole thing. The boy had done nothing.

As the train sped off, Lazzarotti wondered what would happen to the boy if he got caught. Sitting in his office, he couldn't get the incident out of his mind. Finally, he picked up the phone and called the nearest precinct.

The boy had been caught and sent downtown to Juvenile Court. His name was Steve and a lawyer named Fleary would be representing him.

The following Monday, Lazzarotti showed up for the court case. The lawyer briefed him. Bad news! A few years ago Steve had been picked up with other boys on suspicion of stealing a car, but wasn't charged.

When the judge began questioning the girl, Lazzarotti couldn't believe what she was saying. At that point the judge asked her to be more specific, saying, "A witness is present and will be testifying." When she heard this, she grew nervous and and started contradicting herself.

The judge stopped. He called both lawyers forward and huddled with them. Both nodded in agreement: the young woman probably needed psychiatric help. The judge dismissed the case.

Steve grasped Lazzarotti's hand in gratitude, too choked to speak. On his way home, Lazzarotti thought to himself, "How close I came to not getting involved, saying 'It's none of my business.'"

Retold from Sal Lazzarotti: "Why Should I Get Involved?" *Guideposts* magazine

1 Why do people tend not to get involved in cases like Steve's, saying, "It's none of my business"? Evaluate their reasons. Why would/wouldn't you be inclined to get involved in a case like Steve's?

Christian morality

Making my neighbor's *need* "my business" is at the very heart of what Christian morality is all about.

One day a man asked Jesus, "Who is my neighbor?" Jesus responded by telling him this parable.

There was once a man who was going down from Jerusalem to Jericho when robbers attacked him, stripped him, and beat him up, leaving him half-dead.

It so happened that a priest was going down that road; but when he saw the man, he walked on by on the other side. In the same way a Levite also came there, went over and looked at the man, and walked on by on the other side.

But a Samaritan who was traveling that way came upon the man, and when he saw him, his heart was filled with pity.

The Good Samaritan, Van Gogh.

He went over to him, poured wine on his wounds and bandaged them;
then he put the man on his own animal and took him to an inn, where he took care of him.

The next day he took out two silver coins and gave them to the innkeeper.
"Take care of him . . .
and when I come back this way,
I will pass you whatever else
you spend on him."

A regiment of German prisoners was being marched in single column through the streets of Moscow during World War II.

First came the Nazi officers—well fed, well dressed, heads held high. Their demeanor was one of superiority to their ill-clothed onlookers—mostly angry, Russian women who had lost sons and husbands in the fierce fighting.

Next came the German soldiers—young, thin, ill-clothed, hobbling on crutches, heads hanging in pain and shame. The street went deathly silent at the sight.

Then an old woman took a crust of dry bread from her pocket and gave it to a young soldier who could hardly walk. (It may have been her own evening meal.)

Then other women began giving the wounded soldiers bread, cigarettes, and kerchiefs. These soldiers were no longer enemies. They were suffering human beings.

Reported by Donald Nicholl
in *Triumphs of the Spirit in Russia*

And Jesus concluded,
"In your opinion, which of these three acted like a neighbor toward the man attacked by the robbers?"

The teacher of the law answered, "The one who was kind to him." Jesus replied, "Go, then, and do the same." LUKE 10:26–37

2 Why do you think the priest and the Levite bypassed the man? Why do you think Jesus chose a Samaritan to be the hero of the story?

Who is my neighbor?

The priest was probably on his way to Jerusalem to worship in the Temple. Apparently, he feared the man was dead. To touch a dead man would make him unclean and ban him temporarily from temple worship.

A Levite was somewhat like a modern deacon. He assisted the priests. 1 CHRONICLE 23:3–5 But Levites were under a different cleanliness code than priests. They could touch dead bodies.

Possibly the Levite's concern was that the robbers may have been hiding in the underbrush. Perhaps they were using the wounded man as bait to attract and rob another man.

Finally, there was the Samaritan. Jews regarded Samaritans as heretics. In Jesus' day, they were banned from the Temple and the synagogue. Their religious contributions were refused and their testimony in courts was not accepted.

Samaritans were also hostile to Jews. They made common cause with Jewish enemies, often not letting them into their towns. LUKE 9:52

Jesus chose a Samaritan as his hero to teach his listeners that love of neighbor has no boundaries. Every member of the human family is my neighbor, including my enemies. LUKE 6:27

Loving my neighbor

This brings us back to the Ten Commandments. Jesus did not abolish them, but brought them to fulfillment and redefined them in terms of love:

- **God** Commandments 1–3
- **Neighbor** Commandments 4–10

In redefining the Ten Commandments in terms of love, Jesus gave them an entirely new focus and transformed them into:

- **Signs** Of Jesus' love for us
- **Invitations** To love as Jesus did
- **Guides** On how to love

In the last chapter we covered the first three commandments; in this chapter we will take up the final seven: love of neighbor. We will treat them under three headings, respect for:

- **Authority and life**
- **Property and truth**
- **Conscience and Church teaching**

A speaker was giving a talk to parents. He stressed the need for them to reach out more to children, especially teenagers. After he finished, a mother said:

*You've talked a lot
about our failure
to reach out to our children.*

*I've reached out again and again
to my teenage son,
but he rejects my efforts—
often coldly and cruelly.
Tell me what I'm supposed
to do now.*

■ *How would you answer that mother?*

Fourth commandment

Years ago, a popular Hollywood actor, Ricardo Montalban, wrote a highly publicized, fatherly letter to his son. It reads:

*We are father and son
by the grace of God,
and I accept that privilege
and awesome responsibility. . . .
I am not your pal. . . .
I am your father.
This is 100 times more
than what a pal is. . . .
Whatever I ask you to do
is motivated by love.
This will be hard for you to understand
until you have a son of your own.
Until then, trust me.*
—Your Father

3 *Why would/wouldn't you like to receive such a letter as a daughter or son?*

Familial authority

The fourth commandment deals with respect for authority within the building block of society: the family. CCC 2207–13 It also deals with civil authority within society itself. We begin with respect for familial authority.

Years ago, Alvin Toffler made this sobering statement about the family in his book *Future Shock:*

*The family has been called
the "giant shock absorber"of society—
the place to which
the bruised and battered individual returns
after doing battle with the world,
the one stable point
in an increasingly flux-filled environment.
As the superindustrial revolution unfolds,
the "shock absorber" will come in
for some shocks of its own.*

PRAYER
hotline

O Lord, bless all who love me,
and keep 'em lovin me.
And, Lord,
for those who don't love me,
turn their hearts,
or at least turn their ankles
so I can recognize them
by their limping.

Irish blessing

Bill Havens

Bill Havens was a member of the U.S. Olympic canoe team. He was scheduled to compete in the Olympics in Paris. Then he learned that his wife was expecting to give birth to their first child at the very time he was scheduled to compete.

The more Bill pondered the question, the more he thought his place was with his wife, though she urged him to compete. So he dropped from the team.

As it turned out, his wife was late giving birth to a son, and the U.S. team won the gold medal. Bill could have made both events. He never said anything to his son about being disappointed that he missed the Olympics.

Years later, a cablegram arrived from Helsinki, Finland, where the Olympics were in progress. It read: "Dad, I won. I'm bringing home the gold medal you lost while waiting for me to be born." Bill's son Frank had just won the Olympic single's canoe competition.

What Toffler predicted has come to pass. And the shocks to the family community have been so great that some social critics fear it may be heading toward "complete extinction."

Not everyone agrees with these critics; but all *do* agree that the situation is serious. Therefore, all agree that family members have an obligation—more than ever before in history—to contribute to family stability. CCC 2214–33

Concretely, parents must take to heart—more than ever—Saint Paul's words to raise their children "with Christian discipline and instruction." EPHESIANS 6:4; CCC 2221–31

And children must take to heart—more than ever—his words to respect parents. EPHESIANS 6:1–2; CCC 2214–20

God intended the family to be one of God's greatest blessings and gifts. Our gift back to God is to help the family become what God made it to be: the sign and instrument by which human society matures into the Kingdom of God. CCC 2232–33

4 *What do you think is one of the greatest threats to the family today? Explain.*

Civil authority

Closely related to respect for familial authority is respect for civil authority: the authority of the wider civil community. CCC 2234–46

Because we share the blessing of the civil community, we owe it special loyalty and we share in its responsibilities.

Jesus made this clear when he told his disciples "Pay to the Emperor what belongs to the Emperor." LUKE 20:25

Paul made a similar point in his letter to the Romans, saying:

*Everyone must obey
state authorities, because no authority
exists without God's permission,
and the existing authorities
have been put there by God.* ROMANS 13:1

Conversely, the state must also respect the rights of citizens. Citizens do not exist for the state; the state exists to provide a social order in which "we may live a quiet and peaceful life with all reverence toward God and with proper conduct." 1 TIMOTHY 2:2

No state may trample on the God-given rights of individuals and families. If it does, citizens have not only the right but also the obligation to refuse to obey. With Saint Peter they protest, "We must obey God, not men." Acts 5:29

5 *Before engaging in civil disobedience, what are some things you should consider?*

Fifth commandment

Albert Diianni has traveled widely in such places as South America, Central America, and the Philippine Islands. These travels have had a profound effect on him. Writing in *America* magazine, he says:

In my visits to Peru, Brazil, Mexico, and the Philippines, I have seen peoples and lands ravaged by the corruption of political leaders and the uncaring greed of multinational corporations.

I have shivered at the burials of infants who died because their parents lacked the rudimentary education to provide them simple hygienic or medical care.

Diianni's words put flesh and blood on these otherwise cold statistics about the people of the world:

- ■ **Millions are illiterate**
- ■ **Millions have no full-time job**
- ■ **Millions suffer from hunger**

It was with these millions of human lives in mind that the bishops of the Second Vatican Council wrote:

There must be made available to all . . . what is necessary to lead a truly human life: food, clothing, and shelter. . . . We must help the poor, and do so not merely out of our abundance. . . .

This sacred Council urges all . . . to remember the early Christian saying . . . "If you don't feed those dying of hunger, you have killed them."
THE CHURCH IN THE MODERN WORLD, 26, 69

This shocking statement jolts us out of our complacency. It makes us realize that when brothers or sisters are dying of hunger, we have a grave obligation to feed them, inasmuch as we are able.

It is against this disturbing background that we take up the fifth commandment God gave Moses at Mount Sinai: "Do not commit murder." CCC 2258–62

THINK about it

If you can't feed a hundred people, feed just one.

Mother Teresa

HISTORICAL Connection

During the Great Depression, New York's former mayor, Fiorello La Guardia, sometimes presided at court.

Once, an unemployed man was brought before him for stealing bread for his family. La Guardia said, "Sir, I'm sorry! The law excepts no one. I fine you $10."

Then La Guardia opened his wallet, gave the man $10, remitted the fine, and levied a 50-cent fine on everyone in the courtroom for living in a city where a person had to steal to feed his family.

The man left the courtroom with tears in his eyes and $47.50 in his pocket.

Retold from *Reflections for Peace of Mind:* Maurice Nassan, S.J.

**Mankind
must put an end to war,
or war
will put an end to mankind.**

John F. Kennedy

Murder

The destruction of innocent human life is one of the gravest crimes a person can commit. No Christian can question this. CCC 2268–69

Every person has a duty to life and a duty to preserve life. This includes the right to kill an unjust aggressor (someone threatening our life), if this is the only way to preserve our own life. CCC 2263–67

War

What is true of individuals is also true of groups, for example, our nation. CCC 2307–17 Thus, from early on, Christians have tolerated war in certain very serious circumstances.

In modern times, however, many Christians are finding it harder and harder to tolerate war.

This is especially the case now that countries are stockpiling nuclear, chemical, and biological weapons.

It was with this in mind that the bishops of the Second Vatican Council said of modern war:

*Any act of war aimed indiscriminately
at the destruction of entire cities or
of extensive areas
along with their population
is a crime against God and [neighbor].
It merits unequivocal
and unhesitating condemnation. . . .*

*The arm's race
is an utterly treacherous trap for
humanity, and one which injures the poor
to an intolerable degree. . . .
It is our clear duty, then, to strain every
muscle as we work for the time
when all war can be completely outlawed
by international consent.*

THE CHURCH IN THE MODERN WORLD, 80–82

As never before, Christians are becoming aware of their responsibility to be peacemakers in the spirit of the Sermon on the Mount:

Happy are those who work for peace; God will call them his children!
MATTHEW 5:9

Suicide

Closely related to taking another's life is taking one's own life. CCC 2280–83 A question arises, however, concerning such actions as hunger strikes, which involve the possibility of taking one's own life. There are three kinds of strikes.

The first kind is where the striker *intends* his death as a means to an important end. In other words, it involves the *direct* killing of oneself. This is gravely wrong, no matter how lofty the motive.

The second kind is where striker does *not* intend his or her death, but will accept it, if necessary.

The third kind is where the striker does *not* intend death, but uses the possibility of death to "push" the other side.

These latter two cases involve *indirect* killing of oneself. We say indirect because in neither case does the striker intend death. In fact, the striker hopes and prays it won't occur. Both cases, therefore, are morally permissible when the importance of the end is proportionate to the risk to the striker's life.

6 *Can you give an example of an end that is "proportionate to the risk to the striker's life"?*

Capital punishment

Sister Helen Prejean wrote a book entitled *Dead Man Walking* upon which the movie of the same title is based. In it she lists a number of cases of people sent to death row and later found to be innocent.

One innocent man was Randall Adams. The Texas Court of Criminal Appeals overturned his murder conviction in 1989 when it was proven that prosecutors fabricated evidence and used the perjured testimony of the actual murderer.

People have tended to view capital punishment as a "last resort" measure taken by society to defend itself against hard-core criminals. Today, however, many Christians are finding capital punishment harder and harder to justify.

First of all, it risks executing the innocent, especially the poor who cannot afford quality defense (over half death-row inmates are minorities, most of whom are poor and poorly represented by counsel).

Second, it tends to erode respect for life and dehumanize all concerned.

Third, it frustrates the primary purpose of punishment: rehabilitation.

Finally, it leads to incredible court delays that diminish its effectiveness as a deterrent (major reason given for justifying it). CCC 2263–67

7 *How do you feel about capital punishment and why?*

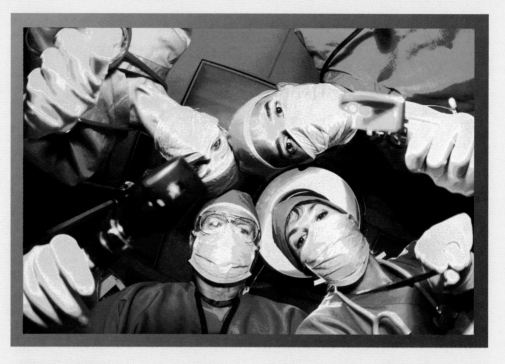

Abortion

A bortion was widespread in ancient pagan society. Early Christian response to abortion was one of militant opposition.

For example, around A.D. 80, the Didache, the oldest known Christian document apart from the Christian Scriptures, says bluntly, "You shall not practice abortion."

Under the influence of Christianity, abortion was eventually outlawed by civil authorities. Not until the twentieth century did it become widespread again.

Today, the Christian response to abortion is still one of militant opposition. CCC 2270–75 This opposition is based on the belief that the fertilized egg will develop into a human person and must therefore be protected. In dealing with the issue of abortion, however, we need to make an important distinction.

First, there is *direct* abortion, which is an action whose direct intent is to kill an unborn fetus. Direct abortion is forbidden by the fifth commandment.

Second, there is *indirect* abortion, which is an action whose direct intention is not to kill the fetus but to save the life of the mother.

For example, let us suppose that to save a pregnant mother's life, a doctor must remove a diseased uterus. The abortion of the fetus that follows indirectly from this operation is totally unwanted and uncontrollable.

To underscore the intent of *indirect* abortion, we might add that every effort to preserve the life of the fetus is made. Removing the uterus in this case is permissible, even though it leads indirectly to the fetus' death.

8 How do you explain the statement that "abortion affects virtually every person in this country to some extent"?

Euthanasia

The word *euthanasia* comes from the Greek word *euthanatos,* which means "easy death." As with abortion, the Christian response to euthanasia is one of militant opposition. CCC 2276–83 But, as with abortion, an important distinction has to be made here.

First, there is direct euthanasia (traditionally referred to as "mercy killing"). This is a deliberate act that brings about the death of someone.

The person is usually someone who is suffering greatly from old age or an incurable illness. Direct euthanasia is always gravely wrong, no matter how noble the motives.

Second, there is what some people refer to as passive euthanasia, which is totally different from direct euthanasia.

It is allowing an aged or incurably ill patient to die naturally, rather than prolonging their death needlessly and indefinitely through the use of *extraordinary* means. In such a situation it is morally permissible to allow the death to occur naturally.

9 *Can you think of a concrete example when so-called "passive euthanasia" would be morally permissible?*

Drugs and alcohol

The danger of alcohol comes when the user abuses or misuses it. CCC 2288–91 It is gravely sinful to deliberately drink to excess, seriously impairing one's ability to function both physically and mentally. The pain and suffering brought on by such irresponsible behavior can be seen daily.

It must be noted, however, that the abuse of alcohol often stems from alcoholism, which the medical profession lists as a disease. Those suffering from this disease have a grave obligation to seek help. Moreover, we have a duty to help them in any way we can.

Related to the abuse of alcohol is the abuse of drugs. Again, the tremendous suffering brought about by drug abuse is one of the horrendous tragedies of our times.

A serious abuse of drugs for mind-altering or recreational purposes is gravely wrong.

As with those who suffer from alcoholism, those who suffer from drug addiction are gravely obliged to seek help, if they are aware of their affliction.

Sixth and ninth commandments

Some people view sex as recreation and sex partners as instruments of pleasure. Today, there is growing rejection of this attitude. More and more, people are agreeing that sex must be responsible: it must be based on love.

But this brings up the question: What is love? In other words, what do we mean when we say of a young husband and wife: "They really love each other deeply"?

10 *How would you answer this question?*

Love versus feeling

There is a lot of confusion about what people mean by love. One writer alludes to part of this confusion, saying that love is not a *feeling* but a commitment.

Feeling
is the high-voltage, circuit-blowing
infatuation we've all experienced
when we connect with someone new.
It is the intoxication
of being accepted and desired.
It is the thrill of taking a leap,
shedding clothes and inhibitions,
being dazzled by the private
magnificence of another. . . .
but in the end, sadly,
it is an emotional sprint. . . .

Commitment,
by contrast, is a marathon of the heart.
It requires training, discipline,
endurance and work.
It is not a spectator sport or an event
whose outcome can be decided in
seconds.

It is pushing up hills and suffering pain
and resisting the temptation to drop out. . . .
When love is viewed as an act of will . . .
it can survive as long as your heart beats.
ART CARNEY

This brings us to the big question: How should we understand the expression *responsible sex?*

11 *How would you answer that question?*

Responsible sex is not yielding to a "circuit-blowing" feeling. It is not taking a "leap" and "shedding inhibitions" because we find each other "exciting."

Nor is it engaging in an "emotional sprint," just to prove to the other that we do really like them very much.

Responsible sex is something much more precious. It is, indeed, "a marathon of the heart." It is the "crown" of a shared commitment that has been won after a journey of mutual discipline, sacrifice, and fidelity.

Responsible sex is a celebration of three great God-given gifts: love, life, and faith.

Sex celebrates love

Responsible sex is a celebration of the mystery of love. It celebrates the flowering of love that is committed to "pushing up hills and suffering pain" as long as the heart beats.

Here we need to keep in mind that sex is not the only expression of love between husband and wife. Rather, it is the *crowning* expression of many expressions of love between the two. These prior expressions take a variety of forms. Saint Paul lists some of them:

Love is patient and kind;
it is not jealous or conceited or proud;
love is not ill-mannered
or selfish or irritable;
love does not keep a record of wrongs;
love is not happy with evil,
but is happy with the truth.
Love never gives up.

1 Corinthians 13:4–7

In other words, Paul is saying that love expresses itself in a multitude of everyday, concrete ways. The crowning expression, however, is the sexual union.

Sex celebrates life

Responsible sex also celebrates the mystery of life. Concerning this point, someone once said that every birth begins with a love story. This is simply another way of describing responsible sex. It is a way of saying that sex joins together in the same loving embrace the two purposes for which God ordained it. God intended the sexual union to be:

■ **Unitive**
■ **Procreative**

THINK
about it

Love your friends and practice on your enemies.

Author unknown

When God
wants a great job done
in the world
or a great wrong righted,
he goes about it
in a very unusual way.

He doesn't stir up his earthquakes
or send forth his thunderbolts.
Instead he has
a helpless baby born,
perhaps in a simple home . . .
[to] some obscure mother.

And then God puts the idea
into the mother's heart,
and she puts it
into the baby's mind.
And then God waits.

E. T. Sullivan

■ *After reading this, what
thoughts occur to you?*

**Lord, help me to see
what I looked like
when you first dreamed of me.**

Author unknown

First, God intended the sexual union to be *unitive.*

This means that God ordained sex to be the way for a married couple to celebrate and strengthen the love bond that unites them.

Second, God intended the sexual union to be *procreative.*

This means that God ordained sex to be the way a married couple cooperates with God to bring new life into the world.

The unitive and the procreative dimensions of the sexual union might be compared to the body and soul of a person.

God joined them together and intended them to work together. In this sense, responsible sex is not just a celebration of love.

It is also a celebration of life.

Sex celebrates faith

Many married couples testify that at the height of sexual union they sometimes soar beyond themselves. They are caught up in an experience that they can only describe as mystical: one that goes to the heart of their marriage.

This "mystical" experience is a deep faith experience of God—especially God's presence in the love bond that unites them.

It is a faith experience of the fact that Jesus blessed the love of a husband and wife in the most remarkable way imaginable. He raised their love to the level of a sacrament. Commenting on this, one author writes:

*In Christian marriage
God covenants with the couple. . . .
God promises to stand by the couple . . .*

*so that they can initiate a union . . .
and bring it to maturity in love.*

LADISLAS ORSY

In brief, then, responsible sex is a "crowning" celebration of God's three greatest gifts: love, life, and faith.

12 *What are some lesser ways you can celebrate these same three gifts?*

Sexual morality

Saint Paul likened the love of a husband for his wife to the mystery of God's love for Israel and Christ's love for his Church. EPHESIANS 5:25–33

It is only against the background of such a mystery that we can appreciate the sixth commandment ("Do not commit adultery") and the ninth commandment ("Do not desire another man's wife").

The traditional teaching of the Catholic Church on responsible sex is rooted in these two commandments. We may sum up this teaching in the following six statements:

1. Sex is a gift from God to be treasured exclusively as the celebration of love, life, and faith between a husband and a wife.

2. Sex involves giving of one's total self to the other. This gift demands such a deep commitment and dedication that it can be made only with the help of the grace that God gives through the sacrament of Marriage.

3. The sexual union between husband and wife must always respect both the unitive and the procreative purposes for which God ordained it.

4. All voluntary sexual activity or pleasure (thoughts, words, and actions) outside of the marriage is objectively and gravely wrong. Subjectively, however, the gravity of an act may be diminished because of circumstances.

For example, someone watching a movie may be caught by surprise by an unanticipated sequence that is sexually exciting. This could result in a powerful sexual reaction that was neither foreseen nor intended.

On the other hand, to watch a movie or read a book simply because it is sexually stimulating and exciting is objectively and gravely wrong.

Finally, we should never forget that God is more compassionate and eager to forgive than we are to ask for forgiveness—no matter how often we fall victim to temptation and sin.

Seventh and tenth commandments

Martin Luther King, Jr., led the struggle for human and civil rights in the United States. A turning point came in 1963 at the Lincoln Memorial in Washington.

There, Dr. King delivered his famous "I Have a Dream" speech. A year later, he was awarded the Nobel Peace Prize. In his acceptance speech, he said:

We have learned
to fly in the air like birds
and to swim in the sea like fish.
But we have not learned
the simple act of living together
as brothers and sisters.

It is only against the background of such a disturbing reality that we can fully appreciate the seventh and tenth commandments (respect for property).

The traditional Catholic teaching on human and civil rights is rooted in these two commandments. It holds that we are all one family under God. And since we are one family, we should treat each other that way.

Treating each other as family means honoring the dignity and the rights of one another as children of God's family. It means treating one another with *justice* and *charity*.

5. Young people, especially, should not lose heart or become discouraged when it comes to the problems and the moral failures they experience in matters related to sex. They should learn to speak maturely and frankly about these problems with a parent, a counselor, or a priest.

6. All Christians should realize that temptations against the sixth and the ninth commandments are not a sign of depravity.

Rather, they are a sign of our humanity and our need for the healing and the forgiveness that Jesus came to bring us.

Self-mastery is a long and exacting work.
One can never consider it acquired
once and for all.
It presupposes renewed effort
at all stages of life.
The effort required
can be more intense in certain periods,
such as when the personality
is being formed during childhood
and adolescence. CCC 2342

Ownership and stewardship

Treating another with *justice* means respecting their right to own property and respecting the property they own. Treating others with *charity* means opening our hearts to those who, for various reasons, do not have adequate material goods for a decent life.

These reasons may be linked to birth: mental limitations, handicaps, sickness, or lack of marketable talents. They may also be linked to culture, such as prolonged exploitation by richer nations. Finally, the reasons may be linked to geography, such as flooding, famine, and limited natural resources.

This brings us to Catholic teaching regarding ownership, stewardship, and the distribution of the material wealth. CCC 2401–14

Jesus recognized that inequality exists when it comes to material wealth. He recognized that some people are more talented and earn more money. Some have more luck and acquire more wealth. Some are simply born into a wealthy family, culture, or country.

But Jesus also made it clear that those who are blessed with wealth have an obligation to help those who are needy. CCC 2443–49 The Parable of Lazarus and the Rich Man makes this clear. LUKE 16:19–31 The Last Judgment narrative leaves no doubt about the gravity of this obligation. MATTHEW 25:31–46

Related to the obligation of those who enjoy material wealth is the responsibility or stewardship of those who operate companies. CCC 2426–36

Catholic teaching has always held the right of companies to make a profit. But it also recognizes the right of workers to make a just wage.

We may sum up Catholic teaching concerning the rights and responsibilities of the workplace in two very general statements:

1. Human labor has always held a special dignity in the Catholic perspective of life.

In the Old Testament, the creation narrative presents God in the role of a worker and an artisan.

And in the New Testament, Jesus himself works as a carpenter for thirty long years. So, too, Saint Paul works as a tent-maker, even while engaged in his preaching ministry.

2. Employers have an obligation to engage in businesses that are moral. In other words, it is morally wrong to engage in prostitution or pornography.

Employers also have an obligation to balance the welfare and needs of employees with their own corporate obligation and right to make a reasonable profit.

Similarly, employees have a moral obligation to work honestly and responsibly for their employers. In other words, they must give a fair day of work for fair pay.

13 *What is your experience concerning the above obligations?*

THINK about it

Life is not lost by dying;
life is lost minute by minute,
day by dragging day,
in a thousand small
uncaring ways.

Stephen Vincent Benet

LIFE Connection

I fear
that we are too concerned
with material things
to remember
that our real strength
lies in spiritual values.

I doubt
there is in
this troubled world today,
a single problem
that could not be solved
if approached in the spirit
of the Sermon on the Mount.

President Harry Truman

Stealing

A camera store in New York City reduced thefts drastically by posting this sign for all customers to see: "Your picture has been taken four times in the last thirty seconds. We have a front view, two side views, and one from the rear."

Stealing is a disturbing problem that stores and banks face. It involves not only customers but also employees.

For example, one reliable survey (documented by lie-detector tests) shows that over 70 percent of store employees and 80 percent of bank employees engage in some form of stealing (often minor).

Technically, stealing may be defined as taking something from another against his or her reasonable will. The phrase "against his or her reasonable will" is important, because it would not be stealing if, for example, we took food to stay alive.

Presumably, the owner of the food would not object if she or he knew of our circumstances. (To object under such circumstances would be "unreasonable.")

The gravity of stealing depends on the:

- **Circumstances involved**
- **Value of what is taken**

An example will clarify what this means. If an employee of a successful business steals five dollars from the cash register, the theft is sinful but not gravely so.

But if the employee intends to continue to steal over a period of time, the thefts can add up to grave matter. CCC 2408

Before we can be forgiven a sin of theft in the sacrament of Reconciliation, we must restore, or intend to restore, what we took. CCC 2487

In rare cases, however, we may be excused from restoring the stolen goods directly to the owner because it would cause hardship substantially graver than that inflicted upon the injured party.

In such rare cases, where it is extremely difficult or impossible to return what we wrongly took, we may give to charity the equivalent of what we stole. CCC 2412, 2487

The willingness to make restitution is a concrete sign of repentance.

14 *What would you recommend to cut down on shoplifting?*

Cheating

A Cornell University study indicates that by the time children today are ten years old they have already developed a "non-condemning attitude" toward cheating. Experts say they pick up this attitude from adults and peers.

Cheating, "whether it be to acquire money, grades, or a scholarship," is doubly sinful. It involves, in some sense, both stealing and lying. We steal and answer from another (stealing) and claim it to be our own (lying).

The gravity of cheating depends on the circumstances of the situation. To knowingly and willingly cheat another out of a scholarship, for example, is clearly a grave sin. CCC 1459 On the other hand, to cheat on a quiz would fall into a lesser category of sinfulness.

15 *What would you recommend to cut down on cheating?*

Gambling

S tate lotteries and betting on sports events are widespread today. They are so widespread that some sources estimate that up to 75 percent of the adult population engages in some form of gambling. We may describe gambling as betting or taking a chance on an uncertain outcome.

When gambling is comfortably within one's means, it may be considered entertainment and, therefore, morally permissible. CCC 2413 But gambling can quickly become immoral when it ceases to be comfortably within our means or out of our control.

When gambling goes beyond our means, it can bring incredible suffering upon people and families. The same is true when gambling ceases to be under our control. When we become aware that it has a compulsive hold on us, we have an obligation to seek help.

Compulsive gambling is so widespread that numerous organizations, like Gamblers Anonymous, have been created to deal with the problem.

Describing the grip that compulsive gambling can hold on us, one person says:

The first time I had a dollar in my pocket
that I could call my own
was when I was forty-six years old.
By that time I had wrecked a business
and put out of work
a couple of hundred people
who depended on me for a living.

16 What are some pros and cons when it comes to state lotteries?

Eighth commandment

Some years back, American and Soviet astronauts docked together 140 miles above the planet Earth. The event made spectacular television coverage.

Yet, a few days later, the *Chicago Tribune* carried a front-page story about people who refused to believe that the event actually took place.

NASA said it was not surprised.

It routinely receives letters from skeptics, like the person who claimed that the first moon walk was "staged on a back lot at Warner Brothers."

17 How do you account for such skepticism?

This brings us to the eighth commandment: "Do not accuse anyone falsely."

This commandment forbids "misrepresenting the truth in our relations with others." CCC 2464, 2482–87

Lying

Human society is built on mutual trust between individuals and nations. Nothing erodes or destroys trust more than lying. When trust breaks down, society breaks down.

The Hebrew Scriptures were especially hard on liars. For example, the Book of Sirach says:

Lying
is an ugly blot on a person's character. . . .
A thief is better than a habitual liar.
SIRACH 20:24–25

Lying is especially destructive when it involves people who have a special claim to our trust, like family or friends.

One of the most destructive forms of lying, however, is lying to oneself. For example, we can deny that we sin. Commenting on the need to be truthful to ourselves, the great poet Shakespeare penned these memorable lines:

This above all— to thine own self be true;
And it must follow, as the night the day,
Thou canst not then be false to any man.
WILLIAM SHAKESPEARE: *HAMLET*

One of the most vicious lies is one that destroys another's good name. Concerning this lie, Shakespeare again writes:

Who steals my purse, steals trash;
'tis something, nothing;
Twas mine, 'tis his,
and has been slave to thousands;

But he that filches from me my name
Robs me of that which not enriches him
And makes me poor indeed.
WILLIAM SHAKESPEARE: *OTHELLO*

A person who injures another's name has an obligation to repair the damage, if possible. But trying to repair the damage is often as difficult as trying to unring a bell.

18 *How might you go about trying to repair the injury to another's good name?*

Detraction

A person's reputation or good name can also be destroyed by detraction. CCC 2477–79 Detraction may be described as broadcasting another's private faults, failures, or sins without sufficient reason.

The most common way this is done is by gossip. A fitting commentary on this sinful practice is this excerpt:

I maim without killing.
I break hearts and ruin lives. . . .
The more I am quoted
the more I am believed. . . .

My victims are helpless. . . .
I topple governments
and wreck marriages. . . .
I make innocent people cry
in their pillows. . . .
I am called Gossip.

Office gossip. Shop gossip. Party gossip. . . .
Before you repeat a story ask yourself:
Is it true? Is it fair? Is it necessary?
If not—SHUT UP. ANONYMOUS

19 *List two or three reasons why you think people engage in gossip.*

Recap

Jesus did not abolish the Ten Commandments, but brought them to fulfillment and redefined them in terms of love:

- **God**   **Commandments 1–3**
- **Neighbor**   **Commandments 4–10**

In redefining them in terms of love, Jesus gave them a new focus and transformed them into—

- **Signs**   **Of his love for us**
- **Invitations**   **To love as he loved us**
- **Guides**   **On how to love**

The latter seven commandments deal with matters relating to love of self and neighbor in areas of reverence for:

- **Authority**   **Commandment 4**
- **Life**   **Commandments 5, 6, 9**
- **Truth**   **Commandment 8**
- **Property**   **Commandments 7, 10**

Review

1 Explain briefly how love acts as a (a) sign, (b) invitation, (c) guide.

2 Briefly explain when we have a right and an obligation to oppose civil authority.

3 Explain (a) when it is permissible to kill in self-defense, (b) why Christians are finding it harder to justify capital punishment.

4 Using the example of a hunger strike, explain (a) the difference between direct and indirect taking of one's life, (b) when the indirect taking of one's life is permissible.

5 Explain the difference between (a) direct abortion and indirect abortion, (b) direct euthanasia and passive euthanasia, and when they are permissible.

6 List and briefly explain (a) when the misuse of drugs or alcohol is gravely sinful, (b) the twofold end of the sexual union, (c) the six statements that summarize traditional Catholic teaching on responsible sex.

7 Explain briefly what it means to treat another with (a) justice and (b) charity; and give three reasons that may keep people from having the adequate material needs for a decent life.

8 List and explain (a) the technical definition of stealing, (b) the two factors that determine the gravity of stealing, (c) restitution and when we are obliged to make it.

9 Explain (a) when cheating becomes gravely sinful, (b) two conditions that make gambling immoral, (c) the difference between lying and detraction, (d) the obligation we have to repair this injury from lying or detraction.

Reflect

1 Sexual curiosity, questions, and fantasies can plague us. The healthy way to deal with these common problems is to discuss them with a counselor or confessor. But the Internet is easier. At first, we are tempted to explore everything available, rationalizing that we're "educating" ourselves. Inevitably, however, it ends up generating all kinds of problems.

■ *How serious a problem among your friends is Internet pornography?*
■ *What advice would you give a friend who is concerned about spending a lot of time visiting unhealthy sites on the Internet?*
■ *Why do these unhealthy sites tend to erode faith?*

2 A high school boy was working for a drugstore. He got caught stealing. He writes:

The owner called my parents
and I got killed.
Worse yet, they won't trust me anymore.
How can I get my parents
to believe me and to trust me again?
I just don't feel like I belong
if I'm not trusted.
I want to be trusted again,
but how do I go about it?

■ *If this student were a friend, what advice would you give him?*
■ *Recall a time when something similar happened to you.*

3 A report in *USA Today* says that "alcohol claims 100,000 lives a year" and costs our nation "more than $117 billion a year in everything from medical bills to loss of time in the work place." Commenting on ancient abuse of alcohol, poet William Shakespeare said:

O God.
That man should put an enemy
in their mouths to steal away their brain.

■ *On a scale of one (not much) to seven (very much), how big a problem is alcohol abuse among your friends? Drug abuse?*

4 A survey of over one hundred universities showed that over half of the students cheated regularly. Even more alarming was that they seldom had any sense of wrongdoing. This raises a question: Besides being against the seventh commandment, why is cheating wrong?

■ *Answer on an unsigned sheet of paper: (a) how often you cheat on quizzes: (i) never, (ii) occasionally, (iii) whenever the opportunity arises; (b) why you cheat.*
■ *On a scale of one (not very) to ten (very), how guilty do you feel when you cheat? Explain.*

PRAYER TIME
with the Lord

May the Lord bless you.
May he make you
glad you are alive,
because it gives you a chance
to love and to look at the stars.

May you be satisfied
with what you have,
but never with what you are.

May you despise nothing
in this world
except falsehood and meanness.

May you be governed always
by your admirations,
and never by your irritations.

May you desire nothing
that is another's,
except their gentleness of spirit
and greatness of heart.

May you think
kindly of your enemies,
often of your friends,
and every day of Jesus Christ.

And may Almighty God
bless you now and forever,
in the name of the Father, and
of the Son, and of the Holy Spirit. M.L.

■ *Compose a blessing for a very special person in your life.*

PRAYER Journal

Albert Schwietzer was a concert pianist who gave up his career in music to become a missionary doctor in Africa. He once said,

It's not enough to say,
"I'm a good father.
I'm a good husband." . . .

You must do something . . .
for those who have need of help,
something for which you get no pay
but the privilege of doing it.

For remember,
you don't live in a world all your own.
Your brothers and sisters are here too.

■ *List one or two concrete things you have done recently to help (a) your family or a family member, (b) someone outside your circle of family and friends.*

SCRIPTURE Journal

1	Lying	Ezekiel 13:6–16
2	Cheating	Amos 8:4–10
3	Stealing	Exodus 22:1–14
4	Illicit sex	Deuteronomy 22:13–30
5	Adultery	John 8:1–11

■ *Pick one of the above passages. Read it prayerfully and write out a brief statement to Jesus expressing your feelings about it.*

Discerning Love

Gentiles do not have the Law;
but whenever they do by instinct
what the Law commands . . .
their conduct shows
that what the Law commands
is written in their hearts.

*Their consciences
also show that this is true,
since their thoughts sometimes accuse
them and sometimes defend them.*
ROMANS 2:14–15

*All of us—from a talk-show host
to a student—have something in
common. Each has a nobler
person within them.
The proof? When we are
tempted to do wrong, the nobler
person speaks up. The name we give
to that nobler person
is "Conscience."*

Conscience

Bubba Smith was a pro football star. In the early 1980s he became famous for his beer commercials: "Tastes great! . . . Less filling!" In October 1985, Michigan State honored Bubba by making him the grand marshal of their homecoming parade.

Bubba was thrilled to be back at his alma mater. As he rode through the student-lined streets, one side started shouting, "Tastes great," and the other side shouted back, "Less filling." Bubba smiled broadly.

But then Bubba became deeply disturbed. He saw that a number of students were "drunk out of their heads."

That experience did it! Bubba quit making beer commercials. The decision cost him a small fortune, but he thought something greater was at stake.

1 *What was the "something greater" that "was at stake" in Bubba's case?*

All of us have experienced what Bubba did. It is an "inner voice" speaking to us in the depths of our being. It is our conscience. Cardinal John Henry Newman described our conscience in these words:

It praises,
it blames, it promises, it threatens. . . .
It is more than man's own self.
The man himself has no power over it,
or only with extreme difficulty;
he may not make it,
he cannot destroy it,
he may refuse to use it, but it remains.
Its very existence
throws us out of ourselves,
to go see him in the heights and depths,
whose Voice it is.
APOLOGIA PRO VITA SUA

2 *In what sense may we speak of conscience as God's "voice"?*

Responding to the conscience

Our conscience is a judgment of our reason. It empowers us to determine whether a certain act is morally good or evil. And it obliges us to follow faithfully its verdict.

If we are to hear and follow the voice of conscience, we must place ourselves in God's presence, and listen. Saint Augustine puts it this way:

Return to your conscience, question it. . . . Turn inward . . . and in everything you do, see God as your witness.

When we make every effort to hear the "voice" of conscience clearly and correctly, we have *both* the *obligation* and the *right* to follow the judgment of our conscience. The Church assures us:

Man has the right to act in conscience and in freedom so as personally to make moral decisions.

He must not be forced to act contrary to his conscience.
Nor must he be prevented from acting according to his conscience."
VATICAN II, *DIGNITATIS HUMANAE*

Let us now take a look at the process of moral decision making. It will show how our conscience and the Church's authority work together.

Moral decision making

A 15-year-old boy and his father were driving past a tiny airport in Ohio. Suddenly, a low-flying plane spun out of control and nose-dived onto the runway. The boy yelled, "Dad! Dad! Stop the car!"

Minutes later, the boy was pulling the pilot out of the plane. It was the boy's twenty-year-old friend. He had been practicing takeoffs and landings. He died in the boy's arms.

That night, the boy was too crushed to eat supper. He went to his room, closed the door, and lay on his bed. He had been working part-time in a drugstore. Every penny he made he spent on flying lessons. His goal was to get his pilot's license when he turned 16.

The boy's parents wondered what effect the tragedy would have on his decision to continue flying. They discussed it with him, but they told him that the decision had to be his.

3 *Recall a time when your parents left a final decision up to you.*

Avery Dulles

Avery Dulles was the son of John Foster Dulles, Secretary of State under President Eisenhower. A convert to Catholicism, Avery became a Jesuit priest. He writes:

*The search for God
can appropriately begin
from a reflection
on the voice of conscience.*

*Anyone who has experienced
the fact of moral obligation
has the makings of a belief in God
and has the prerequisites
for hearing God's word fruitfully.*

*But the hearing of that word
will not result in faith
unless it is accompanied
by prayer.*

Quoted in *How Can I Find God?*
edited by James Martin

Two days later the boy's mother noticed an open notebook in her son's room. It was one he had kept from childhood. Across the top of the page was written, "The Character of Jesus." Beneath it was listed a series of qualities:

- **Jesus was humble**
- **Jesus was a champion of the poor**
- **Jesus was unselfish**
- **Jesus was close to his Father**

The mother realized that in her son's hour of decision he was turning to prayer and to Jesus for guidance. Later, she asked him what he had decided. He responded, "With God's help, I must continue to fly."

That boy was Neil Armstrong. And on July 20, 1969, he became the first human being to walk on the moon.

The millions of people who watched him on television had no idea that one reason why he was walking on the moon was Jesus. They had no idea that it was from Jesus that he drew the strength and guidance to make the decision that was responsible for what he was now doing.

The story of Neil Armstrong illustrates an important point. Responsible moral decisions are not always easy to make. There are times when we are not sure what love invites us to do. When such a decision arises, we should do what Neil Armstrong did. We should:

- **Consult Jesus' teaching**
- **Seek competent advice**
- **Pray for guidance**

Three kinds of decisions

In general, there are three different kinds of moral decisions. We may describe them as:

- **Clear-cut decisions**
- **Clouded decisions**
- **Contrary decisions**

A *clear-cut* decision is one in which it is clear what we must do. A *clouded* decision is one in which the right decision is not clear to all. A *contrary* decision is one that involves acting contrary to traditional authority

4 *Cite an example to illustrate each kind of decision.*

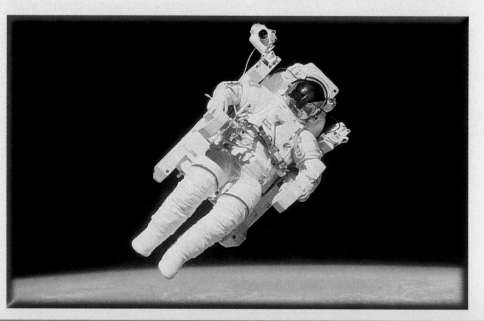

Clear-cut decisions

The movie *A Man for All Seasons* is based on the life of Saint Thomas More. He rose to prominence when King Henry VII appointed him chancellor of England in 1529. But tragedy soon struck his life.

Henry divorced his queen and remarried. To combat civil and religious opposition to his remarriage, he ordered high dignitaries of the state to sign a document swearing that the marriage was valid.

Henry also let it be known that if they refused to sign the document, they would be tried for treason.

A dramatic scene occurred when Lord Norfolk asked Thomas More to sign. When he refused, Norfolk appealed to him to reconsider in the light of his love for his family and his friends.

But Thomas More knew that a more important love was at stake: his love of God. He could not swear to something he knew to be false.

Shortly afterward, he was arrested, imprisoned for 15 months in the Tower of London, and then executed for treason.

The decision More faced was as clear-cut as it was difficult. He was aware of the facts of the case. He knew the Church's teaching on divorce and remarriage. He knew what God's love invited him to do.

Meeting the challenge

More's greatest need, therefore, was for the moral courage to do what his conscience told him he must do.

The role that prayer played in More's decision is clear from a letter he wrote to his daughter Meg. In it he described what he would do if fear threatened his resolve:

I shall remember how Saint Peter
at a blast of wind began to sink
because of his lack of faith,
and I shall do as he did:
call upon Christ. . . .

And then I trust
he shall place his holy hand on me
and in the stormy seas
hold me up from drowning.
And therefore my dear daughter,
do not let your mind be troubled.

The first kind of moral decision, therefore, is one that is clear-cut. It is one in which it is perfectly obvious what we must do.

Such a decision, however, can be extremely hard to make because it can exact such a great personal price from us, as it did for Thomas More. As such, it requires great moral courage.

5 *Can you give examples to illustrate the difference between moral courage and physical courage? Which would be the harder for you? Explain.*

PRAYER hotline

O God,
grant me
the serenity
to accept what cannot
be changed,
the courage to change
what can be changed,
and the wisdom
to know the difference.

Reinhold Niebuhr (adapted for AA use)

THINK about it

The strength of a man consists in finding out the way God is going, and going that way.

Henry Ward Beecher

All of us—whether we are a child, an astronaut, or the Holy Father himself—have something remarkable in common. As noble as we may be, we have a "nobler person" within us.

When we are tempted to do something less than noble, the nobler person "speaks" to us. The name we give to this "nobler person" is *Conscience.*

The "voice" of our conscience speaks to us in our most inner core or "sanctuary" of our being. It calls us to love, to do what is good and avoid what is evil. When we listen to it, in a real sense, we hear God "speaking" to us through it.

■ *In what sense do we hear God speaking to us through our conscience?*

Clouded decisions

When Hitler came to power in Nazi Germany, Franz Jäger-statter was a young Austrian farmer. He had a wife and two small children.

Franz also had the distinction of being the only man in his village to vote against Austria's political merger with Nazi Germany.

In February 1943, Franz was ordered to report for military service in the German army. He faced a dilemma. How could he fight in what he believed to be an immoral war?

Franz consulted his parish priest and his bishop. Both suggested the possibility of serving in the medical corps. It would excuse him from bearing arms.

But Franz felt that just wearing a uniform could be interpreted as a sign that he approved of the Nazis and the war.

When a state-appointed lawyer asked Franz why he was having such a problem with military service, when millions of German Christians had no problem, he responded:

I guess they don't have the grace to see it. But I do have the grace to see it, so I cannot serve in the army.

So it happened that, after pondering Jesus' teaching, seeking competent advice, and praying for guidance, Franz felt compelled to follow his own conscience.

On August 9, 1943, Franz was executed. History has since honored him as a hero and a saint.

Franz's decision is a good example of what is meant by a clouded decision. Commenting on this kind of decision the *Catechism of the Catholic Church* says:

Man is sometimes confronted by situations that make moral judgments less assured and decisions difficult. But he must always seriously seek what is right and good and discern the will of God expressed in divine law.

To this purpose, man strives to interpret the data of experience and the signs of the times assisted by the virtue of prudence, by the advice of competent people, and by the help of the Holy Spirit and his gifts. CCC 1787–88

6 *Why do/don't you think Franz made the right decision?*

Consider yet another example, closer to home, of a *clouded* decision.

The case of Granny

Imagine you are the mother of three children, ages six, nine, and eleven. Your eighty-eight-year-old grand-mother lives with you. She is mentally alert and loved by your children.

But she has severe arthritis and is beginning to need more and more attention. It is also making her more and more demanding. This is starting to take its toll on you, your husband, and the children.

One day, after a very trying experience, your husband reluctantly suggests it might be time to move Granny to a

Contrary decisions

The most difficult and serious moral decision of all is one that puts us at odds with the traditional moral teaching of the Church on a particular point. To illustrate why it is so serious, consider two of Jesus' statements to his disciples:

I tell you, Peter: you are rock,
and on this rock foundation
I will build my church. . . .

I will give you
the keys of the Kingdom of heaven;
what you prohibit on earth
will be prohibited in heaven,
and what you permit on earth
will be permitted in heaven.
MATTHEW 16:18–19

home that offers assisted living. Now, you are faced with a clouded moral decision. It is not clear what love invites you do.

The correct procedure for making such a decision is to follow the three steps mentioned earlier. You should:

■ **Ponder the Church's teaching**
■ **Pursue competent advice**
■ **Pray for guidance**

The second step in this process is especially critical in Granny's case. It involves consulting not only with Granny and the children, but also with professionals, like the family doctor, and your pastor.

Once you have taken these three steps, you may choose with a clear conscience whatever your intellectual judgment, guided by grace, seems to indicate.

7 *Create a list of pros and cons for assisted living in Granny's case. What advice and guidance will you seek?*

On another occasion, Jesus makes this statement to his disciples:

I have much more to tell you,
but now it would be too much
for you to bear.
When, however, the Spirit comes,
who reveals the truth about God,
he will lead you into all truth.
JOHN 16:12–13

These two passages illustrate why a moral decision that is contrary to the official teaching of the Church is so serious. It is because of the twofold charism that Jesus bestowed upon his Church.

First, he authorized and empowered his Church to teach in his name. Second, he assured his Church that the Holy Spirit would guide it in its teaching role.

In other words, to act contrary to the official teaching of the Church is to act in opposition to the twofold charism that Jesus bestowed upon it.

Having said this, however, we must understand that the Church is made up of human beings, and the Holy Spirit guides it accordingly.

This means that the Holy Spirit does not short-circuit human intelligence, insight, and learning. The Holy Spirit guides the Church in keeping with the laws of human nature.

Thus, it happens that the Church receives clarity on certain moral and doctrinal matters gradually and by stages.

Two levels of Church teaching

Because the Church does not enjoy the same clarity on all moral and doctrinal matters, it teaches at different levels.

At one level, the Church teaches as one with full certitude. For example, when it teaches that the Eucharist is really the Body of Christ, it does so with absolute certainty.

Consequently, we give this teaching a full *faith assent*. If we did not, we would no longer be Catholic. CCC 891

At the second level, the Church teaches as one possessing less than absolute certitude on a particular matter. A kind of biblical parallel to this second-level teaching occurs in Paul's First Letter to the Corinthians. He writes:

Now, concerning what you wrote
about unmarried people:
I do not have a command from the Lord,
but I give my opinion as one
who by the Lord's mercy
is worthy of trust. 1 CORINTHIANS 7:25

An example of this level of teaching is one "that leads to a better understanding of Revelation in matters of faith and morals." To this level of teaching, we must give a *religious assent*. CCC 892

The Church has the responsibility to give guidance on moral issues—just as Paul had the responsibility to give guidance to the Corinthians on a question that was bothering them.

Likewise, we have the responsibility to give *religious assent* to these teachings

of the Church. Giving a *religious assent* means we accept the reliability of the Church's teaching.

It was Jesus himself who authorized his Church to teach in his name, and assured it that the Holy Spirit would guide it in its teaching role. For these two religious reasons, we accept the reliability of this teaching—hence, the expression "religious assent."

Forming our conscience

Nonetheless, the Church also teaches that individuals have not only a right, but also an obligation to form our own moral conscience in accord with right reason and divine law.

A human being must always obey the certain judgment of his conscience. If he were deliberately to act against it, he would condemn himself. CCC 1790

The Church also recognizes that we could make an "erroneous judgment" in forming conscience. CCC 1790–94 Such an error could result from either:

- ■ **Vincible ignorance   Our fault**
- ■ **Invincible ignorance   Not our fault**

Vincible ignorance can occur when we "take little trouble to find out what is true and good." It can also occur when, through sin, we allow our conscience to become "blind" to truth. In both of these cases, we are morally responsible for the evil we commit.

Invincible ignorance occurs when an "erroneous judgment" is not due to our fault. For example, it could be due to incorrect information given us by another.

If this be the case, we are not responsible for the error. In other words, we are not guilty of any sin when we do what we thought was morally right.

Nonetheless, it remains an evil or disorder. It becomes important, therefore, to "work to correct errors of moral conscience." CCC 1793

In conclusion, to act contrary to the Church's moral teaching is a grave matter. For it means we act in opposition to the twofold teaching charism that Jesus bestowed on his Church to assist its teaching ministry.

It is also a grave matter because it is so easy for us to delude ourselves into believing what we would like to believe.

The Church's teaching is a "light for our path," given to us by Jesus himself. Therefore, we should strive by faith, study, and prayer to make it a part of our every moral decision. CCC 1802

LIFE Connection

At one point in the movie, *The Alamo,* "showdown time" comes and the defenders have to vote their consciences. John Wayne stands up and says:

Now I might sound like a Bible-beater yelling up a revival at a river-crossing camp-meeting, but that don't change the truth none.

There's a right and there's wrong. You gotta do one or the other. You do the one and you're living. You do the other, and you may be walking around but you're dead as a beaver hat.

■ *Describe a time in your life when "showdown time" came, and you had to choose between the hard right and the easy wrong.*

Recap

Moral decision making has to do with deciding what is the morally right thing to do in a given situation.

A *clear-cut* decision is like the one Thomas More had to make. A *clouded* decision is like the one Franz Jägerstatter had to make. A *contrary* decision is one that puts us at odds with the twofold charism that Jesus bestowed on his Church.

The Church teaches at two levels. At one level, the Church teaches as one having full certitude on a matter. Consequently, we give this teaching a full *faith assent*.

At the second level, the Church teaches as one possessing less than absolute certitude on a particular matter. We give this teaching a *religious assent*. That is, we accept the reliability of this teaching because Jesus gave to his Church the charism (gift) to teach in his name and the assurance that the Holy Spirit would assist it.

Nevertheless, the Church teaches that we have the right and the obligation to form our moral conscience in accord with right reason and divine law.

The Church also recognizes that we may make an "erroneous judgment" in forming our conscience. CCC 1790-94 Such an error could result from vincible ignorance (our fault) or invincible ignorance (not our fault).

In the latter case, we would not be morally responsible for the evil we commit. It nonetheless remains an evil and we need to work to correct it.

Review

1 List, briefly explain, and give an example of the following moral decisions: (a) clear-cut, (b) clouded, (c) contrary.

2 List and briefly explain, the threefold procedure for making a clouded decision.

3 List and briefly explain the twofold charism Jesus bestowed upon his Church to assist it in its teaching ministry.

4 List and briefly explain (a) the two levels at which the Church teaches, (b) the kinds of assent we must give to each level.

5 List and briefly explain (a) the two kinds of "erroneous judgments" that could result from forming our conscience, (b) which one we would not be morally responsible for and why.

6 List and briefly explain the twofold reasons why acting contrary to the official moral teaching of the Church is a grave matter.

Reflect

1 The *Louisville Courier-Journal* carried a story about a seven-year-old who accidentally swallowed a crayon while playing on a school bus. It lodged in the windpipe and was slowly choking the child.

Seeking a speedier ride to the hospital, the driver tried to flag down a motorist. When no one stopped, the driver blocked the traffic lane, forcing the next car to stop. The motorist replied, "I don't want to be late for work."

When the child finally reached the hospital, surgery was ordered. But it was just minutes too late to save the youngster.

■ *Into which of the three groups of moral decisions did the motorist's decision fall? Explain.*

2 You are the mother of three children, ages five, seven, and nine. Your eldest has a poor self-image and needs a lot of support. Your husband Bob spends about 10 hours a day at the office just to make ends meet. You are offered an excellent 40-hour-a-week job.

■ *Why would/wouldn't you take the job?*

3 Bill Quinlan and his 18-year-old nephew David sailed out of San Diego Harbor for Ecuador. Ten days later, a tropical hurricane destroyed their sailboat, leaving them with a rubber raft that began losing air.

It became clear that the two together had no chance of survival. Bill scratched a message to his wife and children on an empty water can. Then he handed his wedding ring to David, saying, "Give this to my son when he's old enough to understand." David accepted the ring, too exhausted to argue.

Bill slipped into the water and swam off. David became overwhelmed with guilt and began to cry hysterically. Then he lapsed into a deep sleep. Sometime later a fishing boat spotted him and picked him up.

■ *Granted that Bill's action was courageous, was he guilty of suicide? Explain.*

■ *In which of the three groups of moral decisions did Bill Quinlan's action fall?*

PRAYER TIME
with the Lord

Father, grant that I may be a bearer
of Christ Jesus, your Son.
Allow me to warm
the often cold, impersonal scene
of modern life
with your burning love.

Strengthen me, by your Holy Spirit,
to carry out my mission
of changing the world or
some definite part of it, for the better. . . .

Make me more energetic
in setting to right
what I find wrong in the world
instead of complaining
about it or myself.

Nourish in me a practical desire
to build up rather than tear down,
to reconcile more than polarize,
to go out on a limb,
rather than crave security.

Never let me forget
that it is far better to light one candle
than to curse the darkness,
and to join my light, one day, with yours.
CHRISTOPHER PRAYER: AUTHOR UNKNOWN

■ *What are one or two things I have complained about recently?*
■ *What might I do to set these things right, rather than complain about them?*

PRAYER Journal

Pearl S. Buck won the Nobel Prize in literature for her novel *The Good Earth*. Deeply concerned about the direction of our nation, she wrote:

*This country is divided into two halves:
the people who build,
and the people who break down.*

*It's time for each of us to stand up and
be counted on the side of the people
who add to our spiritual health
rather than subtract from it.*

*Each day things happen
which make the wheel turn.
And it's up to each one of us
which way it goes.*

■ *Compose a prayer asking for the courage to stand up and be counted on the side of people who build, not tear down.*

_____

_____

_____

_____

_____

_____

_____

_____

_____

_____

SCRIPTURE Journal

1	Clear-cut decision	1 Corinthians 5
2	Clouded decision	1 Corinthians 8
3	Clouded decision	Romans 14
4	Postponing a decision	Acts 5:27–39
5	Landmark decision	Acts 15:1–21

■ *Pick one of the above passages. Read it prayerfully and write out a brief statement to Jesus expressing your feelings about it.*

_____

_____

_____

_____

_____

22
Witnessing to Love

Since we are surrounded
by so great a cloud of witnesses,
let us rid ourselves
of every burden and sin that clings to us
and persevere in running the race
that lies before us
while keeping our eyes fixed on Jesus,
the leader and perfecter of faith. . . .

Strive for . . . that holiness
without which no one will see the Lord.
HEBREWS 12:1–2, 14 NAB

*Early Christians
referred to one another as "saints,"
but not in a self-righteous way.
Rather, they did it in the sense that
this was what they were called to be.
A saint is simply someone who
follows the Gospel invitation
to live and love as Jesus did.*

CHAPTER
at a Glance

Saints today
Saints are models
Saints are witnesses

Two kinds of saints
Canonized saints
Communion of saints

Queen of all saints
Mother of God
Immaculate Conception
Assumption of Mary
Apparitions of Mary

Model saint
Spirit of service
Spirit of prayer

Saints today

The catacombs were underground burial places used by early Roman Christians. They consisted of a maze of underground passageways cut through soft clay that hardened when exposed to the air.

The sides of the passageways contained "shelf graves," in which the dead were buried one on top of the other. Early Roman Christians also met in the catacombs to celebrate Mass together.

Some years ago, five boys were playing in a catacomb outside Rome. Suddenly, the battery in their flashlight died. For two days they groped about in darkness in the passageways which went off in various directions like an underground road system.

Then one of the boys felt a smooth path running along the rough floor of the passageway. He reasoned that it had been worn smooth by the feet of ancient Christians filing in and out of the tunnels for Mass. The boys followed the path. It led to safety.

This story might be used as a kind of parable to illustrate the fact that saints who lived centuries ago can still serve as guides for modern Christians.

1 *What are some examples of how saints of centuries ago serve as guides to us today?*

After Francis was released, it took him a good year to regain his health. Then he left the wealthy surroundings of his family, put on a peasant's garb, and set out to find God. His new home was an abandoned church on the outskirts of Assisi. There he spent hours alone in prayer.

Two biblical teachings, especially, began to haunt Francis. The first was that every person is created in God's image. The second was that whatever we do for the least person, we do for Jesus himself. MATTHEW 25:45

Saints are models

Saint Francis of Assisi was born into a wealthy Italian family. As a youth, he was free-spirited and somewhat irresponsible.

In 1202 he became a soldier and marched off to battle. He was taken prisoner and spent the next year of his life in prison. That experience changed his outlook on life forever.

2 *Why would such an experience change someone's whole outlook on life?*

As a result of profound meditation on these two teachings, Francis developed a deep love for the outcasts of society.

One day, he came upon a leper. Although Francis had a dreadful fear of leprosy, he embraced the man. This moving incident dramatized the extent to which the teachings of Jesus had taken root in his heart.

Not long afterward, Francis was attending Mass. The Gospel reading recalled Jesus' instruction to his disciples to go forth into the surrounding towns to preach the Good News. Jesus told his disciples not to take any money with them, but to trust in God for their material needs. MATTHEW 10:5–15

This instruction touched Francis deeply. He lived in a time like our own, when people were drifting from the teachings of Jesus. So Francis went forth into the towns of Italy to preach the Gospel anew.

HISTORICAL
Connection

Ultimately, Francis attempted no more than to live out the teachings of Christ and the Spirit of the Gospel.

His identification with Christ was so intense that in 1224, while praying . . . he received the "stigmata," the physical marks of Christ's passion. . . .

He died October 3, 1226. His feast is observed on October 4.

Robert Ellsberg: *All Saints*

SAINT FRANÇOIS D'ASSISE

His charismatic personality inspired other young people to follow his example. And so it happened that the Franciscan order was born.

3 *What passage or story in Scripture ranks as one of your favorites? What do you like about the story?*

Saints are witnesses

Besides being guides and models for us to follow and imitate, saints are witnesses of what we are called to be.

In the novel *Anthony Adverse*, Hervey Allen says of Francis and of other faith-witnesses like him:

*Brother Francis and his kind . . .
have always made Christianity
a dangerous religion.
Just when the Church
is about to be taken as a decorative
and snugly woven cocoon . . .
poof!—that cocoon bursts
and the beautiful psyche
of Christianity emerges.*

4 *What do you think Hervey means by "beautiful psyche of Christianity"?*

A saint may be described as a person who follows the Gospel's invitation to love and live as Jesus did.

A saint is a living witness to the fact that God's grace can work miracles in us, if we but open our hearts to it.

Two kinds of saints

The word "saint" derives from the Latin word *sanctus,* which means "holy." Literally, the word *saint* means "holy one" and is translated that way in some Bibles.

The words *holy one* recall God's command: "Keep yourselves holy, because I am holy." LEVITICUS 11:44

Early Christians referred to one another as "saint." They did this not in a smug, self-righteous sense, but in the sense that this was what they are *called* to be.

Thus, we find the word *saints* used over sixty times in the New Testament. Saint Paul used it frequently in the salutation of his letters. An example is his Letter to the Colossians:

Paul, an apostle of Christ Jesus
by the will of God,
and Timothy our brother,
to the holy ones . . . in Colossae:
grace to you and peace from
God our Father. Colossians 1:1–2 NAB

Canonized saints

With the passage of time, however, the word *saint* was reserved exclusively for those Christians who were martyred for their faith or who had lived extraordinary, holy lives.

At first, a person was declared to be a saint by those who had seen the person martyred or who had witnessed the person's holy life.

Around the year 1000, Pope John XV set up a more exacting and objective process for declaring a person a saint. Called *canonization*, it involves an investigation of every aspect of a person's life. CCC 828, 1173

Communion of Saints

A question that people not of the Catholic faith sometimes have is this: "Why do you Catholics pray to saints? Why don't you pray directly to God?"

5 *How would you respond to these two questions?*

Catholics do pray directly to God in every Mass celebrated daily in every nation throughout the world. No relationship is more important than our relationship with God.

But our relationship with one another is also tremendously important. We profess this since earliest Christian times in the Apostle's Creed: "I believe in . . . the communion of saints." This phrase refers to two things:

Many rural villages in India are totally without electricity. People use tiny oil lamps, much like those used in Jesus' time, to light their homes.

The temple in one of these rural villages has a large frame hanging from its ceiling. Cut into the frame are a hundred slots into which tiny oil lamps can be placed.

When the people go to the temple after dark, they carry their oil lamps from their homes to guide them through the darkness.

Upon arriving in the temple, they place the lamp in one of the slots in the frame. By the time the last villager arrives, the darkness of the temple has been transformed into a glorious sea of light.

■ *What important spiritual point does this story make?*
■ *What might it be saying to our world, right now?*

THINK
about it

The blood of martyrs is the seed of the Church.

Tertullian

First, it refers to the three groups that make up the Church, those members:

- ■ On earth
- ■ In purgatory
- ■ In heaven

- ■ In pilgrimage
- ■ In purification
- ■ In perfection

Second, it refers to the "spiritual gifts" that the members of the Church share in common:

- ■ Love for God and one another
- ■ Sacraments, especially the Eucharist
- ■ Readiness to share with the needy
- ■ Praying for one another

In brief, the phrase "communion of saints" refers to: a communion of "persons" (*sancti*) and a communion of "gifts" (*sancta*). CCC 946–62

Queen of all saints

From the dawn of Christianity, one saint has stood out above all others. That saint is Mary, the mother of Jesus. CCC 494–95, 721–26 Mary's specialness flows from the fact that God chose her to be the mother of Jesus:

NARRATOR   *God sent the angel Gabriel to a town in Galilee named Nazareth.*

He had a message for a young woman promised in marriage to a man named Joseph, who was a descendant of King David. Her name was Mary.

ANGEL   *Peace be with you! The Lord is with you and has greatly blessed you!*

NARRATOR   *Mary was deeply troubled by the angel's message . . .*

ANGEL   *Don't be afraid, Mary; God has been gracious to you. You will become pregnant and give birth to a son, and you will name him Jesus. . . .*

MARY   *I am a virgin. How, then, can this be?*

ANGEL   *The Holy Spirit will come on you, and God's power will rest upon you. For this reason the holy child will be called the Son of God. . . .*

MARY   *I am the Lord's servant, may it happen to me as you have said.*
LUKE 1:26–31, 34–35, 38

Mother of God

Mary's words, "I am a virgin," testify to her virginity. CCC 496–507 The child she conceived in her womb was not of human origin, but of the Holy Spirit. Thus, Mary is traditionally referred to as the "Virgin Mother of God."

6 *How can Mary, a human person, be called "Mother of God" in the literal sense of the title?*

The title "Mother of God" does not mean that Mary is God's mother from all eternity. It simply means that Jesus is God *according to the flesh*. It is in this sense that we honor Mary with the title "Mother of God." CCC 495, 507

Historically, the title "Mother of God" dates from the Council of Ephesus, A.D. 431. The council faced the problem of declaring that Jesus had two natures (divine and human) but was not two persons, as some theologians erroneously taught.

In stressing that Jesus was only "one" person, the council added that Mary, therefore, could be called the Mother of God. For, indeed, Jesus is God *according to the flesh*. CCC 495

Immaculate Conception

Catholics also honor Mary under the title "Immaculate Conception." To understand this title, we need to recall that the first sin "flawed" the human race. We refer to this flawed condition as the state of original sin. CCC 390–400

The title "Immaculate Conception" expresses Catholic belief, handed down by tradition, that, from the instant of her existence as a human person, God preserved Mary from original sin in preparation for her calling to be the mother of Jesus. CCC 488–94

Tradition also teaches that Mary remained sinless throughout her life. CCC 411 She was "most blessed of all women." LUKE 1:42 In the words of the poet William Wordsworth, she is "our tainted nature's solitary boast."

Assumption of Mary

One of the Marian feasts celebrated in the Church is that of the Assumption. This feast celebrates Catholic belief—handed down by tradition—that Mary was taken up to heaven at the end of her life in the totality of her person. CCC 966

In other words, she went directly from an earthly state to a heavenly state, without her body undergoing decay, the penalty of sin. GENESIS 3:19 Belief in Mary's assumption is a corollary of her Immaculate Conception. Because she was sinless, she did not fall under its penalty.

Mary's assumption is a beautiful reminder that we are all destined to be in heaven someday in the totality of our person, soul and body, just as Mary is now. CCC 966

Connection

Marine Cyril J. O'Brien tells the following story:

*In my missal
there's a holy picture
to remind me
always to say a prayer
for the man who left it for me—
a Japanese
whom I saw only once,
as he died on Guam.*

*He was trying
to sneak into a bunker
behind a little knoll.
A patrol flushed him
and two companions
from the thicket.*

*They ran into us and were killed.
As a matter of routine,
the Marines searched them
for grenades,
intelligence material, souvenirs.
I put my hand into a wet,
sticky pocket.
It contained a picture
of our Blessed Mother.
It was the pocket over his heart.*

Catholic Digest, January 1, 1949

Touching on this mystery, Paul compares our body before death to a seed; he compares our body after death to the plant that emerges from the seed. 1 CORINTHIANS 15:36–38 Continuing this metaphor, Paul says:

*When the body is buried, it is mortal;
when raised, it will be immortal. . . .
When buried, it is a physical body;
when raised, it will be a spiritual body.*
1 CORINTHIANS 15:42, 44

Apparitions of Mary

In 1858 a fourteen-year-old French girl, Bernadette Soubirous, reported having a vision of Mary at a hillside in Lourdes, France. Civil and religious authorities scoffed at her claim. When she continued to visit the hillside to pray, she was threatened with punishment.

One day, Mary told Bernadette to dig into the ground with her hands. She did and a spring bubbled up. Miracles began.

One of the miracles involved a mother who bathed her paralyzed child in the spring waters; the child was restored to health. Fifty-four years after Bernadette died, that same child, then a 77-year-old man, was an honored guest at her canonization ceremony in Rome.

Today, the Medical Bureau of Lourdes has on file records of over 1,200 recorded cures that have taken place there. Before a cure is accepted by the bureau, it must be certified by an international commission of doctors and surgeons of all faiths.

A highly publicized cure took place in the 1970s.

It involved a former serviceman, twenty-three-year-old Vittorio Micheli of Italy. He had contracted bone cancer, and doctors had given up hope of his recovery.

In desperation, his family and friends took him to Lourdes.

There he was washed in the spring waters. Within a week, his pain vanished and the bone repaired itself.

There have been reports of other apparitions or visions of Mary over the centuries. Because of the possibility of deception, however, the Church exercises extreme caution in dealing with such reports.

Each case is investigated thoroughly (sometimes for years) before it is declared worthy of credibility.

7 *Why do you think some people seem to be drawn more to apparitions and "messages" than to Scripture itself?*

Model saint

Catholics look upon Mary as the model disciple or saint. This means that they look upon her as being the model of what they should strive to imitate.

Two traits, especially, stand out in Mary's life, her:

- **Spirit of service**
- **Spirit of prayer**

Phyllis McGinley

Phyllis McGinley is a modern American poet. She wrote a book called *Saint-Watching*. In it she confesses:

*When I was seven years old
I wanted to be
a tight-rope dancer
and broke my collarbone
practicing
on a child-size high wire.*

*At twelve
I planned to become
an international spy.*

*At fifteen
my ambition was the stage.*

*Now in my sensible
declining years
I would give anything . . .
to be a saint.*

Spirit of service

A young believer said, "My life turned around when I stopped asking God to do things for me and asked God what I could do for him." Mary had this same kind of *spirit of service*.

Her spirit of service is illustrated in her response to the angel's announcement that she has been called to serve as the mother of Jesus. She answered, "I am the Lord's servant; may it happen to me as you have said." LUKE 1:38

Mary showed this kind of spirit when she learned that Elizabeth was pregnant with John the Baptist. She went immediately to help her cousin. LUKE 1:39

Mary's spirit of service also showed itself in a touching way at a wedding in Cana. When she learned that the newly married couple had run out of wine, she immediately sought Jesus' help. JOHN 2:1

Spirit of prayer

A second trait was Mary's spirit of prayer. It showed itself shortly after the birth of Jesus. Some shepherds showed up to tell Mary and Joseph what an angel had told them about the child.

*[Mary and Joseph] were amazed
at what the shepherd said.
Mary remembered all these things
and thought deeply about them.* LUKE 2:19

Mary's spirit of prayer also showed itself in her anticipation of Pentecost. Luke says that she and Jesus' disciples "gathered frequently to pray as a group" to prepare for the coming of the Holy Spirit. ACTS 1:14

In brief, then, Mary is an inspiration and a model to all believers, especially in her spirit of prayer and service. CCC 2673–82

8 *What is one of the biggest obstacles that keeps me from making a more serious effort to make prayer a daily part of my life? To make service to others a part of my life?*

PRAYER hotline

**God grant me courage
not to give up
what I think is right
even though
I think it is hopeless.**

Admiral Chester Nimitz

Recap   Review

A saint may be described as a person who follows the Gospel invitation to live and love as Jesus did. For this reason, saints become for us:

- **Models**
- **Witnesses**

There are two groups of people who enjoy the name "saint": canonized saints, and the communion of saints (members of Christ's Body, the Church):

- **Members in pilgrimage**   **On earth**
- **Members in purification**   **In purgatory**
- **Members in perfection**   **In heaven**

Of all the saints, the Virgin Mary is special. Her specialness flows from the fact that God chose her to be the mother of Jesus. We therefore give her the title "Mother of God."

We also honor her with the title "Immaculate Conception," because she was preserved from original sin.

Finally, because Mary was sinless, she did not fall under its penalty, but was assumed into heaven in the totality of her person.

Mary's assumption is a pledge that we too will join her in heaven in the totality of our person, if we strive to be like her, especially in her spirit of service and prayer.

1 Explain (a) what ordeal changed the life of Saint Francis of Assisi, (b) what two Scripture readings gave him a love for society's rejects, (c) what Scripture reading inspired him to preach the Gospel, and (d) how the time in which Francis lived was similar to ours.

2 Explain (a) how a saint may be described, (b) the Latin word from which our word "saint" is derived and its meaning, (c) how the word "saint" changed in meaning over the passage of time, and (d) what the process for declaring a saint is called and what it involves.

3 Briefly explain: (a) the twofold meaning of the phrase "communion of saints," (b) the three groups of "persons" it includes, and (c) three groups of "gifts" it includes.

4 In what sense is (a) Mary "special," (b) the "Mother of God,"(c) the "Virgin Mother of God," (d) the "Immaculate Conception," and (e) the "model disciple" of her Son?

5 Explain (a) what we mean by Mary's "assumption," (b) how it is linked to the title "Immaculate Conception," and (c) how it speaks to us of our own destiny.

6 What two characteristics, especially, of Mary should we try to imitate? Give two examples from Scripture to illustrate each characteristic.

7 Explain (a) the origin of the springs at Lourdes and (b) how Lourdes became a place to which people came for healing.

Reflect

1 Some years ago, Dr. Alexis Carrel, a New York surgeon and Nobel Prize winner, went to Lourdes to investigate firsthand the cures that were being reported there. He himself had no religious faith at all.

While en route by train to the French village, Carrel was called several times to treat an extremely sick girl on the same train. He said that if she were cured at Lourdes, he would become a believer.

When the train arrived at Lourdes, Carrel accompanied the girl to the shrine. In his book *The Voyage to Lourdes*, he describes what happened at a prayer service after the girl was bathed in the famous spring waters. (For professional reasons, he changed all names and called himself Lerrac.)

Suddenly,
Lerrac felt himself turning pale.
The blanket which covered
Marie Ferrand's distended abdomen
was gradually flattening out.
He watched the intake of her breath
and the pulsing of her throat.
"How do you feel?" he asked her.
"I feel weak, but I feel I am cured."
Lerrac stood there in silence, his mind a blank.

Later, Carrel and two other doctors examined the girl carefully. Their conclusion was unanimous: she was cured.

Carrel still did not believe, even though he had seen everything with his own eyes. That night, he went for a long walk. He ended up in the back of a church and prayed for the gift of faith.

At about three o'clock in the morning, he returned to his hotel. As he sat down to record his thoughts before going to bed, he "felt the serenity of nature enter my soul. All intellectual doubts vanished."

At that moment Dr. Alexis Carrel became a believer. He went on to become a prominent Catholic.

■ *Why do you think Dr. Carrel doubted, even after seeing the miracle?*
■ *Why do you think fewer miracles are apparently taking place at Lourdes today than there once were?*

2 Elizabeth Ann Seton was the first native-born American saint. At nineteen, she married into a wealthy family. Before her husband died at the age of twenty-nine, they had five children.

Two years after her husband's tragic death, Elizabeth and the children embraced the Catholic faith. She became a teacher and opened a school for girls in Maryland in 1808.

The following year she founded the American Sisters of Charity, which pioneered the Catholic school system in the United States.

Elizabeth Ann Seton was canonized in 1975. Other U.S. saints include Mother Frances Xavier Cabrini, Bishop John Neumann, and Mother Katherine Drexel.

■ *What made Elizabeth Seton an unlikely candidate for sainthood?*
■ *Why do you think God often chooses unlikely candidates?*

PRAYER TIME
with the Lord

Dr. Tom Dooley was a legendary doctor to Asia's poor. He died of cancer at age 34. Like all of us, he had his faults. But more importantly, he had a great heart.

On his deathbed in Hong Kong, China, he wrote a letter that is now engraved on a plaque at the Grotto of Our Lady of Notre Dame University, his alma mater. Here's an excerpt from it:

Whenever my cancer acts up,
and it is certainly "acting up" now,
I turn inward a bit. . . .
And inside and outside the wind blows.
But . . . the storm does not matter.

How I long for the Grotto. . . .
especially now
when there must be snow everywhere. . . .
If I could go to the Grotto now,
then I think I could sing inside.

Knowing that prayers from here
are just as good as from the Grotto
doesn't lesson my. . . . passion to be there.
That Grotto is the rock
to which my life is anchored. . . .

I must return to the states soon,
and I hope to sneak into that Grotto—
before the snow has melted.

■ *Describe your special prayer place.*

PRAYER *Journal*

Today I saw a water lily
growing in a pond.
It had the freshest yellow color I'd ever seen.
The lily—a precious treasure—
was unconcerned about whether
anyone noticed its astounding beauty.

As I sat there,
watching it unfold its petals noiselessly,
I thought of Mary pregnant with Jesus.
She, too, was a precious treasure.
She, too, was unconcerned about whether
anyone noticed her astounding beauty.

But to those who did, she shared a secret.
Her beauty came not from herself,
but from the Jesus life within her,
unfolding its petals noiselessly.

■ *Do a "pencil meditation" on something you
saw or heard recently.*

_____
_____
_____
_____
_____
_____
_____
_____
_____

SCRIPTURE *Journal*

1 **You will bear a son**   Luke 1:26–38
2 **You will be called blessed** Luke 1:39–56
3 **Your heart will break**   Luke 2:22–35
4 **Do what he tells you**   John 2:1–12
5 **Behold, your mother**   John 19:23–27

■ *Pick one of the above passages. Read it
prayerfully and write a short statement to
Jesus expressing your feelings about it.*

23 Rejoicing in Love

I saw a new heaven and a new earth.
The first . . . disappeared . . .
And I saw the Holy City,
the new Jerusalem, coming down
out of heaven from God. . . .
I heard a loud voice speaking. . . .

"Now God's home is with people!
He will live with them,
and they shall be his people. . . .
He will wipe away all tears from their
eyes. There will be no more death,
no more grief or crying or pain."

REVELATION 21:1–4

Is death a leap into a void?
Of course not.
It is to throw yourself
into the arms of the Lord;
it is to hear the invitation,
unmerited,
but given in all sincerity,
"Well done,
good and faithful servant . . .
come and enter the joy
of your master."

PEDRO ARRUPE, S.J.

End of the world

Author Tom Blackburn was about to begin work on a script about the end of the world. He went to the Bible and read:

The Day of the Lord will come like a thief.
On that day the heavens
will disappear with a shrill noise,
the heavenly bodies will burn up
and be destroyed,
and the earth with everything in it
will vanish. 2 PETER 3:10

After reflecting on this passage, he decided to begin his script just minutes after the world ended. He would have someone in heaven interview several people about what they were doing when the world ended. Here are two responses:

A San Francisco housewife said,
"I had just put the coffee on . . .
when I felt the whole house start to shake.
Then there was this terrific flash
of lightning and the whole sky lit up.
And I thought, my heavens!
The children are going to get soaking wet!"

A real-estate man from Florida said,
"You know when you come right
down to it, the whole thing happened
just like they said it would."

SENSE AND INCENSE

1 *What would you do today, if you knew the world would end tonight? If you would do it then, why do you neglect doing it now?*

Regardless of how we imagine the end of the world, this much is sure. It will be sudden, catching many people unprepared. The end itself will involve four events, the:

- **Return of Jesus** CCC 669–79
- **Resurrection of dead** CCC 1059
- **Last Judgment** CCC 1038–41
- **Entry into glory** CCC 1042–50

*The great trumpet
will sound,
and he will send out his angels
to the four corners of the earth,
and they will gather
his chosen people
from one end of the world
to the other.*
MATTHEW 24:30–31

Return of Jesus in majesty

Scripture describes Jesus' return in dramatic, poetic language, designed to capture the emotion and the majesty of that awesome hour. Matthew says:

*Then the sign of the Son of Man
will appear in the sky;
and all peoples of the earth will weep
as they see the Son of Man
coming on the clouds of heaven
with power and great glory.*

Resurrection from the dead

More than any scientist, Wernher von Braun deserves credit for putting astronauts on the moon. He wrote in *This Week* magazine:

*Many people seem to think
that science has somehow made
"religious ideas" untimely
or old-fashioned.
But I think science has a real surprise
for the skeptics.*

Werner von Braun

Wernher von Braun's career began in Germany. He developed the famed V-2 rocket that devastated British cities during World War II. Toward the end of the war, as the Russians advanced toward Germany, von Braun and his staff fled to Bavaria, where they surrendered to the United States.

Toward the end of his life, von Braun wrote:

*Science and religion are sisters. Through science
we strive to learn more
of the mysteries of creation.
Through religion,
we seek to know the creator.*

■ **Why is religion often held in less regard than science?**

---

*Science, for instance, tells us
that nothing in nature,
not even the tiniest particle,
can disappear without a trace.
Nature does not know extinction.
All it knows is transformation. . . .*

*Everything science has taught me—
and continues to teach me—
strengthens my belief in the continuity
of our spiritual existence after death.*

2 *Explain von Braun's statement: "Nature does not know extinction. All it knows is transformation." How does it apply to the resurrection of the dead?*

Saint John says about life after death and the resurrection of the dead:

*Time is coming
when all the dead will hear his voice
and come out of their graves;
those who have done good
will rise and live,
and those who have done evil
will rise and be condemned.* JOHN 5:28

Judgment after death

There's an ancient play called *Everyman*. In it God sends Death to the hero to tell him that his life is over.

When the hero recovers from shock, he asks Death to give him a few minutes to invite his friends—Money, Fame, Power, and Good Works—to accompany him into the afterlife. Death obliges.

To the hero's dismay, however, the only person who accepts his invitation is Good Works. The rest refuse.

The play makes an important point. As we pass through death from this life to the next, one thing alone will matter. Jesus alludes to it this way in his Sermon on the Mount:

Your light must shine before people, so that they will see the good things you do and praise your Father in heaven.
MATTHEW 5:16

ART Connection

Michelangelo was an Italian poet, architect, sculptor, and painter. One of his greatest artistic achievements is the Sistine Chapel of the Vatican. Begun in 1508, it was completed in 1512. Shown here is a detail of the ceiling's "Last Judgment."

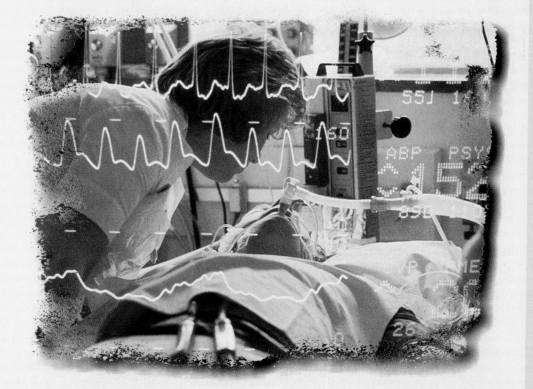

A prisoner in a Nazi death camp was standing next to a barbed-wire fence. Suddenly, the sun bloomed gold against a clear blue sky. Then it happened. His heart soared and he sang:

The sun has made a veil of gold
so lovely that my body aches.
Above, the heavens shriek
with blue—
Convinced I've smiled
by some mistake.
The world's abloom
and seems to smile.
I want to fly, but where, how high?
If in barbed wire
things can bloom
Why cannot I? I will not die.

Author unknown

■ *When did the world "bloom" and wake within me new faith and new hope?*

Dr. Elisabeth Kubler-Ross of the University of Chicago has interviewed hundreds of people who have been declared clinically dead and then revived.

These people commonly report experiencing a kind of instant replay of their lives. Dr. Kubler-Ross quotes them as saying:

When you come to this point,
you see there are only two things
that are relevant:
the service you rendered to others,
and love.
All those things we think are important,
like fame, money, prestige, and power,
are insignificant.

3 *Can you think of any passages or parables in the Bible that suggest or state that "love" and "service" are, indeed, the only two relevant things that count in the end?*

The play *Everyman* and the research of Dr. Kubler-Ross lead us to a major theme of Scripture: judgment after death. Commenting on judgment after death, Saint Paul says:

All of us must appear before Christ,
to be judged by him.
Each one will receive what he deserves,
according to everything he has done,
good or bad, in his bodily life.
2 Corinthians 5:10

The Scriptures speak of two judgments. They will take place at the end of:

■ **Our life** **Particular** CCC 1021–22
■ **Our world** **Last** CCC 1038–41

4 *Why do you think there will be two judgments, rather than just one at the end of each person's life?*

Let us now take a closer look at each judgment.

The deeds we do,
the words we say,
Into still air
they seem to fleet.

We count them ever past;
But they shall last—
In dread judgment they
And we shall meet.

John Keble

LIFE
Connection

I shall pass through this world
but once.

Any good therefore
that I can do,
or any kindness
that I can show
to any human being,
let me do it now.

Let me not delay it
or defer it,
for I shall not pass
this way again.

Attributed to Stephen Grellet

Particular judgment

Each person will experience a particular judgment immediately after death. CCC 1020–22

Jesus refers to such a judgment in his Parable of the Rich Man and Lazarus. The rich man lived in a fine home and feasted on fine foods. The poor man, named Lazarus, used to be brought to the rich man's door to beg for food. But the rich man ignored him.

Eventually, both men died. The rich man ended up in a place of torment. Lazarus ended up in "the bosom of Abraham," a place of honor and comfort. The rich man pleaded with Abraham:

*Take pity on me, and send Lazarus
to dip his finger in some water
and cool off my tongue,
because I am in great pain in this fire!*
LUKE 16:24

Abraham explained that a "deep pit" separated them. Then the rich man pleaded with Abraham to send Lazarus back to earth to warn his family, saying, "If someone were to rise from death and go back to them, then they would turn from their sins." LUKE 16:30 But Abraham replied:

*If they will not listen to Moses
and the prophets,
they will not be convinced
even if someone were to rise from death.*
LUKE 16:31

5 Why won't they be convinced?

Last judgment

One day Jesus was talking to his disciples about the end of the world. He used this dramatic imagery to describe it:

*"When the Son of Man comes as King
and all the angels with him,
he will sit on his royal throne,
and the people of all the nations
will be gathered before him.*

*"Then he will divide them into two groups,
just as a shepherd separates
the sheep from the goats. . . .*

*"The King will say
to the people on his right,*

*" 'Come, you that are blessed by my Father!
Come and possess the kingdom
which has been prepared for you
ever since the creation of the world.*

*" 'I was hungry and you fed me,
thirsty and you gave me a drink;
I was a stranger
and you received me in your homes,
naked and you clothed me;
I was sick and you took care of me,
in prison and you visited me.'. . .*

"Then he will say to those on his left,

*" 'Away from me. . . .
Away to the eternal fire
which has been prepared
for the devil and his angels! . . .*

*"I tell you, whenever you refused to help
one of these least important ones,
you refused to help me."*
MATTHEW 25:31–32, 34–36, 41, 45

Jesus' dramatic description indicates that the entire human race will face a last judgment.

Three destinies after death

In summary, then, a particular judgment will take place immediately after death. It will result in one of these three destinies.

Whatever the destiny, it will not be postponed, but will take effect immediately following the particular judgment:

- **Hell**   CCC 1033–37
- **Heaven**   CCC 1023–29
- **Purgatory**   CCC 1030–32

Hell

One day Jesus told this Parable of the Weeds among the Wheat:

A man sowed good seed in his field.
One night, when everyone was asleep,
an enemy came
and sowed weeds among the wheat
and went away.

When the plants grew
and the heads of grain began to form,
then the weeds showed up.

The man's servants came to him. . . .
"Do you want us to go
and pull up the weeds?" they asked him.
"No," he answered,
"because as you gather the weeds
you might pull up some of the wheat
along with them.

"Let the wheat and the weeds
both grow together until harvest.
Then I will tell the harvest workers
to pull up the weeds first,
tie them in bundles and burn them,
and then to gather in the wheat
and put it in my barn."
MATTHEW 13:24–30

6 *What is the point of this parable?*

The Parable of the Weeds and Wheat raises two questions. First, what did Jesus intend to teach about hell? About the punishment of hell?

Why shouldn't you believe
you'll exist again
after this existence,
seeing you exist now
after not being? . . .

Is it harder for God . . .
who made your body
when it was not
to make it anew
when it has been?

Saint Irenaeus

FILM

Connection

Near the end of *The Great Dictator*, Charlie Chaplin cries out:

*Look up, Hannah!
The clouds are lifting!
We are coming out
of the darkness
into the light. We are coming
into a new world—a kindlier
world, where men will rise
above their hate
and their greed and brutality.*

*Look up! Hannah!
The soul of man
has been given wings,
and at last he is beginning to fly.
He is flying to the rainbow . . .
into . . . the glorious future
that belongs to you—to me—
and to all of us!
Look up! Hannah! Look up!*

Literal interpreters hold that Jesus intended to teach that hell is an actual *place*. Contextual interpreters hold that since hell exists outside of time and space, hell is best understood as a *state* of separation from God and the saved.

This brings us to the second question: How did Jesus intend us to understand the punishment of hell: fire? Bible interpreters tend to fall into groups in answering this question. Jesus meant the word *fire* in a:

- **Literal sense**
- **Dramatic sense**

Literal interpreters hold that Jesus used the word in a literal sense: real *fire*. Contextual interpreters hold that he used the word in a *dramatic* sense: to dramatize metaphorically, the urgency with which we should avoid hell. We should avoid it as we would eternal, physical fire.

In other words, the essence of hell is eternal separation from God and whatever suffering that involves, whether it be physical "burning" or spiritual "burning with shame and remorse."

This leads us to the traditional teaching of the Church about hell. It may be summed up in three brief statements. Hell:

- **Exists**
- **Is eternal**
- **Involves separation**

7 *Which of the interpretations of fire do you feel is correct?*

Purgatory

Someone once asked Samuel Johnson, the great British writer, what he thought about the Catholic teaching on purgatory.

He surprised them, saying that he thought it made good sense. He explained that it is obvious that most people who die aren't bad enough to be sent directly to hell; nor good enough to be sent directly to heaven.

So it makes sense to conclude that there must be a kind of middle state after death, in which a purgation, or purification, takes place.

8 *How do you feel about Samuel Johnson's conclusion?*

The traditional biblical passage cited as evidence of purgatory is in the Second Book of Maccabees. There Judas Maccabees takes up a collection for an "offering to set free from sin those who had died." 2 MACCABEES 12:45

This brings us to the traditional Catholic teaching on purgatory. CCC 1130–32 It may be summed up in three brief statements. Purgatory:

- **Exists**
- **Is temporary**
- **Involves purification**

9 *How does the passage from the Book of Maccabees imply that purgatory exists, is temporary, and involves purification?*

Entry into glory

This brings us to heaven or "entry into glory." Scripture uses a variety of images to describe it. Consider just three:

- Life in God
- Vision of God
- Union with God

Life in God

In a beautiful letter to the Christians of his time, John exhorts them in these words:

Keep in your hearts the message
you have heard from the beginning.
If you keep that message,
then you will always live in union
with the Son and the Father.

And this is what Christ himself
promised to give us—eternal life.
1 JOHN 2:24–25

Vision of God

Concerning the image of heaven as the vision of God, Saint Paul wrote to the Christian community at Corinth:

What we see now
is like a dim image in a mirror;
then we shall see face-to-face.
1 CORINTHIANS 13:12

Theologians call the vision of God the "beatific vision." The word beatific comes from the Latin word *beatus*, meaning "happy." The heavenly vision of God results in happiness beyond words. CCC 1023–29

Union with God

Concerning the image of heaven as union with God, Saint Paul wrote to the Christian community at Colossae:

Your life is hidden with Christ in God.
Your real life is Christ
and when he appears,
then you too will appear with him
and share his glory! COLOSSIANS 3:3–4

Our union with God is the culmination of the destiny for which God made us. Saint Augustine expressed this destiny in these memorable words:

Our hearts are made for you, O Lord,
and they will not rest until they rest in you.

Recap

Regardless of how we imagine the end of the world, this much is sure. It will be sudden, catching many people unprepared. The end itself will involve four events:

- **Return of Jesus**
- **Resurrection of the dead**
- **Last judgment**
- **Entry into glory**

Scripture describes Jesus' return in dramatic, poetic language, designed to capture the majesty of that awesome hour.

Saint John says of the resurrection of the dead: "All the dead will hear his voice and come out of their graves." JOHN 5:28

Finally, Scripture speaks of two kinds of judgment after death:

- **Particular**   **End of our life**
- **Last**   **End of the world**

A particular judgment awaits each of us at the end of our life on earth. It will take place immediately after our death and result in one of these destinies:

- **Heaven**   **Union with God**
- **Hell**   **Separation from God**
- **Purgatory**   **Preparation for union**

A last judgment also awaits each one of us. It will manifest to the world what we have become and end with Jesus leading the faithful into glory, where there will be no more death, no more grief or crying or pain. REVELATION 21:4

Review

1 List and briefly explain the four events that will take place at the end of the world.

2 List and briefly explain (a) the two kinds of judgments that will take place after death, (b) where and how Jesus refers to each, and (c) when each will take place.

3 List and briefly explain the two positions Bible interpreters take concerning Jesus' teaching on hellfire.

4 What three brief statements sum up the Church's teaching on (a) hell and (b) purgatory?

5 List and briefly explain three images that sum up the Church's teaching on heaven.

Reflect

1 There is a story of a merchant in ancient Baghdad who sent his servant to the market to buy supplies. The servant returned, trembling.

"Master!" he shouted. "Someone jostled me. When I looked, I saw it was Death. He gave me a threatening look. Lend me your fastest horse that I may flee to far-off Samarra. He will never think of looking for me there."

After giving his servant the horse, the merchant went to the market to buy the rest of the supplies. Who should he see but Death. He said to Death, "Why did you give my servant a threatening look this morning?"

"That wasn't a threatening look," said Death. "It was a surprise look. I was surprised to see him in Baghdad, for I had an appointment with him tonight in far-off Samarra."

■ *What is the story's meaning? Suppose you knew that you had only 24 hours to live. What would you do and why?*
■ *Compose a brief message you'd like read at your funeral Mass. Why choose this message?*

2 While operating on a woman, Dr. Wilder Penfield, a famous neurosurgeon, accidentally touched the temporal cortex of her brain with a weak electric current. The woman, who was under local anesthesia and able to talk, reported reliving the experience of bearing her baby.

Other similar experiments then followed. They confirmed what Dr. Penfield had discovered. Patients felt again the same emotion that the original situation produced and were aware of the "same interpretations" they gave the experience.

Some scientists are now convinced that the brain has recorded every sensation it has ever received.

■ *Why is it significant that the patients were aware of the "interpretations" they gave to their experience at the time it occurred?*
■ *What event would you like to relive in your life and why this event?*

3 A king with no heirs was conducting interviews for a gifted youth to become his son and rule after him. A peasant named Kriston felt "called" to apply.

He worked hard to buy good clothes for it. Putting them in his backpack, he began the week-long journey in tattered clothes. When he got to the palace, he saw a shivering old man in thin sack cloth sitting at the gate.

Moved to pity, Kriston gave the man his good clothes. As Kriston mounted the palace steps he began to panic. Had he ruined all chances of being chosen?

At first, the guards wouldn't admit him. But after consulting with the king, they took Kriston to the throne room. He was stunned at what he saw. On the throne sat the beggar in Kriston's clothes. Before Kriston could speak, the king embraced him and said, "Welcome, son!"

■ *What Bible story does this story recall? Describe a time you sacrificed a good deal to help another.*

PRAYER TIME
with the Lord

Once twins were conceived. As they grew, they explored the womb. When they found their mother's life cord, they said, "How great is our mother's love that she shares her life with us." Soon the twins began to change rapidly.

"What does this mean?" said the one. "It means that our life in the womb is coming to an end," said the second.

"But I don't want to leave the womb. I want to stay here forever," said the first. "We have no choice," said the second. 'Besides, maybe there's life after birth."

"How can there be?" said the first. "We will shed our mother's cord. Life isn't possible after that. It's the end."

The first twin fell into despair, saying, "If life in the womb ends in death, what's its purpose? Maybe we don't even have a mother." "If we have no mother," said the second, "how did we get here and stay alive?"

Finally, the moment of birth arrived. When the twins opened their eyes, they cried for joy. What they saw exceeded dreams:

What no one ever saw or heard,
what no one ever thought could happen,
is the very thing God prepared
for those who love him.
1 Corinthians 2:9

■ *How is the situation of the twins in the womb parallel to our situation on earth?*

PRAYER Journal

When just a young man, Benjamin Franklin composed this inscription for his gravestone:

> The body
> of B. Franklin, Printer,
> Like the Cover of an old Book,
> Its Contents worn out
> and Stripped of the Letter and Gilding,
> Lies here, Food for Worms.

> But the Work shall not be wholly lost:
> For it will, as he believed,
> appear once more,
> In a new & more perfect Edition
> Corrected and amended
> by the Author.

■ *Compose a ten-line inscription for your gravestone that reflects your feelings about death and the afterlife.*

_____
_____
_____
_____
_____
_____
_____
_____
_____
_____
_____
_____
_____
_____

SCRIPTURE Journal

1	Future judgment	2 Corinthians 5:1–10
2	Future glory	Romans 8:18–30
3	Future coming	Acts 1:1–11
4	Future destiny	1 John 2:26–3:3
5	Future home	Revelation 21:1–7

■ *Pick one of the above passages. Read it prayerfully and write out a brief statement to Jesus expressing your feelings about it.*

_____
_____
_____
_____
_____
_____
_____
_____

Index

Share Your Meditation

Think About It

Photo credits

Notes